To my beloved husband, I thank you for your willingness and boldness to declare 'whatever it takes' to love the Lord. As your wife, to watch you live this declaration every day has been life's greatest testimony for me of God's love, grace and acceptance of who we are in Him.

My hope is that whoever may have a chance to read Johns journey with the Lord will see a glimpse of hope and receive a revelation of God's love.

Clare Davidson
Wife and Partner

John has a gift for communicating God's truth and love with illustrations that penetrate the heart and capture the imagination. His hunger for intimacy with the Lord and his desire to bring others into an awareness of who they are as sons and daughters of Father God saturates all that he teaches and writes. I praise God that he is a part of our ministry school and my life.

Pastor Shawna Diehl
New Life Christian Fellowship

Great Lakes Supernatural Ministry School
Founder

My dad has always been there for me. He's one of a kind. He's that great loving father figure in my life, and I am truly blessed. As time passes by, we all do our share of growing up, both of us. We have learned from our mistakes, and taken on each experience as a great life lesson learned.

Fortunately for myself, I have a dad who is there for me 24/7, always there with a positive word of knowledge from the Bible. He keeps me strong. To this day, I look at my dad and I can say that I see the love of the Father. I'm proud of my dad. He's encouraging and it's inspiring to me to come home to a joyful household in which I can hear praise and worship at all hours of the day and night. I know I can either find my dad singing in the basement, pouring his heart out to God or reading the multiple passages in the bible, in order to reach out with uplifting words to others around him. I can see how much love he has for my mom, my brother, and myself.

Knowing that I won't go a day without a hug or kiss on the forehead is a warm heartfelt feeling I'm fortunate to have. I'm blessed to have such a wonderful family, and to have a smart encouraging dad to guide me in my life tribulations.

Thank you Papa Bear,
I Love You

Rachael Lynn Davidson
Loving Daughter Baby Bear

John reveals Gods work in his heart, after his declaration of "whatever it takes" .This book is for those whose heart echo's John's cry, "God I want more of you" Join with John in his adventure with our heavenly vinedresser as God cuts away all that stands between Him and us. Jesus words of John 15:1-17 come alive in the pages of this book as The Godhead prepares our hearts to be His Dwelling Place and His glory revealed.

Blessed of God,
Vicki Krupiczewicz –Servant of the Living God

I just completed reading a remarkable story reflecting a life and a vision that was life transforming. John Davidson did something that few ever really do; he meant it when he told the Lord "whatever it takes". I personally know the price that John has paid. I also know that now John sees that it was well worth the price. The back of manmade religion and tradition is forever broken for John and many who will read and reflect on this book's meaning, while mediating on the Word of God.

John, through the clear anointing and direction of the Holy Spirit, has made some of the invisible visible. John's story is clearly one of the Father's love in full action. Jesus is always there in the full regalia of love, mercy and grace, never condemning, but ever patient, ready to fully save us from all (especially ourselves). This is a compelling and convicting story. The story is full of the scripture and will release fresh meaning for each reader in their own life without violating the truth of God's Word.

Read the "Dwelling Place" while keeping a box of Kleenex and a Bible handy. I truly believe that if you are a God seeker, this book (The Dwelling Place) will capture, convict you and open your dwelling place to great joy. I truly encourage you to read this book. It will do a transformation in your view of the wondrous Triune God that we love and long to serve.

Daniel Avery, Founder and President of Abiding Faith Ministries

I got the Dwelling Place ...and could not put it down, but I am pausing at page 70 for we have been in the rooms of the house... Yes, repenting, repenting, repenting. I wanted you to know as I discern even now this is a clear word for the NOW. I mentioned to you the book, *Discovering the depths of Jesus Christ*, by Jeanie Guyon in the late1800's. I think this strong message reminds me of her fellowship with the LORD which she wrote about.

Evermore,
Dawn Marie Payment
Friend

I don't know how to thank you for the gifts of your two books. I feel as though I am a changed person because of them. I have waited all my 80 years to hear these words. God continue His word in you

Love
Mary Watson
New friend

This book is good stuff. It will take you on a journey showing you why you are here and were you are going. If you wonder where you are and where you hope to go with God and you want to create more hunger and understanding of how God fits in your life this is the book for you.

John Scafe
National Director
Bible for Mission Thrift Centers

The Dwelling Place

Journey from the

Heart of God

to the

Heart of Man

JOHN M DAVIDSON

Scripture quotation marked (KJV) are from the King James version of the Bible.

Scripture quotations marked (NKJV) are from the New King James version, © 1979, 1980, 1982 by Thomas Nelson, Inc. Used by permission. All rights reserved.

Scripture quotations marked (NIV) are from the Holy Bible, New International Version, ©1973, 1978, 1984 by the International Bible Society. Used by permission

Scripture quotation marked (NKJV) are taken from the New King James Version. Copyright © 1982 by Thomas Nelson, Inc. Used by permission. All rights reserved.

Scripture taken from *The Message*. Copyright © 1993, 1994, 1995, 1996, 2000, 2001, 2002. Used by permission of NavPress Publishing Group."

Take note that the name satan and related names are not capitalized unless they start the beginning of a sentence. We choose not to acknowledge him even to the point of violating grammatical rules.

THE DWELLING PLACE: Journey from the heart of God to the heart of man

For speaking engagements you may contact the author at:

John M. Davidson
Casa Royale Ministries
3804 Michael Ave SW
Wyoming, Mi 49509
e-mail; supernaturalroyalty@gmail.com

ISBN: 978-0-557-71412-4
Printed in the United States of America
©2011 by John M. Davidson

Library of Congress cataloging-in-Publication Data (pending)

No part of this book may be reproduced or transmitted in any form or by any means, electronic or mechanical, including photocopying, recording, or by any information storage and retrieval system without permission in writing from the publisher.

This book is lovingly dedicated to my precious daughter,

Rachael Davidson

Her heart is one of pure gold. She understands what it means to love God and to love others. She pours out her heart to others and is an atmosphere changer. She truly is a beautiful person from the inside out. I am so proud to be your father

Table of Contents

		Introduction	9
Chapter	1	The Living Room	15
Chapter	2	The Kitchen	25
Chapter	3	A Clean Heart	33
Chapter	4	The Bedroom	45
Chapter	5	The Throne Room	59
Chapter	6	The Powder Room	65
Chapter	7	The Bridal Chamber	71
Chapter	8	The Pantry	79
Chapter	9	The Halls of Shame	89
Chapter	10	The Halls of Faith	97
Chapter	11	The 'Whine' Cellar	113
Chapter	12	The Worship Center	121

Chapter	13	The Trophy Room	131
Chapter	14	The Water Treatment System	145
Chapter	15	The Furnace	157
Chapter	16	The Old Library	173

PART 11   THE FULNESS OF GODLINESS   191

Chapter	17	The Kitchen	193
Chapter	18	The Closet	201
Chapter	19	The 'Living' Room	223
Chapter	20	The Fence and the Tree	229
Chapter	21	The New Library	245

PART 111   THE FRUITFULNESS OF GODLINESS   279

Chapter	22	Lady Wisdom	281
Chapter	23	Eli John	291
Chapter	24	Addicted to Worship	313
Chapter	25	The Nursery	227
Chapter	26	The Conclusion of the Beginning	233

Acknowledgements

A book like this would never have been possible without the input and involvement of a myriad of people in my life. I would not be here today without my wife of almost 23 years. My favorite part of the day is the morning where we usually can be found in the living room drinking fresh cups of coffee as we share about all aspects of our lives; our hopes, dreams, visions, children and work. I can honestly say I love Clare more now than ever and I know she would say the same. The experiences of *The Angel and the Vision* and *The Dwelling Place* have made that all the more real.

I will be forever grateful to Ed Kerkstra who I affectionately call Father. He spent hundreds of hours praying with me. Without his tireless and patient work of teaching me to hear the voice of the Lord, I would not have been able to receive this amazing vision, nor write this incredible story of God's love. I cannot say enough about this man. All I can say is that I have learned to see, feel and hear the voice and the love of God in a way I never thought possible.

And then there is Vicki Krupiczewicz who pushed me beyond my comfort zone to fulfill the call of God on my life. She has been like iron sharpening iron as she challenged me to pursue my heart cry of "Whatever it takes". She is a true prophet of

God who is not afraid to speak the truth. She was the inspiration for Lady Wisdom in this book and the one who gave me the input for the description of the fruit.

I am so thankful to the Pastors in my life who have poured themselves into me. For Pastor Randy Vruggink of River of God Church who personally discipled me and gave me a safe place to grow for six years.

Thank you Pastor Lonnie Shields of New Life Christian Fellowship, my home church, in Grand Rapids Michigan for never stop laughing. You make me smile. Your sound Bible teaching and passion to see the power of God flow in healing of body, soul and spirit have deeply imprinted this book. You and Pastor Jon Hazeltine are pioneers cutting a path through the jungle of religion to release a fresh light of the love of God.

I will be forever thankful to the Grand Rapids branch of The End Time Hand Maidens who gathered around me and poured a mother's' love in me that was so strong that it brought about a remarkable healing within me. The things that broke off me were life changing.

And finally thank you to Pastor Shawna Diehl, my worship leader and founder of Great Lakes Supernatural Ministry School who taught me that Jesus is a fun person to be with and someone who loves to laugh. You taught and demonstrated "drinking in the Spirit" in the most undignified way that cut through the fog of religion that shrouded my life for so long.

I could mention so many others but suffice it to say none of us can reach our destiny without linking our arms and pouring out ourselves to one another with God's love

Introduction

I reflected back over the brief time I had been in this house. It was moments before when I had asked the angel to pierce my heart with the sword. I knew the sword represented the Word of God. I had watched the eight eyes that rotated on the sword slide easily into my heart. I had been amazed at how kind, loving and compassionate they were. I knew they were the eyes of the Lord. But why four pair? I simply had no clue but I had a clear sense that this was about new beginnings and these four pairs of eyes had everything to do with it. I knew they were going to clean house and torch all that was worthless and needed to be burned yet a calm and peace had settled over me like the morning dew.

As soon as my heart had been pierced by the flaming sword I found myself immediately in this house and I knew instantly that it represented my heart.

The house was totally trashed and it took quite a while for the angel and I to find Emmanuel, Comforter and Rhema*

I looked over to Emmanuel, Comforter and Rhema who were positioning their buckets, shovels and trash cans in the family room as they got ready to get to work. I had already figured out by this point that

The Dwelling Place

Emmanuel, which means God with us, was Jesus and Comforter was the Holy Spirit. I was still trying to figure out who Rhema was.

Now that I was concentrating on the work at hand, it truly did seem daunting at best. The family room was a maze of brick work with pathways up to four feet tall. The walls were a complicated maze of stone work that was securely cemented in. At the time I did not know what all this meant but I would discover in time that it had to do with complications with family. It was about relationships gone bad, trust broken, offenses taken and hurts, wounds and rejection that had happened for decades.

Emmanuel was all enthusiastic and had already begun cleanup. He seemed totally unfazed by the immensity of the situation. As He whistled a worship tune, I stood amazed at his cheerful attitude. He really seemed to enjoy His work.

I was amazed that these guys were not offended that I had kept them contained to a six by six area in the front porch for twenty years if not double that. I could not see even a hint of them holding an account of my wrongs. They were already treating me as most valuable and precious. How could they do that? Why would they want to do that?

I was learning already that when you tell these guys something they go ahead and do it. There are no games just action. They don't manipulate you; there is no one up? They were just sincere. This was the hardest room because it involved more than just me.

I noticed that Rhema was doodling on his notepad. As he did I got a strong impression that I needed to exercise forgiveness. This room was about me forgiving myself and those who had hurt me.

I noticed crumpled up pieces of paper all over the floor and everything about the room seemed either partially finished or partially made. For example, the end table was there but it had no stain or finish

Introduction

on it. The walls were dry walled but not finished sanded. There was no trim on the walls or floors.

I picked up one of the wadded up pieces of paper. It was a letter of condemnation and shame from a family member exhorting me to right religious behavior. I had better do what they believed I should do because judgment day was coming.

I picked up another and another and it was more of the same. One of them exhorted me to witness to everyone because if I didn't their blood would be on my hands. I felt a sense of shame and anger rise over me. A vice seemed to settle over my head.

Emmanuel and Comforter both came over to me and placed their arms around me. "Do not fear and don't be angry. This is why we are here. These letters and words are not from us. These letters and words have caused what you see here in this family room. They have caused broken relationships, separation, guilt and shame. You have set us free to help bring order to this chaos. We will help you sort through all this. Your fight here is not against your flesh and blood." "But first we must find the culprits who are creating chaos in your life and put an end to the devastation caused here. "

"We believe you when you said, "Whatever it takes." Do you still feel that way now that you are getting a clearer idea of what your house looks like?" Emmanuel looked sincerely into my eyes with a warm compassion. Expectantly He held my gaze as I pondered the little I had seen.

Breathing deeply, I responded with deep fervor, "Yes, whatever it takes. I make you Lord and Master over everything."

Slapping me on the shoulder and giving me a huge grin, Emmanuel responded enthusiastically, "Ok then let's get to work then. We need to find some intruders and critters that have no right to belong here. It

The Dwelling Place

suddenly dawned on me that six of the eight eyes I had seen on the sword were these three guys. I had just made the connection as I looked into their eyes. It was the same love, kindness and compassion. It would take some time, though, before I would be able to draw the connection to the last pair of eyes.

Introduction

Notes

1

THE LIVING ROOM

It didn't take long for the workers to come upon the living room where the fat man and his three cohorts were hanging out. The fat man was belching out orders left and right and the other three friends were doing everything possible to cater to him. Open containers of food, pizza boxes, candy and every kind of fast food container was everywhere. The TV and radio were both blaring at the same time, and all sort of violent images, seductive bodies, and enticing things were coming from the TV. I placed my hands over my ears to drown out the hideous noise.

"Who is this arrogant and nasty person and what are these other people doing here?" I shouted over the noise.

"That is Fat man who is the <u>old man</u>;" the angel said pointedly "and those other three men with him are worldly Wendy, Freddie fleash, and damien devlin. He goes by devlin for short."

The angel stepped quietly back into the shadows as the three workers walked boldly into the living room and walked straight to the fat man, looking him squarely in the eye, and said,

The Dwelling Place

"We have a message for you from the owner of the house. He no longer is extending an open invitation to you. He says you have to die."

"What!!!" the fat man shouted with a loud snarl. "This is my house and I'm not going anywhere." "We are not going anywhere either," the other three chimed in unison. The atmosphere became a clamor of loud laughter, cursing and leg slapping.

"I'm afraid you don't have a choice," the workers responded in unison. "You have to be invited to stay in this house and these are your marching orders," the head worker said, as he handed an official document signed with the owners seal.

The fat man snatched the document and ripped off the seal. "Go to hell," fat man sneered. You have no power or authority here.

"I've already been to hell and I hold the power of life and death." Emmanuel, the head worker, declared authoritatively. Fat man snickered as He began to nonchalantly read the words on the document. It didn't take long for an overwhelming fear to come over him. Suddenly, the bravado was gone and his hands began to shake profusely. In the document were two passages of scripture. The first stated boldly:

> He is as dead as you want him to be, the angel responded

> "So put to death the sinful, earthly things lurking within you. Have nothing to do with sexual sin, lust and shameful desires. Don't be greedy for the good thing of this World—for that is idolatry. God's terrible anger will come upon those who do such things? You used to do them when your life was still part of his world. But now is the time to get rid of anger, rage, malicious Behavior, slander and dirty language. <u>Strip off the old nature and all its evil deeds</u>"

The Living Room

. (Colossians 3:5-9) NLT

The fat man read that his power and authority had been stripped off along with his three cohorts and was getting the sense that the owner was claiming the authority of this Word for himself.

I watched as his face turned purple with rage, and then turn to complete disbelief as he continued to read on.

> *"I am crucified with Christ, I myself no longer live, but Christ lives in me. So I live my life in this earthly body by trusting in the Son of God, who loved me and gave himself for me."*

(Galatians 2:20) NLT

The fat man realized that his legal right had been stripped, and that I now had firmly grasped it in my heart. Although He had already known this, he had trying to bluff his way through things all along. I watched in amazement as the fat man began to shake uncontrollably and his eyes slowly rolled back in his head as he began to choke. Suddenly, he fell over backwards on the floor, and a death rattle began to gurgle from his throat.

> *Your obedience and faith without doubting in God's promises gives them all the tools and authority to clean house.*

"Is he dead?" I asked in complete amazement as I kicked him with my toe. "He doesn't seem to be moving".

"He is as dead as you want him to be," the angel responded. "As you can see, these three worker men are more than willing and able to do your dirty work. Your obedience and faith without doubting in God's promises, gives them all the tools and authority they need to clean house. Up until now, everything in this house has been fed by rebellion and pride. Since that attitude is now out; they have nothing to feed on.

The Dwelling Place

Emmanuel turned to look at the other three menacing men. "As you can see the love of the Father is here and your authority has been stripped. You must leave. You have been stripped of all authority and been made a spectacle."

I laughed, as the three men (worldly Wendy, Freddie fleash, and damien devlin) ran as if their tails were on fire. I marveled that with just a "Word" they scattered like rats to their holes. I shook my head reflecting on all the lost time I had wasted giving these nasty men the ability to have the authority to live and control my heart. They sure had made a mess of my heart, but I had let them. I was responsible for this mess. I had given my authority to the wrong people. Why had I done that? I turned to look back as Emmanuel, Comforter, and Rhema were now hauling out more trash to the front yard to burn. "They certainly don't waste any time," I said, nodding in approval.

Every piece of trash had a name on it (rage, lust, bitterness, anger, gossip, discontent, worry, ungratefulness, lack of forgiveness, slander, pride, spiritual pride, to name a few).

I noticed Emmanuel grabbing a favorite rocking chair. Across the back of the chair was the words "laziness". It had been etched into the wood with great care.

"That's my favorite chair," I quipped.

Emmanuel paused, and began to set down the chair.

Suddenly, I heard a gasp and gurgle come out of fat man. Emmanuel looked expectantly at me to see what my decision was.

"Whatever you choose to hang on to from Freddie fleash, worldly Wendy or damien devlin, gives life and strength to the fat man. He is your "old man". And he must be continually put to death. No longer can you view things through fear, doubt and unbelief. Any pride or rebellion is

The Living Room

the kind of odor that invites these nasties back. Do not fear though," Comforter replied.

"Greater is He (Jesus) that is in you than he that is in the World."

(1 John 4:4) KJV

It was a couple of days later, and I had awakened from a very restless night of sleep. Outside it was a cloudless day and the sky was a beautiful blue. There was absolutely no wind. Although the day was gorgeous, I found no enjoyment in its beauty. My body seemed to ache all over and a burning sensation lay like a deep heaviness in my heart. It was as if someone had taken a blowtorch to my insides.

I found myself immediately back inside my house which represented my heart. Emmanuel, Comforter and Rhema were sitting in various chairs, and had stopped the work of cleaning up the house. Somehow during the night, more trash and worthless junk had piled up on the floor. Holes had been punched in the walls, and it looked like there had been some kind of fire because some of the walls were charred and the house smelled like smoke. I noticed more pictures that were etched on the walls of my heart. In the kitchen "Freddie Fleash" and "Worldly Wendy" were busy stocking the refrigerator with groceries that they had just gotten from the store.

> *Whatever you choose to hang on to from your Flesh, World or the Devil, gives life and strength to the fat man*

I turned with an irritated face to look at Comforter and complain but noticed that he had a very strange look on his face. He opened His mouth to speak, but I seemed to have a hard time hearing Him. There was such a grieved look on His face. His hands were clasped over His heart as if in great pain. I put my finger in my ear to try and stop the incessant ringing. "Why was I having such a hard time hearing Rhema and Comforter?" I

The Dwelling Place

asked myself? I continued to rub my index finger inside my ear hoping to jar something loose to stop this awful ringing.

Rhema sat quietly in the corner writing words on a notepad. I walked behind him to see what he was writing. As I looked over his shoulder, I read the words. Well, I tried to read the words. It was so fuzzy that I had to grab my bifocals because even my contacts wouldn't focus to read.

I squinted and adjusted my glasses as the words came into focus:

> *Don't store up treasures here on earth, where they can be eaten by moths and get rusty and where thieves break in and steal. Store your treasures in heaven, where they will never become moth eaten or rusty and where they will be safe from thieves. Your eye is a lamp for your body. A pure eye lets sunshine into your soul. But an evil eye shuts out the light and plunges you into darkness. If the light you think you have is really darkness, how deep that darkness will be. No man can serve two masters. Either he will hate the one and love the other or he will despise the one and be devoted to the other you cannot serve God and money (sin).*
>
> *(Mathew 5:19-24) NLT*

I wondered what a teaching on money had to do with me and all this trash in my house and how terrible I felt. I scratched my head and reached for a mixed drink. I needed something to take the edge off. Ooooahhhghh!. I felt so bad. The inside of my chest felt like it was burning.

I glanced through the front window and saw fat man on a gurney. "I thought he was dead," I said to myself, feeling a slight confusion. "Why is someone giving him oxygen? It looks to me that he is getting new life." A sudden panic began to overwhelm me.

The Living Room

Fat man began to cough and sputter, and struggled to get up on one elbow while grasping the oxygen mask and taking deep breaths. He wheezed, hacked and coughed, causing his big fat belly to jiggle. In but a few moments he had gone from a dark blue to a light blue. He seemed to be going between not breathing and breathing. It looked like Freddie fleash was holding an IV bag and was also administering mouth to mouth; one thousand one, one thousand two, and one thousand three. Freddies voice echoed through the air with an eeriness that sent shivers down my spine. Freddie Flesh suddenly stopped counting and began greasing up the defibrillator, and was waiting for the charge so he could give fat man a jolt and attempt to fully bring him back to life. "Why was my flesh trying to bring back Fat Man," I wondered.

What a difference a few hours had made in my heart. The total atmosphere had changed from joy to a foggy heaviness that hung heavy in the air. Already, I was having some trouble with my hearing, and my eyesight was a little blurry. After sneezing and drying my nose on a Kleenex®, I began to reflect over the last few hours starting with getting home from work. I rubbed my knee which had developed a dull ache in it. What had I done to cause such a destructive commotion in my heart? All I had done was watch a favorite TV series that one of my family members had given my wife for a Christmas present six months ago. I had watched six or seven episodes. I had become so engrossed that it was 2:00 a.m. before I fell to sleep in exhaustion. The Lord had convicted me that the TV and internet were the two things that wasted the most time. The Word says, "If your eye (TV and internet) offend you, cut it out."

Suddenly, it dawned on me that I had come home with full expectation to spend an invited few hours in the Lords presence, but had convinced myself that instead I need some "me" time. God had known what my idols were, and I had gone in the backyard and dug up what I had buried. I was piecing together what I had just burned, and I looked down at my hands to see them all sooty black.

The Dwelling Place

Revelation began to flood my mind as the written Word began to become the Rhema Word. It was as if Rhema's true purpose and assignment in my house had just come to light for me. Rhema was here to give me revelation. He brought scriptures of what Emmanuel and Comforter said to me come to light in my mind so I could understand it. He was the embodiment of revelation. Rhema was revealing to me that this scripture was about devotion. It was about one hundred percent and absolute surrender to The Lord Jesus Christ. The priority is heavenly treasure. The focus is a single and pure eye. It's all about knowing Christ and making Him known. That means that I am to walk in faith without doubting—to know the mind of Christ.

I am to choose to either be completely devoted to Christ twenty-four/seven, or to be totally committed to this worldly system which is so obsessed with money, personal pleasure, pride, and lust. There could be no sitting on the fence for you would not find God there. This was satan's domain. Satan owns the fence. Although I felt a lot of thoughts working their way through my mind, Rhema was helping it to become real in my heart. I fell on my face and began to weep. I had ignored my Lord and Savior and grieved the Holy Spirit. Rhema was writing words of loving discipline to reveal to me, rather than revealing His wonderful plan of destiny for me.

In the past, I would have cried legalism, but now my heart had changed. Now, I called it devotion. I had grieved the Trinity Three because I had promised them my time, and instead had filled my mind with worthless treasure.

The Living Room

Notes

2

THE KITCHEN

"I ignored your still quiet voice and allowed all this worthless junk back into my life," I cried out in deep anguish. "Now Worldly Wendy and Freddie Fleash have hope in their eyes and are stocking the refrigerator for the old Fat Man. Even devlin is outside giving Fat Man oxygen in an attempt to bring him back alive."

It had just dawned on me that devlin had just switched places with Freddie Fleash and with all the commotion; had just now jump started his heart.

"By my choice I have given the enemy access and tools to use against me." I cried out despairingly.

I looked inside the refrigerator to see what Worldly Wendy and Freddie Fleash had brought in. There were containers that were labeled "spirits" and all kinds of various fruits. I was feeling real anxious and felt a strong impulse to nibble on something. Without thinking and putting two and two together, I picked up what looked like a muskmelon. I probably should have known, but my recent revelation in one area had not yet

The Dwelling Place

made me fully aware in other areas (I also never asked Emmanuel's opinion either). I took a small bite and immediately my mouth dropped wide open as if I had touched a fire with my tongue. I felt a burning lust rise up within my heart. The atmosphere of the kitchen suddenly became thick and musky and I found myself becoming agitated and even more anxious.

"What did I just do?" I exclaimed in total disbelief. I felt like I had just jumped out of the pot and into the fire. I ran in circles and then into the other room calling out, "Emmanuel, Emmanuel! Help me! Help me! Fire! Fire!" I was frantically wiping my tongue with both forefingers trying to remove the taste and the burning sensation.

Emmanuel ran into the room as I yelped in an anxious voice, "I was curious what Freddie Fleash and Worldly Wendy had put into the refrigerator and I saw this delicious muskmelon. I picked it up and took a bite out of it and felt this burning lust inside me. What happened? What did I just do?"

My tongue was already starting to turn numb, and I was wondering if Emmanuel could even understand me. "I'm stlartinng toou feeaal nummmb num," I blubbered. I stared blankly at Emmanuel as saliva started drooling out of the corners of my mouth and splashed down on the hardwood floor.

Emmanuel pulled the tongue depressor out of my mouth after doing a serious examination and responded quickly by saying, "You must guard your heart. Do not let your curiosity lead you into sin. You cannot listen to your flesh even though it screams out for gratification. The pain of denial will eventually subside. You must choose to believe the truth of what God says about your abilities and make your flesh obey what God's Word says,"

> "Every man is tempted when he is drawn away by his own lust and enticed (sees it). Then when sin has conceived it brings forth

The Kitchen

sin (eats it) and sin when it is finished (completes itself) brings forth death."

(James 1:14-16) KJV

Again, I burst out in tears. As I wept, I felt an arm slide gently across my shoulders. It was such a comfortable feeling of love and acceptance. "Aii'm shooow sharry," I said mumbling the words, as my tongue and lips kept growing to three times their normal size. My eyes were becoming itchy and were starting to see seductive girls walking by in bikinis. I reached out my hands to grab one of the seductive mirages in front of me.

"Whoa, boy!" Emmanuel said, as he tried to hold me steady. "You're not thinking straight. You just bit into a *Lust melon*, not a juicy tasty muskmelon. Your flesh is in hyper-drive right now."

> *We only want you to be the best of what Your heavenly Father created you to be*

Comforter came along side and whispered in my ear as He began to give me reassurance and teaching from the Word of God. In one hand, He had the notebook from Rhema, and in the other hand, He had a scroll which was titled the <u>Written Word</u>. He turned to look me square in the eyes and began to read both Words at the same time.

The Written Word and Rhema Word began to minister to my heart with a tenderness and sensitivity I had never before experienced,

I listened as Comforter spoke of Jesus' plan and purpose for my life. "God has a destiny for you," He said. "When you make a promise to God that He can do whatever it takes, He hears that devotion, but He is a jealous God and wants all your time. However, He will never force Himself on you to obey Him. He wants a loving willing heart. His jealousy for your love will not keep you from eating this fruit or free you from being held captive to it unless you receive His love.

The Dwelling Place

All of your life you have lived afraid of Me and have tried to live your life out of duty and obligation. You have been told what you should do and been manipulated into doing what others thought you should do. This is a new day for you will now see us in a whole new light. We only want for you to be the best of what your heavenly Father created you to be. Look around this house and answer this question. Has the old way helped you?" I nodded my head from side to side.

"Only one thing can do that," Emmanuel spoke with a calm reassurance.

"And whut ish thaat?" I mumbled quietly as I looked at the clutter and devastation in my house while hanging my head in shame.

"It is my love. The more revelation you get of My love, the more it will lead you to experience My love. The more you experience My love the less you will find yourself drawn away by your own lust. You have already discovered that giving in to this lust does not satisfy. It only fuels your flesh and brings even more dissatisfaction." Emmanuel reached out with both arms fully extended. "Come experience my love."

I looked at Emmanuel for a moment but saw nothing but warmth and tenderness in His eyes.

For a moment, I looked cautiously at Emmanuel. "No spanking?" I said meekly.

"No spanking," Emmanuel said with a hearty laugh. "This is a new day. This is the beginning of a whole new way of life. In fact, if you stay teachable and humble, you will find that it will only be my goodness that brings you to repentance." Emmanuel held me tight, yet I still had the feeling I could pull away and run after devlin if I wished...or Worldly Wendy...or my flesh. For a moment the lure of those possibilities tugged at my thinking. My head was spinning as a vision of being controlled, manipulated and dominated into doing what was right and being forced

The Kitchen

to obey God flitted across my mind. My thoughts were pulled back to the present as I heard...

"I have given you a good heart here, but you have believed lies about how your house is to be maintained. You have become proud and rebelled against my design and plan. You are living in this world, but should not be accepting and receiving it into your life," Emmanuel spoke firmly, yet tenderly. "Receiving the world into your life pushes out My love. You are just passing through this life, but you are to bring the kingdom of heaven to bear on this world. If you want the deepest revelations from the heart of God, your eye must be single, but this must be a choice that you, yourself, are willing to make."

"If you really want to be free of Fat Man, Worldly Wendy, devlin and Freddie Fleash's broken down wall mentality, then you must choose. The price to pay is absolute and total devotion of your thoughts and time to me. Making Emmanuel your absolute Lord and Savior means exactly that," Comforter shared in a loving, but firm tone. "By making that commitment, you are on the road to discovering real living." No matter how you feel, you must choose to walk in what is right. By right, I am talking about believing what the promises in the Word say and taking them to heart. I love you my son. Life and death are before you, but I encourage you to choose life."

Emmanuel held me close to His chest as Comforter taught me and read the words on the notepad from Rhema. He instructed me that I had no obligation whatever to the fat man who constantly urged me to listen to him. If I continued to listen to him, I would perish and die, but if I would lean on (Comforters) power and turn from my wicked deeds, I would live (Romans 6:18).

"Rest in my love," Emmanuel whispered quietly into my ear.

I had heard enough and cried out, "I turn from my wickedness. I renounce every agreement and all communications I have made with that

The Dwelling Place

spirit of lust, and I command that spirit to be loosed from me and go to the foot of the cross. I repent from believing the lie that these spirits can protect me, or that they are a part of my identity, and I command them to leave me now in the name of Jesus"

Immediately my vision was restored and I began to understand. I was back! I could see again! The blurriness was gone and my vision was sharp and clear. My lips and tongue returned back to their original size. A loud popping noise happened in quick succession in each ear and suddenly the ringing was gone and everything sounded normal again.

"Thank you, Lord Jesus, for forgiving me," I cried out. "You are so faithful, loving and kind!"

I took out a piece of paper and wrote down my words of surrender to the Lord. After putting my seal on them, I handed them back to Emmanuel and said emphatically, "Would you be willing to give this back to Fat Man. I notice he is getting some color back in his cheeks."

> *Emmanuel would help me, but it would be through me*

Emmanuel handed the letter back to me and smiled, "I have already put fat man to death once and for all at the cross, but for it to be real to you, and you must deliver this letter and stab him in the heart.

I gave Emmanuel a startled look. I guess I thought that Emmanuel would do all the dirty work and I would just sit back and watch.

"I will go with you and be the strength within you" Emmanuel said giving me a reassured glance as He handed me a small dagger. On its handle was a scripture verse with the inscription (Col 3:5) KJV. As I gripped the handle, I heard the verse resound in my ears,

"Put to death the old man."

The Kitchen

Revelation began to flood my mind. Rhema began to teach me that it was not solely about dos and don'ts; it was about an intimate and deep relationship with Emmanuel, Rhema, and Comforter. Certainly Emmanuel would help me, but it would be through me. I had to step forward and believe. Hmmmmm!

I began to remember back to an earlier time when this old man and his henchmen were a real hindrance to that depth of intimacy. Whenever I pursued after intimacy, it was like this hook would grab me by the back of the neck and drag me down into its quicksand of death. These guys were tenacious and once they got their hooks into you they were not satisfied until they destroyed you completely. They always promised you peace and made you feel that there would be no consequences. When you gave in though, they would pound you until you were totally bloody and bruised. I was discovering that when I'm double minded, I stop the good guys' ability to work effectively in my life.

"What is that hook? What is it that seems to have such power over me?" I was not sure of the answers at this point, but I had to admit that it troubled me greatly. What I had discovered though, was that I did like the love that I had experienced with Emmanuel. I thought deeply about that for a moment. "You really cannot have it both ways," I thought. "You grow or you die. You choose or you slide." I had just had my first encounter with the love of God. I really liked the fact that He was straight forward with me and cared about my well being. I did not sense that He was manipulative or did a double talk. That in and of itself put an awe in me.

I felt a new love permeating the bottom of my soul. As a new trust began to develop, a steely look began to settle in my eyes. Snapping out of my musings I cried out, "Let's put Fat Man out of his misery," I growled resolutely as a fierce determination and courage built within me. Emmanuel proceeded to give me a high five as we headed out to the gurney.

3

A CLEAN HOUSE

Emmanuel opened the refrigerator door and held His breath. All the fruit that was in the refrigerator was either rotten, moldy or stinking.

"Would you bring me a waste basket?" Emmanuel asked me pointedly. "This had only appeared to be delicious fruit, but when Emmanuel had opened the door; its true nature had been exposed. I brought the waste basket and immediately gagged, falling to my knees and barfing profusely into the waste basket. This fruit was absolutely nasty smelling.

"You need to stay close by my side so I can shine a light on the things in your heart that are toxic and stinking. If you let these kinds of fruit that worldly Wendy and Freddie fleash bring in when your defenses are down or you're not paying attention, they will defile you."

The Dwelling Place

Emmanuel was holding a heavy duty flashlight and was peering intently into the refrigerator. "If you noticed," Emmanuel continued. "It was not the fact that the fruit was in your refrigerator that defiled you, but it was when you put it to your lips and digested it. That is when it defiled you. You are going to see things and hear things all day long, but it is not until you covet it for your own fulfillment and eat of it that it will corrupt you. Do not covet these things. Do not consume them. You can be easily fooled unless you walk in My presence. These fruit are notorious for giving indigestion and diarrhea. They will also make your lips and tongues swell up and will give you itchy eyes."

While Emmanuel was talking, Rhema's pen was racing faster than the Indie 500 across his notepad. A verse came to my mind from James 1:14-15 (NKJV) that stated that:

> *"Each one is tempted when he is drawn away of his own desires and enticed. Then when desire has conceived it gives birth to sin and sin when it is full grown brings forth death."*

> I was learning to stay close To Emmanuel

"Ahhh!" I thought, "The conceiving is in the eating."

"Rhema and Comforter are a part of me," Emmanuel spoke quietly but firmly, "and we will teach and enlighten you, but you must be fully devoted to us, and by devotion, I mean completely. Did you see how easily and quickly worldly Wendy and Freddie fleash came back in? It can happen that fast," Emmanuel said, as he snapped his fingers. "You must be sober and vigilant and stay on guard at all times. I need you to stay focused."

"This is why you must keep Rhema, Comforter and I within touching distance. We will instruct and protect you. Do not fear for I have overcome the world, the flesh and the devil. Your agreement with Me gives you that same power for I live in you and I am your strength and protector."

I got a very clear picture that Emmanuel, Rhema and Comforter had no intentions, or even a remote desire to be friends with fat man or his cohorts. I wasn't sure how things would pan out with Freddie fleash because I needed my physical flesh but I was sure it would all work itself out in time.

I was learning fast, but more importantly I was learning to stay close. I remembered that sheep only see from up to six feet away. They need to stay close to the shepherd. (Psalm 23:4) "I must stay close to the Lord and listen to His voice," I said with new eagerness. I was still feeling a little cautious from being religiously abused as a child, but already I could see a huge difference by staying close to Emmanuel.

"If your aim is to enjoy worldly Wendy and cater to Freddie fleash in his present state, you can't be a friend of God," Comforter said. "It is not about God rejecting you. It's the fact that the two are polar opposites and can't dwell together (James 4:4). We jealously long for you to be faithful (v.5). That is why you are given more strength and grace to stand against worldly Wendy, Freddie fleash, and damien devlin. It is very important that you humble yourselves before God, draw close to Emmanuel, purify your hearts and let there be strong tears for the wrong things you have done. You must bow down before God and admit your dependence on Him. When you do that, He will lift you up and give you honor." (James 4:6-10).

"What do you mean, 'in his present state', 'I asked a little perplexed.

Emmanuel began to explain that Freddie fleash has been under the control of fat man for a long time. If fat man is gone he will be looking for a new Master. The flesh will eventually follow the desires of the heart. The flesh is neutral in and of itself. There is nothing evil in your body. It can however yield itself to evil to do evil deeds and cater to itself. God

The Dwelling Place

created something beautiful when he made you. Your body was made to give glory to God. Through My death on the cross, I have made that possible again. Like a fly on a white wall, it was now crystal clear. A favorite verse from my childhood suddenly became crystal clear,

> *"Therefore, I urge you, brothers, in view of God's mercy, to offer your bodies as living sacrifices, holy and pleasing to God-this is your spiritual act of worship"*

(Romans 12:1).

God was discerning my motives—not for what would give me pleasure, but rather what would please Him. What pleased Him was a humble heart of dependence on Him.

I began to see that I was to believe in Him and His promises without doubting and obey Him without question (at least until I could question without being disobedient). I was beginning to understand that there was a difference between God's love and God's pleasure. God loves me unconditionally, but He is not always pleased with my behavior, but if I offer my body to him as a living sacrifice in a holy and pleasing way, He is very pleased.

"God, I will love you with all my heart and all my soul and my entire mind," I responded fervently.

I found that I was still too prone to believing lies. I needed to believe and obey without question until I had revelation and full understanding. God didn't make stupid people. He gave me a good mind and a good heart. I just needed to tap into it.

It would take me a long time to realize that a good mind was nothing like I was experiencing right now. It would prove to be a totally different thing. I was trying so hard to reason things through with my own understanding.

A Clean House

I watched as Emmanuel pulled out the bottles of spirits from the refrigerator and threw them into the trash. "These are a great counterfeit," Emmanuel said with a grimace. "They will dull your mind and weaken your resolve. I want you drunk all the time...just not like this."

He grabbed the rotten fruit, which made me almost vomit. "I had taken a bite of that," I thought with disgust as I wrinkled my nose in disgust. It had appeared so good before. I watched it fall apart as Emmanuel picked it up and tossed it. Maggots and fruit flies tumbled from the core. Fortunately, the moment Emmanuel touched the fruit, the whole thing started to wither and dry up and all the flies and maggots became dust.

"What kind of fruit is that?" I asked, shuddering from the repulsiveness and smell.

"Well this fruit here is hate, and this long skinny fruit here is slander, and this one is anger. Oh, and this one that looks like a lemon, is bitterness and you have already experienced the lust melon," Emmanuel responded as He shook His hands off.

> I now understood there was good fruit and bad fruit and I could see I would definitely need Comforters help to discern between them

I noticed an apple and was about to ask what it was when I felt words of knowledge flooding my mind. That one was deception. The one that looked like a watermelon was gossip; it was so juicy and sweet and went down easily and was so satisfying. A bunch of banana looking fruit was at the back. As Emmanuel pulled it out to toss it, I stepped back in horror as words of knowledge flooded my mind. This was deception, depression, worthlessness, death, and suicide.

How often I had eaten of this fruit and savored its flavor only to find myself bitten by its taste of death. Even though it was the taste of death one could quickly acquire the taste and you would crave it to the point of addictive behavior even though it was killing and numbing you inside.

The Dwelling Place

That's what following after fat man, worldly Wendy and devlin would give you.

I was so grateful I had run immediately to Emmanuel. I would need to be careful to look who stocked my refrigerator next time, and make certain to have Emmanuel examine the fruit first. I now understood there was good and bad fruit and I knew I would definitely need Comforters help to discern between them for it appeared I had eaten counterfeit fruit.

"Please give me help to discern what good fruit is and what is bad fruit," I cried out to Comforter.

With a deep loving smile, Comforter replied, "I have just the person to help you. At the right time she will reveal herself."

I did not want to be out of fellowship for one minute if at all possible. It was so awesome to walk within an arms distance of the Trinity Three. I would never had known or seen these fruits and bottles of spirits for what they were, had I not been walking close to them. Surely I was blessed.

Emmanuel reached for a big saucer that was full of milk. In the milk was Rusk. The Rusk was saturated and pretty much falling apart.

"What does that mean?" I said as a frown turned down the corners of my lips.

Comforter paused and began to teach me, "This is one of the greatest tools of the enemy. He has convinced pastors and teachers to tell people what they want to hear. They cater to itching ears rather than preach and teach the truth. As a result we have a generation full of milk toast Christians.

"Millions who think they are my children are not my children at all," Emmanuel replied sadly. They have fooled themselves into thinking that

A Clean House

because they prayed a simple prayer, that they are saved. They prayed a little prayer and then never gave us a second thought. They think reciting a few words that involve no relationship is what salvation is all about. They are sadly mistaken. However, a prayer without relationship is not salvation. It starts by faith in Jesus Christ; you live your life daily by faith in Jesus Christ. You overcome by faith in Jesus Christ, and you die as an over comer having faith in Jesus Christ. Be careful of what I am saying though," Emmanuel spoke with much fervor. "I am not talking about working for your salvation by your own human effort (Ephesians 2:8-9). What I am saying is that salvation involves relationship and that salvation includes turning from sin. You cannot have salvation without relationship.

"This generation does not know the fear of the Lord because it has not been taught it. Security comes from absolute surrender and faith in Jesus Christ. It comes from an intimacy with the Father. Intimacy comes from obedience.

As Rhema wrote on His pad, I began to recite a verse I had memorized as a child.

> *"Those who continue to (practice) sin have never known Jesus or understood who He is."*

(1 John 3:6) The Message

Preachers today are preaching a soft message of salvation but if you read the whole Word of God. It is those who endure to the end who will be saved (Mathew 24:15). You only need to casually study Revelation 21:8 to see the seriousness of all this:

> *"But the fearful, and unbelieving, and the abominable, and murderers, and whoremongers, and sorcerers, and idolaters, and all liars, shall have their part in the lake which burneth with fire and brimstone: which is the second death "*

The Dwelling Place

As I studied this, I came to understand that "the fearful," were those Christians who gave in under persecution and turned away from their faith. When the rubber met the road, they denied their faith in exchange for trying to save their life. A scripture verse came to mind:

> *"He that loveth his life shall lose it and he that hateth his life in this world shall keep it unto life eternal."*
>
> *(John 12; 25) KJV*
>
> *"He that endureth until the end shall be saved"*
>
> *(Mathew 1:22) KJV*

The unbelieving were those who had no faith in God or His promises. The abominable was that person who caused others to turn from him because of his own stench Then there were those who practiced murder. I would latter tie this in with those who refused to forgive someone, they would not be forgiven and be able to enter heaven:

> *And his lord was wroth, and delivered him to the tormentors, till he should pay all that was due unto him.*
>
> *So likewise shall my heavenly Father do also unto you, if ye from your hearts forgive not everyone his brother their trespasses*
>
> *(Math 18:34-35).*

These verses became even more embedded in my spirit as I read about the Resurrection of Pastor Dan of Nigeria who died in a car accident and was dead for three days and was miraculously raised from the dead, even though he was partially embalmed. When he came back to life, he told how an angel had taken him to the gates of heaven but had told him that had this been his time, he would not have not been allowed to enter heaven because of unforgiveness towards his wife. He had refused to forgive his wife over an argument and because of her

A Clean House

slapping him on his face on the morning of his death. He was so angry he vowed to get even with her. The angel said that as he was dying and was confessing his sins, they were not being heard because he refused to forgive his wife. To read the full testimony goes to this link

www.heavensfamily.org/ss/ressurrection-from-the=dead=pastor-daniel-ekechukwu

Then there were those who practiced sex without being married yet called themselves Christian. These are what the scriptures called fornicators and whoremongers and that they would have their place in the lake of fire. There were also those who cast spells or dabbled in black or white magic. As I studied, idolaters were those who loved the things of this world and worshipped false gods. Material things were more important than a relationship with God. Finally, there were the liars who practiced deceiving people from believing the truth.

I began to squirm as the truth of this settled in my spirit.

"I am looking for men and women who will preach My Word with Spirit and truth, live what they preach, and not fear man but fear me," Emmanuel said with deep conviction.

"I don't understand what you mean by 'fear'?" I questioned. "Am I supposed to be afraid of you...like scared? That is how I had seen God the Father all my life and look how messed up things have gotten for me."

I felt the air of the room become electrified as the warmth of Emmanuel's presence filled the atmosphere and penetrated right through me. With deep love in his eyes, Emmanuel placed a reassuring hand across my shoulder and said, "I want you to be so filled with the knowledge of my love, the beauty of my presence and to experience my love in everything you do; I want this to such a degree that when things that used to tempt you cross your path, you will choose life over death; you will choose to live in my love rather than indulge in sinful pleasures

The Dwelling Place

for a season. That is the meaning of fear. It is a culture of honor that comes from learning to walk through your day and including me in all you do, awe in honoring Me. I want you to live more aware of my love than anything else that is tangible around you and seeing everything around you through my love. As you stay close to me and walk with me, I will begin to give you the power to understand how wide, how long and how deep my love is. As you start to live this out, you will experience my love more and more. The more you experience it, the more you will be filled with the power and fullness that comes from me. This will result in running from the evil I listed above."

After the refrigerator was cleaned out and washed thoroughly, Emmanuel walked over to the walls and examined the pictures that were painted, etched, or built into the walls.

"It is one thing to see things as you go through the day that will pass you by. It is another thing to desire them or even be captivated by them by opening your heart and mind to them. When you open your heart like that, you can see the results." Emmanuel pointed out to the pictures, as He traced them with his finger. "You opened your heart to these pictures. We will need to apply a very special paint to these pictures or the image will bleed through. This special paint is able to not just cover, but actually repair the damage to the walls where these pictures have etched themselves into the interiors of your heart. The paint goes on red, but when it dries it turns a pure white. We call this paint 'Life'. You probably used 'Kilz®' before to cover things over, but in this realm that paint won't work.

"Wow! That is really cool," I said, laughing a jovial laugh, "A red paint that turns white." As a builder, I had seen white caulk that turned clear, but I had never seen a red paint that turned white. I watched Emmanuel as He took a paint roller and a pan of red paint and began to paint the walls of my kitchen. When He finished, I felt so clean and new again. What a wonderful paint," I said. Almost immediately it was dry,

A Clean House

and the blackness and damage caused by the images was gone. This paint did not just cover, but it somehow removed the stain and dissolved the images into nothingness. I felt like a new man.

"If you walk in the light of my presence you have nothing to fear for my blood will be continuously cleanse you and you will have relationship with me and others," Emmanuel explained lovingly (1 John 1:5-9). "Do not let devlin bring condemnation to your heart. I will convict of sin and it will always be through my goodness. As you can already see, I do not manipulate, dominate, or control. Everything is done out of my everlasting love. Whatever I bring to your attention, I encourage you to quickly repent of it so your joy may be full."

I looked at the fresh red paint and before you knew it the paint had dried and looked as white as fresh fallen snow. I was so glad that I had invited the trinity three into my house. After reading about Revelation 21:8, I would have hated to think where I would have been spending eternity if I had died with the Trinity three contained in the front porch. I had so many questions.

Of one thing I was sure. The problem was not of Emmanuel, Rhema and Comforter wanting to be in my house/ heart. There was no hesitation on their part. They did not want me to perish but to live and enjoy life to its fullest. It had all to do with the invitation on my part. They always, loved, always hoped and always believed. They were not willing for one to depart this life without God in their life as Savior and would fight until the end, for ones fate was not sealed until they died. I was done practicing sin. Standing near the precipice and seeing how close I could stand without falling in was no longer my cup of tea.

I was grateful that I had received that love and repented.

4

THE BEDROOM

I was really enjoying the peace and joy from having a clean heart when Emmanuel grabbed me by my arm and said, "Come we have a lot of cleaning still to do. You made a promise of "whatever it takes" and we take your promises seriously just as we expect you to take our promises seriously. The more cleaning we do the more freedom you will experience. Isn't this fun?"

"My word is my bond," I said. "I have put my total faith in you. Do whatever it takes."

I wasn't sure what He meant yet by "cleaning my heart," but I was thankful for Him giving me the grace and strength to let Him change me no matter how much it hurt. "

I'm not sure I would call this fun yet, though. I do feel a lot better."

Emmanuel put His hand on the door, seeming to ignore my last statement. Pausing for a moment, he turned to me with warm smile and said, "What I am about to show you is a revelation of your heart in your

The Dwelling Place

most private area. This is your secret place. Every person has a secret place that nobody knows about. We are currently in the deepest part of your heart. Because you want my presence so bad, you are not only willing to do whatever it takes, but also to believe all my promises as I reveal them to you and practice them. I believe you are ready to have Rhema, Comforter and I come in to this area. Again, this is your heart in the secret place. This is what happens when you take those right angle turns, practice sin and allow yourself to be under the power and control of the evil one (1 John 5:18-21). This is the area you are most vulnerable in and you will need a sustained special revelation of my love," Emmanuel spoke soothingly, as He gazed squarely in my eyes.

The more cleaning We do the more freedom you will experience

I let out a nervous sigh and looked to my left. I was in a hallway and I noticed two closed doors side by side that were facing me. One had the title, 'Throne Room', and the other one right next to it said, 'Powder room'. A puzzled look crossed my face. "Interesting title for the bathroom," I thought. "And why would I need a powder room? Well, that one would have to wait." Emmanuel had turned the doorknob and stepped into the bedroom.

Emmanuel turned to look back as I prepared to follow Him into the bedroom. "Remember, you are seeing all this through the eyes of the Lord. You must see these things through my eyes or it will consume you. Come, stay right next to me. What you will see today is going to help set you free. Emmanuel reached out his arm to draw me close to His side."

I entered the room to see the most hideous thing I had ever seen in my life. In the spiritual realm what I saw looked nothing like it would have looked like in the natural realm. In the natural realm, I would have been captivated by the perceived beauty of this event... but this was repulsive.

The Bedroom

The room was in pure darkness, but by some miracle I was able to see everything. I saw what looked like five creatures on the bed. By a spirit of knowledge, I knew that the large one was devlin. The other three were Worldly Wendy, Freddie fleash and Fat Man. A sickening sweet smell of lust filled the air, but because I was standing next to Emmanuel, sheltered by His strong arm, it did not seem to affect me. It was like I was seeing things with my heavenly body. The person in the middle looked strangely familiar. He was bruised, bloated, cut and had massive wounds on himself. He looked almost unrecognizable. It was obvious that it was an orgy of some type, but yet it did not appear the same as if it would be in the natural world. It was hideous.

The individual on the bed was worshiping devlin, kissing and hugging him. As the man was enthralled in what he was doing, what looked like a long tail with sharp arrow-like barbs on it curled along behind the man and stabbed him in the back.

The person was so delirious with lust that he did not seem to notice or care. The other three cohorts were offering fruits to satisfy his hunger. "It must have been fruits from the refrigerator before Emmanuel threw them away," I pondered to myself. "Maybe they got them out of the garbage can. That can't be. Everything in the garbage can had turned to dust."

I turned my thoughts back to the scene before me. A TV screen was attached to his forehead and scene after scene was being burned into his head. He had an almost zombie look in his eyes. He had this numb look about himself and seemed lethargic and unmotivated. Devlin was nibbling on his ear whispering syrupy things that he wanted to hear. "I will give you power, wealth, status, women, men, whatever you want if you will just worship me."

All around the room were evil looking bat like creatures hanging off the edge of the ceiling. They had long fangs and in their hands were

The Dwelling Place

arrows and darts dipped with poison. When the individual was not looking, they would throw a dart or shoot an arrow at his backside. The darts had names on them like hypocrisy, religious spirit, bitterness, lust of the eyes, pride, doubt, performance, shame, suicide, and burning lust to name a few. I noticed that it wasn't enough for devlin to have an orgy with this man. He had to throw a whole bunch more things at him to complicate and suck in him further.

Because the room was in pure darkness, the captive on the bed did not seem to notice or care that devlin and His bat like creatures where creating such massive wounds. In fact, he seemed to think that he deserved it. He didn't think he deserved to be treated right or to even be happy and free for that matter. He had just accepted that this was his lot in life. The wounds did not seem to hurt him at first. In fact it did not seem even to dawn on him until the life blood within him had oozed out. He hardly even noticed devlin whispering in his ears. It seemed to him that this was part of his own thoughts. I suddenly had a word of knowledge that the wound would not hurt until the completion of sin. "Ah," I said.

It was fast becoming apparent that rebellion was a key word and central to Devlin's strategy

"Sin when it is finished brings forth death."

(Romans 6:23) KJV

Emmanuel looked at me sadly and said, "This is what happens when you give place to devlin and you make it your aim to enjoy this world. <u>You are having an affair with the devil.</u> Damien devlin has become your lover.

"Those who are mine I hold securely and touch them, but those who turn from me in rebellion open themselves up to the evil one."

The Bedroom

(1 John 5:18; 1 John 2:16-18) The Message

Again I saw that word 'rebellion' come up. It was fast becoming apparent that this was a key word and central to devlin's strategy. I coiled back in horror as I watched the sickening spectacle before me. I was repulsed that anyone would want to have such an intimate closeness with one who found it his greatest pleasure to kill, maim, and destroy. Despite this repulsion, I felt such an overwhelming and amazing love for this individual. In spite of the fact that he looked so unlovely, I felt a deep love and compassion for him.

I observed that when you have an affair with Devlin you open yourself up to the worst torture and abuse. It is true that pain seeks pleasure. He will lure you into sin and when it is over accuse, condemn, and bring shame for the very things he has lured you into. He then spits you out and tosses you on the garbage pile. He promises you everything and gives you nothing but pain and misery. He will dominate, manipulate and control you then, belittle you for letting him do it.

> *I was repulsed that anyone would want to have such an intimate closeness with one who found it his greatest pleasure to kill, maim, and destroy*

Small little tentacles with hands on them were playing with his head. Some tentacles were covering his ears, some his eyes. Some tentacles were able to reach right into his head and mess with his brain. Any good Word or Word of God that was deposited in his head or heart was immediately snatched out and thrown away.

The noise in the room was deafening, like a thousand magpies feasting on the carcass of an elephant as the little minions and cohorts screamed and chanted in unison. It seemed, from what I could see that the noise dulled the pain that was etched on this man's face. His eyes had a deeply pained look and drool poured from his mouth. His eyes were deep pools of emptiness and misery. It looked like the thing that

The Dwelling Place

captivated him, that which he craved for so much had become his own personal, private hell.

"Is this a fore shadowing of what hell will look like," I wondered. A person's hell on earth would seem to only increase exponentially after he died. There would be no peace or joy only your conscience accusing and condemning you. That for which you craved for so much on earth would torture you for eternity and you would experience no satisfaction or release. I shuddered at its implication.

I noticed dark spirits coming and going to and from his body. On his hands and feet were heavy shackles. Sickness and disease were already beginning to manifest themselves in areas where he had yielded to their power. You could almost taste and feel the aches and pains in his body.

"Who is this man?" I asked Emmanuel.

Emmanuel looked me full in my face and said with a remarkable compassion, "This is your heart; this is your bedroom!"

> My disobedience and my form of godliness were in reality having a love affair with Devlin and an orgy with Worldly Wendy and Freddie fleash

I groaned a deep groan as the realization hit me. My bedroom? My heart? You mean I am having a love affair with devlin? I am having a love affair with the devil? I didn't equate my unwillingness to be fully obedient to God and completely surrender to Emmanuel's Lordship the same as having a love affair with the devil.

I had slowly given devlin this power over my life and had made Him my master. My disobedience and my form of godliness were in reality having a love affair with devlin and an orgy with worldly Wendy and Freddie fleash. I was having a love affair with myself. "So this is self love," I said as I squirmed uncomfortably. I was denying the power of godliness and was caught up in a delusion of a form of godliness. I shook

The Bedroom

my head in disbelief while trying to deny my own conclusion. This shocking revelation greatly disturbed my 'religious thinking'.

While pondering deeply this seemingly contradiction, Comforter entered the room and stood behind me. I was totally caught off guard as he said, "You cannot serve the Lord and devlin. You cannot serve two Masters. You must hate the one and love the other or be devoted to the one and despise the other. You must choose who your lover will be. Do you understand?" Comforter spoke gently and tenderly, while testing my perception. "If you make money, relationships, power or pleasure in the things of this world your god, you choose to make devlin your lover." Comforter cupped my cheeks in His hands, looked me square in my eyes, and with much emotion said, "We want to be your exclusive lover."

I found myself blushing at the unabashed intimacy that Comforter was displaying towards me. I regained my composure and reasoned through what I had just been told.

I now was beginning to understand why the angel kept referring to Jesus as the 'Master'. It was not for His benefit, it was for mine. It was all about whom I was going to love. That thought sickened me. I fell on my knees before Emmanuel and cried out, "What must I do to be saved from this retched existence? I feel the depth of Your love, and I repent. Be merciful to me a sinner."

Comforter placed His hands around my shoulders and Emmanuel got down on His knees before me. He cupped my face in His hands while quietly and soothingly whispered His love to me. "Even though you have been unfaithful to me I have always been faithful to you. (2 Tim 2:13). I am your patient lover always wooing you back to myself. If you confess your sins, I am faithful and just to forgive you your sins and to cleanse you from all unrighteousness. (1 John 1: 9)"

The Dwelling Place

"There is no reservation of hope in My love. It is all freely given and available; Emmanuel interjected as He reassured me. "I will never hold myself back from you no matter how bad it looks to you. This is and has already been forgiven. I am the faithful lover and will teach you how to love by my example. You will always find Me to be faithful to you. I will teach you how to love...that is if you wish for me to do so."

All I could do was to nod my head up and down. Emmanuel reached down and unscrewed the top off a little container that was on top of the dresser. Dipping His fingers inside, He scooped up some salve. Reaching over to me, He put a soothing salve on my eyes. I felt a deep warmth and a soft light. The salve moved through my eyes and melted down into my heart. The chains snapped off as if they were twigs.

> It suddenly dawned on me that although I was always forgiven because of the finished work of the cross, I needed to say it and embrace it for it become real in me

"You are forgiven. Go and sin no more." Emmanuel said with a deep tenderness.

"Every sin you or anyone else has ever committed is forgiven at the cross. When I died, I took every sin and paid the price so that you could live in freedom. You can walk in my love and in my presence with total abandonment. Everything you see here in this room or have embraced is a lie. You no longer need to look to these spirits to meet your needs or find your identity in them. But you need to receive my forgiveness to experience my forgiveness and cleansing and that is what you are experiencing right now."

I heard what seemed to be a great tearing sound. There was a great screeching and flapping of wings. I turned to look back into the room. Devlin had jumped back in horror as if a holy fire had enveloped me and I was off limits. Worldly Wendy and Freddie fleash jumped out of bed as if it was on fire, grabbed their clothes, and ran screeching out of

The Bedroom

the room. The room was clean and swept. I had rendered my heart before God and again he had come through, as He always does when you call on Him with a humble heart (Joel 2:13). I had repented and had a change of thought.

It began to dawn on me that Emmanuel and Comforter had been here all along and they had seen this affair that I was having. Even though I had been having this affair (on and off for more than thirty years, I felt no condemnation, no guilt and no shame. The deception that had clouded my mind was gone and in its place was complete clarity. There is no condemnation when you are in the sphere or area near Emmanuel.

Because I was standing right next to Emmanuel and was staying close to Him, I felt a strong desire to turn from this type of behavior. I knew this with a deep conviction and felt a hope and a freedom opening up inside me.

> Emmanuel took in a deep breath of air as if savoring the very atmosphere of my heart

This was the first time I had ever felt this way. New hope began to filter up from the depths of my heart. I could do this; I wanted to do this; I will do this. My eyes were open to the liar that devlin was. Rhema was behind me writing furiously on His notepad. I felt a great conviction that I was giving my affection, time, and love to the wrong person. Just standing next to Emmanuel and Comforter and being open to Rhemas revelation made me cry out prayerfully, "Forgive me Jesus; cleanse me from all sin. I don't want this."

It was all so clear to me. "Ahhhh! This is beautiful," I breathed out. I felt so clean and free." It suddenly dawned on me (thanks to Rhema), that although I had always been forgiven because of the finished work of the cross, I needed to say it and embrace it for it to become real in me. It was my absolute devotion to Emmanuel, and drawing close to Him that opened me up to receiving this life changing work.

The Dwelling Place

Just being with Emmanuel in this room had given me freedom. His very presence in my life was bringing life. I was so free. Rhema's words were now filtering through and becoming revelation in my mind. When I walk in or with the Spirit, I have no desire to fulfill or practice evil. My sin nature was finished and put to death at my salvation, but I needed to agree with what was already finished. Wow! I felt free and I am free because God says so.

I felt a comforting hand on my shoulder. "Emmanuel took in a deep breath of air as if savoring the very atmosphere of my heart. "So much cleansing has been done in your heart. I am so pleased. This would be a great time to worship the Father and give glory to God for the great things He has done."

We both fell on our knees as Emmanuel smiled as He pulled out a bottle of red wine. In cursive signature were the words, 'Forgiven and Free'. "I'll drink to that," I blurted out with a laugh, as Emmanuel opened the bottom drawer and pulled out two crystal wine glasses that were lying in a purple velvet lined box. He poured us each a glass, and we began to worship and thank the Father for freedom and forgiveness.

As I worshipped the Father, a great joy and peace filled my heart. "I love my Creator," I whispered. He had put a place in me only He could fill and He had filled that place with Himself. When I sinned, He so generously and compassionately forgave me. He did not hold anything against me, as bad as it was. How could I not but continue to give Him my all? I was so fulfilled.

As we drank, I heard a thumpity thump in the other room. I looked around slightly distracted for a moment wondering what it was. Emmanuel laughed, as his arm slid across my shoulders.

"Do you know what is different now?" Emmanuel said with a twinkle in His eye.

The Bedroom

. I thought about it for a second and said, "I know, my heart is getting softer."

Emmanuel grinned, as I suddenly realized that the thumping sound was the result of several stones that had fallen off the wall. The mortar had turned to liquid and could no longer sustain the rocks in place.

I had always thought of my worship as being from myself to God. This was an incredible experience that I was having... Emmanuel was worshipping with me and we both were worshipping the Father and giving thanks for the Holy Spirit together. I was enjoying the Holy Spirit, (Comforter) who was in me and around me. I was enjoying intimate worship with the one who forgave me. I wept as I worshipped. All around me, I felt the presence of Comforter as His soothing love enveloped me. Rhema sat on the edge of the bed with paper and pen resting on His lap. He just smiled in restful contentment. No words needed to be spoken at this time. We just enjoyed each other's love. I would remember this moment later on and wonder how this special moment could be sustained all the time.

You are not your junk

Sometime later after being refreshed in exhilarating worship, Emmanuel brought me a glass of cool refreshing water. "Drink," He said. "This is the living water. My wine makes you thirsty for more and My water quenches your thirst. It will not only quench your thirst, but will strengthen you as We continue to clean house. I am so pleased that you are so quick to want all the junk cleaned out of your heart. Many people never get this far because they believe that I can only have access to limited parts of their heart. They are afraid that they will lose something or everything. They do not realize that if they just yielded it all, they would gain it all."

The Dwelling Place

Emmanuel sighed, as He continued, "They don't realize that by loving their life, they actually end up losing it."

"You are already beginning to understand, know, and touch My love. I love everyone the same as I am no respecter of persons, but you are learning to get more of Me because you are finding more and more freedom and are pressing into Me. Your pure and holy heart enables you to see and hear clearer."

"My heart is pure and holy?" I asked with a slight doubt. "I only see this one room clean right now."

> *They do not realize that if they just yielded it all, they would gain it all.*

"What you see and what I see are not the same yet," Emmanuel said enthusiastically. "The end and the beginning are the same to me. I do not tie your identity of who you are to whether your house (heart) is dirty or not. You are not your junk. This will all make sense as we continue to clean house and put all the junk to the fire. Come on, we can't stop now. (Hebrews 12:28-29) The Message. I will have some exciting things to show you here in the bedroom now that it is swept and clean. But first we need to take care of the throne room.

The Bedroom

Notes

5

THE THRONE ROOM

As we exited from the bedroom, Emmanuel placed his hand on the door to the throne room. Holding His hand to my chest, He paused, and with a gentle motion and said, "You may want to stand back. This is the room were either Jesus is Lord or you sit on the throne."

I stepped back as Emmanuel turned the doorknob and tried to push it open. The door would not budge. It seemed to be sealed shut.

Emmanuel turned to me and said, "Help me lean into this door. It's not moving. Maybe the both of us can push it open. After many attempts, Emmanuel said with a fierce determination, "We will have to pull the whole door off, frame and all. I smell a real stink in there." I could only nod in agreement that he could do whatever it took to open the door. I too smelled something funny. This door had been sealed shut for a long time and the smell, even with the door closed, was overwhelming. Even though I was holding my nose closed with my thumb and fore finger, my eyes got teary eyed from all the ammonia smell that permeated the air. Waste needed to be eliminated from the heart and

The Dwelling Place

showers needed to be taken. The throne room was the central place in the heart and at one time when it was functioning correctly, was the busiest room next to the kitchen. There was definitely something wrong with the bath room. Emmanuel, Rhema, and Comforter took power tools and began to cut the door out. After what seemed like an eternity, the door was finally pulled out.

All of us pulled handkerchiefs out of our pockets and placed them over our noses. I thought the odor was bad before with the door closed, but now that it was torn off, the smell was absolutely overwhelming. The room was filled from the floor to the ceiling with raw sewage-- a sewer of pride. Plastic letters were mixed in with the sewage that formed a wall where the doorway had been. It was packed in so heavy and hard that it didn't even budge or sag when the door was removed. The door was one of those embossed doors, and you could see the imprint from the door in the sewage. The sewage was cached all the way to the ceiling.

> *Pride goes against everything you were designed to be.*

I stood in wonder mesmerized by something that was as solid as rice crispy squares except these were no rice crispies. A sticky sound penetrated the air as I gazed at the mucus covered wall that glistened with a slimy grossness. Goo slowly slid down the opening and formed a sticky puddle on the floor below.

The plastic letters had words on them. I put some gloves on and cleaned off some of the slime from the surface where I had pried some of the letters out with one hand while holding a handkerchief up to my nose with the other. The smell was so bad that my eyes stung from the raunchy smell wafting through the air.

As tears ran down my cheeks from the ammonia smell and I fought a gag reflex, I noted that the words on one of them said, "I", on another

The Throne Room

was the word "me", and another said "myself". One of the plastic letters that I pried out was in an accordion type design. As I finally pried it loose, I pulled on both ends and the words became clear as it straightened out. It said, "It's all about me!"

This definitely was a detestable throne room full of pride; spiritual pride, generational pride, and personal pride. This room was definitely all about me. The stench of this room made me almost gag (and it was my own stink)! I did not dare look at Emmanuel. "If only I had a toilet to throw up in," I said between gag reflexes.

"I hate pride with a passion," Emmanuel said. "It goes against everything that I am, and it goes against everything you were designed to be. As you can see, the shower doesn't work either because the toilet has been backing up sewage all the way to the ceiling. You cannot receive the blessings I am sending when self is in the way gunging everything up. Pride is the worst thing. Your pride has saturated and totally filled this room.

> *You cannot receive the blessings I am sending when self is in the way gunging everything up*

"When you are wallowing in your own pride, you don't notice it, but everyone else can see it," Emmanuel said resolutely. Emmanuel pointed his finger at a myriad of dark spots that were approximately two by four inches in a rectangular shape. "Those are blind spots. You can only see the ends of them because they are totally saturated with this sewage of pride, but they are what keep you from seeing the faults in your own life even though you see the faults in everyone else's life very easily."

"So those are called blind spots?" I asked inquisitively.

"No, those are two by fours that are sticking out of your eyes. Those are the beams in your own eyes that prevent you from seeing your short comings".

The Dwelling Place

Emmanuel looked me square in the eye without flinching and said authoritatively, "I am the Lord Your God and will not share my glory with another. I must be Lord of this room completely. All pride must go. It has to be Me in you not you all by yourself."

I humbly agreed. Emmanuel turned and walked five steps to the left of the throne room and paused as His hand rested on the door knob. I guess we were done with the throne room for the moment. I turned back to take one last look, paused and then turned to follow Emmanuel.

Emmanuel, by this time, was on a mission and was on a bee line for the next room. We were definitely on a mission to clean house. This next room was a particularly peculiar room, and I was right on his heals to uncover its secrets. The brass plate on the door reflected the dark lettering clearly. It was the *Powder Room*.

The Throne Room

Notes

6

THE POWDER ROOM

Being a guy, I had no clue as to why my house and heart sported a powder room. But Emmanuel was quick to reassure me that every man, woman and child had one.

As Emmanuel opened the door, He turned to me with a questioning look and said, "What is a powder room usually used for?"

"My wife would use it to put her make up on," I replied with much self deposed wisdom.

Emmanuel sauntered into the middle of the room and looked up surveying the room to take in its full contents.

"In this realm, this is the room where people put on a mask of make up to make themselves look different than they really are. It is about showing appearances, dressing up and so forth. It's to help make you look spiritually good," Emmanuel said wisely.

The Dwelling Place

"But I don't wear makeup," I protested. "Well, unless you count the two times I dressed up like a woman for a skit, but that was just acting."

"I know your heart," Emmanuel replied with a grin. "This is not what I am talking about, although I did find your skits humorous. I am talking about the mask that you wear to impress people."

Emmanuel walked further into the powder room and lifted his eyes up to gaze on the far wall. It contained a wooden shelf structure that was in a box design. Each box shelf had room for one mask.

"This is your heart and home and your masks are yours alone. The mask you have and wear may be totally different from someone else's mask. We are here, though to talk about yours." Emmanuel reached up pulling one of the masks off the shelf. It was a silly mask.

"Often, when you are around people, you come across as silly. You will say silly dumb things to cover over the rejection you feel inside. You will make jokes about everything. You put people down with your jokes. You say that you really don't mean it, but you speak snide things in a subtle way. You say one thing but mean another. You want people to like you, but this is not the way to make it happen. I want to heal you in this area so that your 'yes' will be 'yes' and your 'no' will be 'no'. You can be a fun, vibrant, colorful person and still be truthful and straightforward. I want people to see your real face. I want you to be genuine. My glory cannot shine through a silly face."

I gulped as Emmanuel picked up another mask. It was a smug mask. This mask had a cocky, prideful look on it.

"You have already seen what the 'throne room' looks like. This is how the throne room of pride expresses itself from your face in this smug mask. The more you know me, however, and learn My love, the more secure you will feel," Emmanuel responded. "My heart is to teach you to be humbly dependant on me. I see you as I created you and accept you

The Powder Room

as you are with all your flaws and weaknesses as well as your strengths and gifting. You don't need to put on airs for me or anyone. I want you to be genuine, kind and loving.

Emmanuel reached over and picked up another other mask. It had a holy, religious look on it. It was the face of a Pharisee. A Pharisee was a religious person in Jesus day that knew all the rules and regulations of the Bible, but they didn't have a personal relationship with God. He was principle driven. The law and rules were far superior to relationship.

"This is the face that you put on the most, my dear son. It is the face of trying to do the right religious thing at all cost. This religious behavior has been devoid of having an intimate relationship with Me. You no longer will need this face. You will find that relationship with Me comes from the inside of you and shines out from your natural face. As you walk with Me and develop a close relationship with Me, what you see in Me will begin to flow out of you."

I stood there stupefied as Emmanuel slowly moved from one face to the other. My mind was spinning as He gently but firmly explained each face to me. He paused for a moment and stood staring at the last box. There was one more face to be looked at and it was a fierce looking face. It had a dark brooding tone to it and looked very angry.

"This mask is the one you put on when things don't go your way. You started wearing this mask when you began pursuing the wrong things. If you put your trust and hope in material things, you will be on quicksand for you cannot depend on these things to always be there. Material things are unpredictable and fleeting. This will promote anger because you are trying to dominate, manipulate, and control something that is not possible to control. You will find that you don't need this mask any more either. My love and joy growing within you will be the purity and holiness flowing out of you."

The Dwelling Place

Emmanuel turned to look at me and opened His arms wide to give me a warm and intimate embrace. As He held me close, He whispered in my ear, "I am more than enough." As He finished saying that, He kissed me tenderly on my cheek while patting my back with His left hand.

I left the room in wonderment. My head was spinning. I reached up and touched my cheeks with both hands. The moistness of Emmanuel's lips left warmth that flowed gently from my head all the way down to the soles of my feet,

Was it really possible? Could I finally live a life without masks? I had mixed feelings over all of this and my emotions were exploding like fireworks on the fourth of July. This exposure by Emmanuel and His candidness left me feeling very vulnerable. In spite of all this, I felt safe. I did not get the impression that He was going to take this stuff that I hid behind and throw it back in my face or rip them off until I was ready.

These masks had protected me from getting hurt. They masked the wounds from years past. So to suggest that I did not need them or to encourage me to take them off would be a monumental accomplishment. To live with my heart on my sleeve (so to speak), would take great courage. To be vulnerable, yet saturated in God's love was still beyond my wildest comprehension, but I was getting a glimpse of what that could look like.

I pondered all this with careful thought. Emmanuel had put hope in my heart, and the love I was beginning to feel was causing me to believe that I could really experience life in a full and satisfying way. I felt warm and safe because of the honor that Emmanuel gave to me in this room. Wow! There was never any condemnation or judgment when I was with Him! It was so different…and refreshing! This hope was actually causing my emotions to thaw out and become pliable and soft.

The Powder Room

As I felt the warmth of His presence shining within, I heard another thumpity, thump resound in my ears and I smiled knowing that more stones were falling off the walls.

I had kind of expected that there would be a power struggle with Emmanuel forcing me to take the masks off. I was pleasantly surprised that this was not that way though. I had always seen God as one who had his thumb on me controlling my every move, yet it seemed that this was not the case at all. He taught me what was right yet left the choices up to me. I was slowing feeling my defenses coming down. It was His love. It was His love!!!

Maybe I could take the masks off. Maybe I could be real and genuine.

As I left the room a single thought was going through my mind. What did my real face look like? Would Emmanuel really like it?

Notes

7

THE BRIDAL CHAMBER

Emmanuel walked out of the powder room and turned towards the bedroom breaking the silence as he said, "Now that the bedroom is clean and swept, let's go back in there and see the awesome bridal chamber I have prepared for you."

As Emmanuel opened the door, I eagerly walked in behind Him. An amazing transformation had started happening since we had been examining the throne room. A holy fragrance filled my senses. Everything in the room from the bed sheets to the drapes was pure white, giving an inviting softness to the atmosphere.

Emmanuel turned to me with a wide smile and embraced me tenderly. For an hour He held me in His arms and said nothing. I had never felt such an intimacy and love before. Truly we were one spirit together. As Emmanuel held me tight, I could feel the heartbeat of God and it became one with my heart. Reservation slowly melted away into a trusting rest. I was beginning to learn to honor His presence. With all the gunk and junk that Emmanuel had seen and touched, I was in awe of Him

The Dwelling Place

because of the care and patient love He had for me. Here He had just exposed my pride and told me how much He hated it, yet two minutes later He was holding me like I was His most precious son. I felt totally accepted in His love and yet at the same time, I wanted to get rid of all this junk I had embraced for so long. I didn't desire it anymore. I was still trying to separate my identity from my junk but it was all becoming clearer. His goodness made me want to confess everything and turn from it forever. His love compelled me. This room was giving me a clear vision of what things should be.

"I love you, Jesus," I whispered reverently.

"I love you too, my son," Emmanuel said. "You are white as snow and most precious to me. I gave my life for you so you could live. I rescued you when you were perishing. I took you from the gutter and gave you a new home, these new clothes and whatever your heart desires. What you don't understand yet, is that I see you as my son filled with all my fullness. I see you differently than you see yourself. You see all the junk and mess in your life and see it as your identity. But in time, you too will see yourself like I see you. I see the junk on you, but not a part of you."

"All you need to do is ask and I will give you anything you ask. All I ask is that you respond in love to me and believe in me. This is not because I need your love but rather because you were designed to receive my love. I love to receive you love. It gives me great pleasure but it actually completes you when you respond back to me the love I have placed within you. So respond with the love and belief I have placed within you. Trust me, for I will never leave you or forsake you. You are my greatest treasure."

As Emmanuel continued to lavish His love on me, I felt more and more doors in my heart opening up. I had told Emmanuel 'whatever it takes', but now I was experiencing the delicious fruits of my choice to

The Bridal Chamber

totally abandon myself and trust Him completely. I felt myself melting into His chest, and the bands of stress that circled my upper body began to melt away.

Through His unending love and tenderness, I felt helplessness, hopelessness, and despair wash off me like dirt in the shower. I continued to open my heart to Emmanuel. The more I yielded the more revelation and understanding of the character of God I experienced. He was worthy to be trusted. I was learning and experiencing that surrender to the Trinity Three had done nothing but give me total life and freedom.

I had expected my surrender to be accompanied by my being made to do things and yet…. these guys were always patient, always kind, and always protecting. I shook my head, and I say almost ….in unbelief.

Already, I was watching what I was saying. It was not because I had to, but because I felt an honor welling up within me. I wanted to please Emmanuel.

"In my life, Lord, be glorified," I breathed out slowly. That had been such a religious stained glass window phrase before, but I was feeling the freshness and the freedom of it now. It was so real to me.

I turned my attention back to Emmanuel. He really did love me…unconditionally. I was learning to trust Him. I couldn't help it as I gave Him an impulsive bear hug. I did not feel like He was asking for anything and yet I wanted to give Emmanuel everything. The fact that He did not need my love but still wanted to be intimate with me because He genuinely enjoyed me was overwhelming, to say the least.

> *The fact that He did not need my love but still wanted to be intimate with me because he genuinely enjoyed me overwhelmed me.*

After an extended time in the bridal chamber, Emmanuel and I opened the door and stepped into the hallway. I was feeling ten feet tall.

The Dwelling Place

"I feel like I'm getting more and more holy," I said to Comforter, as I waved a hand expansively in front of me.

Comforter placed a loving hand on my shoulder and gave it a gentle squeeze, "Don't misunderstand what is happening here, My son. When you invited Father God to be your Father and Jesus to save you, you became a new creation. You became a one of a kind, unique person unlike anyone else. You also became complete in Christ. The dirtiness you see is more your viewpoint of yourself than Ours. When you saw through Our eyes, it was to protect you from temptation from the evil one. It was not how We see you. We see you clean, perfect and holy.

"Your rooms becoming clean is a revelation being opened up to you about how you should see yourself? As the lies are exposed and the truth is established, the junk associated with that lie has to go. We want you to experience yourself the way We see you. We see you without the lies because We are the truth. You are just now getting a glimpse of the reality of the real you!

> *Do not confuse your destiny with your identity. You need to understand you have a destiny but concentrate on what I am revealing to you about your identity*

"You are learning how much I love you and that I can be trusted," Emmanuel said fondly. "Before God you stand righteous and pure. We need to get you to the place where you see yourself the same way God sees you. God sees you as perfect, because of My death on the cross. I took your sin on myself and died in your place. Because I was the substitute for your sin, I paid the price. Now you can stand before a holy God without any fear at all. You need to see this as normal, not something you have attained that makes you superior."

I was beginning to see that the cleaning of my heart was to enable me to see who I already was. As I was mulling this over in my spirit, I

The Bridal Chamber

heard Emmanuel say, "Let's go forward and look at some other areas of your heart."

"What about my destiny?" I questioned.

"Do not confuse your destiny with your identity," Emmanuel said emphatically. You need to understand you have a destiny, but concentrate on what I am revealing to you about your identity. If you don't know how to separate the two, you will fall back into religion. I want to spend more time helping you to discover who you are."

Emmanuel's eyes seemed to pierce deep into the inner most depth of my heart as He said this. Despite His penetrating gaze, I did not look away this time. I felt totally comfortable with His forthrightness.

"I'm ready," I replied eagerly. "I know you will only do what is good for me and reveal it in me in Your perfect time."

Emmanuel smiled as he turned towards the hallway. As I followed, I arched my eyebrows together in a wiggly shape. I kind of was getting it, but I kind of was not. Emmanuel was saying that I am perfect, and yet He is cleaning out my heart. He says I have a new heart, but yet here He is doing all this stuff like cleaning out the dirty rooms and the evilness that was lurking within. And the painting, it seemed like He was always painting the walls...sometimes it was several times a day. I just didn't get it all yet. He says I have a destiny, but I feel like my identity is part of my destiny. Wow! Aaaaarrrggghhh!

Understanding did seem to be softening me as each room was dealt with one by one. The stones were falling off the walls one by one and the heights of the mazes in the rooms had diminished.

In fact as I pondered this, I felt a slight tremor as various stones fell off the mazes and landed on the floor. As I was beginning to walk in humility and teachablitiy the mortar could not sustain itself and started to disintegrate.

The answers still eluded me, but I knew that it would all make sense soon. Sometimes you have to get to the end to see the beginning...or so I thought. I let out a deep sigh! My head was spinning! Where did Emmanuel go? I think I need another drink!

The Bridal Chamber

Notes

8

THE PANTRY

"Before I take you down the hallway of shame, we need to visit the pantry," Emmanuel said in a matter of fact voice while holding two glasses of water in His hand. I did a double take, as if had just taken two punches, a left and a right one. There was a hallway of shame? What was that all about? I have a pantry in my heart? Wasn't having the refrigerator stocked with rotten fruit enough?

I sighed again as a feeling of strong apprehension and panic came over me. Pantries were usually places where you store things for a future time. I was not seeing the glass half full here. Doubt and fear were having a hay day as they gurgled and flip flopped within me.

"Cheer up," Emmanuel chirped, with a broad smile on His face. "It is not at all what it seems. You're going to love what I am going to show you." Emmanuel opened the door for my viewing pleasure. I tentatively poked my nose in seeing a fairly large expansive room. It was about the size of an average bedroom but with shelves from floor to ceiling. The shelves were about ten inches apart and covered most of the room.

The Dwelling Place

A desk was at the end of the room and a young woman was busy marking bottles and mixing ingredients to be put on the shelves. Boxes and bags that were ready to be mixed were on the floor.

Out of the corner of my eye, I saw one of devlin's henchmen dropping off a box and quickly disappearing. Had I not been watching, I probably would not even have noticed.

"What in the world is devlin's henchman doing here?" I muttered to myself." I turned my attention to the room and started wondering, "What did all the canned goods and mason jars represent, and what were all these goodies?"

Everything was categorized alphabetically in sections from A through Z.

I picked up the first jar as it was in the 'A' section. I knit my brows together rather perplexed. The label read 'A*ches and pains*'. "This is odd," I thought, "What am I going to do with that?" I rubbed a spot on my neck that had started to hurt as I moved to the 'C' section. This was quite a large section and I began to read the bottles. The first bottle read 'C*ancer of the lungs*' (subtitled: cigarette smoking), another read 'C*ancer of the throat*' (subtitled: gossip and slander). Another one read 'C*ancer of the left breast*' (subtitled: hating a relative); 'C*ancer of the right breast*' (subtitle: hatred of a neighbor or friend). 'C*ancer of the genitals*' (subtitled: adultery, fornication). In the "E" section was a bottle that said "Ear aches" (subtitled: listening to evil/gossip/slander). Another was "Blurry eyes" (subtitled: lust of the eyes/ lust of the flesh); Throat cancer, (subtitled: gossip); Gall stones (bitterness).

I frowned as I pondered the significance of these bottles that I had stored in my pantry for cancer of the lungs. I didn't have cancer, sickness or any of these diseases. I latched onto the bottle that said, "Cancer of the lungs". I had only smoked a half of a cigarette when I was sixteen.

The Pantry

Was that enough to put this little bottle in my pantry? It didn't seem quite fair.

The girl was working hard to match up diseases and sicknesses to corresponding parts of the body. They were being stored up for a later date. These bottles were like seeds and they seemed to grow in size depending on how I fed my mind with positive or negative thoughts. As the heart had need of these supplies, it could draw upon them for either good or bad.

"Interesting," I thought. "I wonder if there is a medical basis for all this. Everything does seem to have a design and a purpose here. It is as if seeds were being planted or stored up now for a latter time...hhhhmmm!" I was rubbing my chin hard. I could see someone outside of this spiritual realm scoffing at all this. I could see the medical field would have a hay day with this room. "We were not in the 'real' world. At least not the one you could see with your natural eyes. We were in a spiritual realm. How much though, filtered through to the real world." I picked at my lip as I tried to fathom all of this. Could these bottles be removed from this pantry? Could I stop them from getting bigger?

My eye caught the word *'Punishment'* in the 'p' section. Curious, I picked up a bottle of punishment. After the title *'Punishment'* was the words 'terrible' in parenthesis. Under it was the subtitle: stubbornness in turning from sin. (Rom 2:5).

"Wow!" I thought. "I am storing up terrible punishment because I have been stubborn in not turning from my sin." I looked for a wastebasket. Finding one in the corner, I said, "Well, I'm not receiving that one anymore. I have committed myself to turning from any and all sin, and I am following God."

In my preoccupation with all these horrid bottles, I was now realizing that I had been storing up destructive things in my heart. I looked at the

The Dwelling Place

bottle in my hand that said *Cancer of the Left Breast*. Sub title: bitterness towards a relative.

"Is every left breast cancer prone to some kind of cancer because of bitterness towards a relative?" I murmured half out loud as I reached up and squeezed my chest. "Could any of this be reversed?" I would have to ask Emmanuel about this. My train of thought was interrupted as I heard:

"This room has to be cleaned out by faith," Emmanuel said. "Whatever is not of faith is sin. You will need words of knowledge and revelation from Rhema to help you. Comforter will teach you what you need to know. You have to be offensively minded in this room. You have to find out my promises in the Word and root these things out one at a time. You are no longer under the curse, but you must call out to Me to be set free. The important thing here is that you now know what bad ingredients you have been storing up in your pantry."

> You have my permission to become good at knowing Me and my permission is filled with revelation. I deeply want you to experience me in all of your five senses and in every way. This is my heart's desire for you

"I only want you to store up things in this room that give you life, not death. You will be amazed at the wonderful things you can store up here," Emmanuel said as He slipped His arm around my waist and gave me a man squeeze. Some things will be used daily and some will be for different seasons. Repentance is foundational here. Action must be taken. Your life and health depend on it. Everything here can still be reversed."

I noticed a wooden plaque on the wall just inside the door. It had one hook on it. On that hook was one key. As I stood there looking at this key hanging on the hook, I heard a scratching sound behind me.

The Pantry

Again it was Rhema writing on His notepad. Thoughts began to flood my mind.

"Remember the safety deposit box? I (Emmanuel) have already turned my key. You must search the scriptures, and receive revelation from Rhema and Comforter to remove each harmful jar and can one by one."

I began to visualize a small treasure chest. It looked like an ancient security box. I was being handed a magnificent key. It was the key to the kingdom. I saw myself accepting this key and opening up the treasure box. Inside the box was another set of keys. I noticed names that where inscribed on the handle to each key. As I strained to look at the inscription, the picture faded away.

I turned to Emmanuel with a question mark in my eyes as to what this meant. Emmanuel responded. "All that you see is yours. I freely give it to you. The more time you spend in my presence and the more you hunger and thirst after my Word, these deep truths will reveal themselves to you. These are the keys that will bring power and authority into your life. I can see that very soon these keys will be operating fully in your life. You must dive deep into the river of my Presence to find these keys. I am not holding these keys from you but am holding them for you. When the time is right the vision will reveal itself to you and the keys will be available to you. They will be revealed to the one who practices intimacy with me. Be patient for you are on the right path. Each key is linked to intimacy with my Presence. Practice makes perfect; perfect means skilled. The one who is skilled in knowing me is the one who practices my Presence. Include Me in everything you say and do. This is the man who can say that he knows His God and can call Him Friend. You have my permission to become good at knowing Me and my permission is filled with revelation. I deeply want you to experience me in all of your five senses and in every way. This is my heart's desire for you."

The Dwelling Place

I turned back to look at all the canned goods, jars and bottles. "Wow!" I said, "That was an eloquent and powerful Word!"

Emmanuel seemed to ignore my last statement and with great enthusiasm stated, "Do not fear for God has overcome the world and so must you. Never give up! People are dying prematurely all over the world because they do not know God's Promises and claim them. They do not abide in Me and let My Words abide in them. They are not walking in forgiveness. You have a mess here, but you are to be very encouraged. Look at how much we have accomplished in such a short time, and I have given Comforter to you to come along side and help you. He is an awesome help isn't he?" Comforter beamed a radiant smile at Emmanuel as he slid his hand across my shoulder and gave me a big squeeze.

"What about the young girl," I asked.

"She can only hurt you if you give her ingredients to mix that will harm you," Emmanuel replied. "She is grieved when you give her bad ingredients and you can even numb her if you give her enough bad ingredients to mix, especially when the ingredients are given in deliberate rebellion and pride. She is happiest and free when she can stock the shelves with cans and vitamins that bring you life. Her name is *Conscience*. Even though she lives in the pantry, you will feel her presence within you. She will be most useful to you as you obey My words and promises. If you give her good ingredients she will stock the shelves with good things; if you give her bad ingredients then she will stock it with bad things.

> She is happiest and free when she can stock the shelves with cans and vitamins that bring you life. Her name is Conscience

"I am going to give Conscience a new duty though."

Turning to Conscience, Emmanuel spoke urgently, "Your new responsibility will be to let the owner of this heart know when wrong

The Pantry

ingredients are being sent here to be mixed. You are free to express yourself and inform him of bad ingredients coming into this house.

Emmanuel placed both His hands on Conscience head as He said, "You will be governed by truth. I brand it on your heart. Be a help to John."

Emmanuel turned back to me holding two walkie-talkies in His hand. Here is a set of walkie-talkies. One is for you and one is for you," Emmanuel said with a deep intenseness in His eyes as He handed me a walkie-talkie and Conscience the other. You are to communicate with each other. If Conscience beeps you to warn you of something, bring it to Comforter or Myself. We will search the scriptures together with you to make sure all is done in faith and obedience. I nodded in agreement. It sounded like a safe plan.

"On this side of eternity Conscience is designed to work hand and glove together with Comforter. The two are compatible together," Emmanuel said pointedly.

I could see clearly now that one who didn't allow Comforter to work hand in glove would have to try and sear his conscience because self would be trying to do its own thing.

I shuddered to think of the horror of one who had to spend an eternity in hell with conscience accusing you and telling you over and over again where you were wrong without the ability to respond with repentance or being able to correct things. I did not relish that thought even in the slightest bit.

With renewed fervor, I scanned the shelves; I looked under 'L' for life, and picked up a bottle called *'Long life'*. Under it was the subtitle 'honor your father and mother.' Under 'J' was a bottle called *'Joy juice'* (subtitle: strong bones).

The Dwelling Place

Curious, I wondered what kind of vitamins could be listed here. "I need a *strength vitamin*," I thought. "What do we have here? Ah! Yes. I looked approvingly as I saw the subtitle: 'wait on the Lord'."

"Wow!" I said, "Whatever I put in this pantry will ultimately determine my health or my sickness. How amazing is that!" I noticed that 'D', 'F', and 'U' section were quite large. I frowned as I read the titles 'Doubt', 'Fear', and 'Unbelief'. A myriad of subtitles were listed under the hundreds of bottles that were stored here. I growled silently, as I thought to myself, "This is God's house. Why am I storing up these wrong ingredients on the shelves of my pantry? I have been serving God my whole life, but I have been trying to do it my way. Because I have been doing it my own way, I have been storing up ingredients that encouraged and bred all kinds of sickness and disease. It is what I had let my mind dwell upon all this time and now here I could see the results."

> Whatever I put in this pantry will ultimately determine my health or my sickness

I noticed that one of devlin's henchmen was back trying to sneak ingredients back in to introduce more bad ingredients to be mixed.

"What are these dudes doing in here?" I snorted in indignation, as I observed the little thing scurry across the floor leaving a slim trail behind him. I gave him a swift kick, which sent him flying across the floor causing him to bang his head on the wall and fall into a crumpled heap on the floor. Grabbing up a dust pan and broom, I swept him into the dustpan and whipped him out the front door.

I had heard a pastor say that sickness and disease comes from the devil, but I was seeing that my wrong choices and willful disobedience, and to some degree my lack of understanding of the promises of God, had caused a lot of this. I needed to make conscience my ally and let her perform her intended purpose by working closely with Comforter.

The Pantry

I observed that these little creatures were here because they were allowed to, not because they had a right. A door had been opened up that they could pass through. They were like mice in the house; unwanted guests. They did seem to be much smaller than before, and some boxes that they used to be able to carry into the pantry where too heavy for them now. I wondered what that was all about

Notes

9

THE HALLS OF SHAME

I turned from the Pantry as Emmanuel walked past me into the hallway. I was pondering these thoughts when Comforter spoke up. "This is a very critical place to clean up because you have to pass through these halls to get to the other rooms."

Emmanuel had gone to the throne room to do some cleaning. He was zealously cleaning out the sewer of pride and seemed to be enjoying Himself immensely. He was singing at the top of His lungs, "Choose Today". It was one of the songs I had written.

"That's amazing!" I thought. Emmanuel was having a riot of a time singing my song.

> **If you love your life you lose**
> **If this World has a hold on you**
> **If the things you hold dear**
> **Hold your life in deepest fear**

The Dwelling Place

**And your life has lost meaning and hop
Then take it to the cross
Consider all but loss
All my houses and lands
All my dreams and all my plans
What I think, what I say, what I do
Belong to you.**

©2006 Choose Today
Words and Music by John M. Davidson

My feeling good about Emmanuel singing my song was short lived, though, as I began to walk down the hallways of shame. I felt a sense of blame, shame, and condemnation as I meandered down these hallways. On the walls were pictures of all my past failures. I remember so many times devlin bringing me into this hallway to discourage me from relationship with the Lord or stepping out for Jesus. He would point his bony finger at me and rip me up and down about all my failures.

"You're not worthy and you have no right. There is no sense in trying. You're going to fail anyway," he would say.

The walls were covered with business failures, personal failures, bad decisions, broken relationships, bitterness, criticisms, bad memories, and bad experiences. It was a hall of clutter and confusion. It was the hallway of regret. I stumbled as I walked over a pile of clutter that was lying on the floor.

I held my hand up to my heart and clutched my chest as the pain and sorrow of this room overwhelmed me.

Comforter put His arm around my shoulders and began to comfort me as he taught me about the cross and how Jesus had taken the curse on himself. Through His resurrection from the dead, He now had established a new covenant, based on faith, and we could bring all those memories to the Cross to be washed by the blood of Jesus.

The Halls of Shame

"You are worthy and you have a right. It is not a 'self' right but a 'God' right. You have a right to be called a son of God because God has declared it so. You have put your faith and trust in me and confessed your sins. It is worth the fight and I have every confidence that you will be an over comer to the end."

As I looked at all the clutter, it resembled some kind of a material thing. You could pick up each failure, decision, criticism, or memory off the floor and look at it. Each item had a black button attached to it. I tried to pull them off but they would not budge.

"What are these black buttons with a 'd' on them for?" I asked, confused because I couldn't seem to pull the black buttons off.

"Each item has a demon attached to them. Comforter stated emphatically, "To get rid of these you have to confess with your mouth the Lord Jesus and remove that demon's right to function in your life. You must confess that you don't want them to operate their lies in you. You must sever all soul ties with that spirit and send them back to the feet of Jesus,"

> He taught me about the cross and how Jesus had taken the curse on himself. Through His resurrection from the dead, He now had established a new covenant, which basis was in faith and we could bring all those memories to the cross to be washed by the blood of Jesus.

"The Lord Jesus Christ has given you that authority," (Mark 16:18) Comforter exclaimed as He smacked His fist in His other hand. The loud smacking sound startled me, but it had the desired effect of driving Comforter's point home so I would remember it.

"This hall has become devlin's stronghold in your life. He knows that if he can stop you in this hallway, he can shut you off from the rest of your heart. He will have created a bottleneck. Shame, blame, and regret are some of His greatest tools to shut you down so you won't be effective. He will close you down and you will never know your full potential. He wants to drive you towards death and destruction. He will force you to have a heart attack by keeping you from occupying and using the majority of your heart. This hallway is a major artery and must be cleared of the cholesterol of doubt, fear and unbelief. We can't have you experiencing victory in one area and then go to another room and experience regrets; it's onward and upward." Comforter arched His back, stood up straight and pretended like He was marching. Turning back to me, he looked me squarely in the eyes with an infectious smile.

"You know he really is so insignificant and small. If you only knew how powerless and puny devlin really is," Comforter explained patiently. "It is all smoke and mirrors."

Comforter was teaching me to discern that blame, shame and guilt were brought on by devlin. Regret will freeze you and keep you from being productive in the present. I determined from that moment on that I would not give my energy to regret and failure. They definitely were time wasters.

> He now had established a new covenant, which basis was faith and we could bring all those memories to the Cross to be washed by the blood of Jesus.

"The Holy Spirit is the one who brings conviction, repentance and forgiveness," I reasoned. "I was to repent and move on."

"Behold I make all things new," Comforter said. "You must learn to listen to the right voice and learn the voice of your Father.

"You do that by confessing out loud the attributes of the Father and spending time in His presence. The right thing can be said to you, but if you are not listening to the right person, you will hear it wrong and it will come across as blame, shame and guilt. When you feel bad it is a warning sign that you believe some kind of lie about yourself."

The Halls of Shame

Just knowing what I knew in these last few minutes seemed to develop strength and courage within me. I was seeing firsthand devlin's strategy to accuse, blame and shame me into curling up into a ball and feeling sorry for myself. If he could keep me focused on my past failures, I would not look ahead and fix my eyes on Jesus. I would not stay close to Emmanuel and would drift from Him by feeling sorry and depressed. I could already visualize the toilet starting to overflow...

"Not gonna do it!" I said with a southern drawl. "I'm on to your schemes; no more regrets." We would deal with things as they came up and move on.

We were interrupted to see Emmanuel running back from the throne room beaming from ear to ear. "I got the throne room cleaned out!" He said with exuberance. It looks beautiful! I am so excited with the results!"

"That was fast," I said with an obvious admiration.

> *You must learn to listen to the right voice and learn the voice of your Father*

"When you laid it all on the line," Emmanuel said excitedly, "and humbled yourself, it all turned to goo. It was amazing! It was so easy to clean up. You ought to see it now. The toilet is flushing efficiently and eliminating waste. I even put a special red die in a container in the back of the bowl. Whenever you release the lever, it will continually wash things white as snow. The awesome thing is that this container will never ever run out of bowl cleaner."

The look on Emmanuel's face was priceless. If you ever looked in your child's eyes, and saw the unabashed excitement and joy of getting some treasure that they had asked for and dreamed of, that is the closest thing I could compare it to.

Emmanuel was so excited. His joy was contagious.

The Dwelling Place

"He hates pride, but He gets so much joy out of humility. No wonder he lifts up and honors the person who humbles himself before God," I thought to myself.

I looked at Emmanuel and shook my head. He was so unpretentious. He tackled every job with quiet purpose and He did not seem to mind how ugly or dirty the job was. He got such a kick out of cleaning up other people's messes. I looked Him up and down and saw that most of His clothes were soaked in the sewage from cleaning it up. He had taken my pride upon Himself. He who knew no sin had taken my sin upon himself.

Tears welled up in my eyes. The verse in 1 Corinthians 13 came to mind which said that "He seeks not His own way. He bears all things and he believes all things." It seemed that Emmanuel just gave and gave and gave some more. He never stopped giving; He always believed that I would do the right thing and live the way He designed me to be. He had complete and full confidence in me.

As I meditated on this, it dawned on me that because of this revelation of His love it would be a motivation for me to live pure and holy before Him. It would not be out of duty though, but out of love...because I wanted to.

"The tendency for pride, or any sin for that matter, needed to be flushed and eliminated daily," I pondered slowly. " It is just the same as we daily, without a thought, eliminate waste from our lives," (1 John 1:7). I was so happy that I had come to this new diagnosis. I had not yet made the connection that Rhema was busy writing on His notepad off to the side as I continued to sort these things out in my mind.

I determined to make a mental note that I would make this a priority in the future. I really needed to learn how to walk in humility and remain teachable all the time. I hadn't figured it out yet that the thought I had just gotten was from Rhema scribbling on His note pad. Rhema smiled as I continued to try and reason things through. It didn't seem to bother Him

The Halls of Shame

if I took credit for His thoughts. He also knows the end from the beginning.

I looked in the shower and gave thumbs up. It was a body shower and had showerheads coming from every angle. Overhead, a huge twelve inch rain shower was just waiting to be used.

From now on, I would give God all the glory for all the great and awesome things He had done and was doing in and through my life. After all, I was His son now, and that is what sons do, they give honor to their Fathers.

Everything I am and ever will be is because of Him," I whispered with a quiet gratefulness. I was beginning to find my identity as Emmanuel's son.

"This is the greatest," I said beaming from ear to ear. "I can receive blessings from every angle. All I have to do is to ask in faith and make sure all my sins are confessed, and listen to papa Daddy. Then turn on the lever over here and blessings will rain down on me. In fact, this looks so inviting; I am going to take a hot shower right now." The thought of receiving blessings got me really excited.

Emmanuel slapped me on the shoulder laughing as He said, "I think I'll grab a shower of my own when you're finished. I love receiving blessings from Father.

Grabbing a towel from the closet, I grinned back at Emmanuel, proceeded to undress and turned all the body shower heads on. Minutes later I was basking in amazing blessings.

10

THE HALLS OF FAITH

The halls of shame had just been swept and cleaned. Every attachment and defilement had also been removed. You could just feel the freedom in the air and it was breathtaking. It was during this time that Emmanuel said He had an awesome surprise for me. He pointed to a door in the hallway with no door handle and no lock. Emmanuel told me to stand behind Him as He opened the door.

` "What I am about to show you is just the beginning, not just a onetime experience," Emmanuel said in hushed tones. "This is going to rock your socks!"

Emmanuel opened the door just a crack. It could not have been more than a half of an inch, yet the profound impact of what Emmanuel gave me the privilege of experiencing was absolutely breath taking. A light shone through the small crack of the opening, but what hit me sent me falling immediately on my face on the floor. The holiness of God and the light of His presence, like a strong perfume, caught me and literally wiped me out. I immediately sensed a burning within my chest and lung

The Halls of Faith

areas like I had never experienced. The closest thing I can relate it to be, is if I had been drinking too much and breathing in the frigid winter air in Alberta Canada in late January, but the comparison was so absolutely ridiculous. I was almost paralyzed. The purity of the burning was the most awesome thing.

Now, I was not a stranger to feeling a burning inside my chest, but this was very different. My usual experience with burning in my chest was like a blow torch which destroyed my insides. I would feel hollow, empty, and it hurt so bad. This was a whole different ball game though. It was a burning that felt like a fire, but it cleansed, purified and filled me with a sweet Presence.

I began to weep as the holiness of the Father burned within me. "So this is the power of Godliness," I whispered quietly as I breathed out slowly. The greatness and the awesomeness of God were seared within me in that moment. In all of this time, yes, decades of time, I finally had tasted the essence of Father's Presence. I lay still, sobbing before Him. I would forever be changed by this moment. A new respect and awe replaced any cavalier attitude I ever had for Emmanuel, Rhema, and Comforter. Holiness had taken on a whole new meaning

> *I was in shock and awe at the awesome holiness of God*

"What was that?" I gasped as I tried to involuntarily suck in a breath of air.

"You just felt and experienced the very outer edge of the Presence of the Father," Emmanuel exclaimed, with a huge smile. "You have been allowed to get a taste of the Father's Holiness because of the work that I have done in your heart."

"I am undone!" I cried out. Although I was humbled before the Father, I felt a surprising strength and boldness. I was clean and purified

The Halls of Faith

by the Holiness of God. An incredible peace totally enveloped me. I felt no need to do anything but lay there.

"Be still and know that I am God."

Although I did not here an audible voice, so to speak, I knew it was Fathers voice whispering quietly to my spirit.

How long I lay there, I do not know. I do know that when I got up I could hardly walk. All day long this burning was in my heart. I could not seem to stop speaking in tongues the whole day. I was in shock and awe at the awesome Holiness of God. Because of Emmanuel's love and my faith in Him, I could come fearlessly into God's Presence and be assured of His glad welcome (Eph 3:12). God wanted me to come into His Presence, but His revealing Holiness changed me. I had not seen the Father, but had felt His results. Oh, how I longed to see Him! I wanted to know and personally experience the Father. I wanted more!

> *I paused for a moment to enjoy the exhilaration of freedom*

"Thank You, Emmanuel!" I exclaimed. This journey of 'whatever it takes' was having incredible results. I began to have a hunger and thirst for more. My vision and thoughts were clearer.

My desire and resolve were stronger and I wanted more. "Show me more of your glory!" I gasped. "Let me see more of your Holiness. Open the door to your presence and stretch me. Wipe me out with more than I can take."

I began to see that there were levels of revelation about having freedom and boldness to enter the throne room and stand before God. I had been standing boldly before the throne of God, but now I was given the privilege to experience that awesome Holiness of God.

The Halls of Faith

"I want to be able to hear and discern your thoughts and intents," I prayed fervently. I stepped back a minute and paused as I thought about what I had just said. A scripture verse popped into my head that stated:

> "My thoughts are not your thoughts and my ways are not your ways says the Lord"

(Isaiah 55:8) KJV

Feeling humbled by the Word yet undaunted, I responded passionately, "You've given me a new heart and spirit to be able to hear your thoughts and ways. I will not settle for this..." I waited for a response, but it was surprisingly quiet.

A few days later we passed through the same hallway. I paused for a moment to enjoy the exhilaration of freedom. There was no condemnation now in these hallways. Gonzo! This was truly astonishing! Emmanuel again invited me to the same doorway. I braced myself again for the same shock and awe of the holiness of God. This time however, the door opened without a hitch, and we stepped into the very throne room of God. The room was very bright with Roman style pillars. At the end of the long room was a very large marble throne. It had to be fifty feet high. On the throne sat God the Father. I could not see His face because it was so very bright.

"I thought I would feel the Holiness of God like I did a couple days earlier," I said almost complaining. I looked over at Emmanuel with an uncertainty. Instead of the feeling I had experienced the other day, I felt uncomfortable, almost like I was standing before the judgment seat and great fear of abandonment and rejection overwhelmed me. I shivered as a cold dampness seemed to penetrate right through me.

I turned again to Emmanuel whose eyes were filled with deep love and compassion. "What do you see?" Emmanuel asked.

The Halls of Faith

"I am seeing God the Father," I replied.

"I know, but what do you see," Emmanuel stated pressing me further

"I see God the Father sitting on a throne and His face is very bright. All I can see is an outline," I replied plainly.

Emmanuel smiled compassionately as he said, "What you see is your perception of God the Father. The relationship you had with your earthly father has created this image. You are viewing your Heavenly Father through your experience. You see your Heavenly Father as judgmental, cold and out of reach. Your relationship with your earthly father was cold and distant. The love you experienced from him was conditional. When you failed him, or acted out of pride, or you did not reach his expectation, he cut you off."

"You had to perform to a certain level to gain acceptance with your father, and because of that you have projected that on your Heavenly Father. You cannot get a clear picture, because your relationship with your father was not clear. You cannot see the eyes of your Heavenly Father because you are afraid they will contain the same disappointment and pain you felt your earthly father had towards you. That pain is too great for you so you would rather view His face as a non descript bright light. You feel no physical touch or trust because you did not experience that as a child."

> *Your earthly father was human and made mistakes; your heavenly father though is perfect*

A memory of when I was twenty-five years old flashed before me. I had gone to visit my father to tell him I was getting married again. Somehow we had gotten into an argument, and in his anger he told me he was sorry I was his son. I groaned and fell to my knees as I felt the memory and weight of those words crushing me.

The Halls of Faith

"Your earthly father was human and made mistakes. He spoke out of anger and that was not His true intent." Emmanuel said with deep tenderness. "Your Heavenly Father, though, is perfect; but you do not see Him perfectly. Devlin has convinced you to believe lies about what Father God is like. Would you like to see what your heavenly Father really looks like?"

Eagerly, I looked at Emmanuel with a hunger of a starving child who had not eaten in a week. "Yes!" I cried out, nodding my head up and down. "I want that more than ever."

Instantly the scene changed and I was walking up the drive to the most beautiful mansion I had ever seen. As I looked up at all its splendor, I saw a man coming out the front door and running towards me as fast as he could. He was an average, ordinary man who looked like the loving father I had envisioned a perfect father to be like…. but more. He was jumping up and down and waving His arms. As we drew closer to each other, He called out "Son, it is so good to see you. I have been looking for you." He grabbed me in a big bear hug and held me close for several minutes, not saying a word as he continued to kiss the side of my face over and over. "I've missed you so much. How have you been?"

> Son, I am so proud of you. You are all the man I ever hoped or dreamed you would be. I brag about you to all my friends

After a few intimate minutes, he held me at arm's length and looked me up and down with great pride in his voice. "Son, I am so proud of you. You are all the man I ever hoped or dreamed you would be. I brag about you to all my friends. Come! Come! I killed our finest cow. Its prime rib tonight; I've prepared the choicest cuts. The whole family is here to celebrate your coming home. Come, take a shower and change into some new clothes I bought for you. This is going to be the best night of our lives."

The Halls of Faith

I remained mesmerized. He was proud of me? I am all the man He hoped I would be? What was He seeing that I didn't?

As we walked arm in arm, my father brought me up on all the family business and shared his new plans to partner me in. He was so excited. He told me everything he had was mine. He even had a new house planned out to build for me. He had blue prints, but wanted my input on designs to incorporate into it.

"What did my father see in me that I didn't," I mused. Why did He not judge me for the wrong things I had done? Should He not be focusing on my shortcomings? My preoccupation was interrupted as Father said,

"I did the preliminary stuff just the way you like it. But wait, tell me everything. What has been going on in your life lately? How is your family? How is your work?" Father God proceeded to sit down and drop everything. All His attention was on me. It was amazing and wonderful. He did not seem to mind that I had spent the last few years in the bars; had lived my life only for myself and had abused my body, or even that I had told Him a few years ago I wanted nothing more to do with Him. He only had eyes for me and they were filled with His amazing love. For hours we talked. Well, it was more like I talked, and He listened. Time did not seem to matter at all.

My heart melted as the love that never failed was poured out on me. I got a clear picture that I was a son and nothing could separate me from that relationship. What I did or didn't do had nothing to do with my being a son. Even though I had briefly disowned Him, he never disowned me. Even in my dream, I was having a hard time wrapping my thoughts around that one. "What about my performance or lack of it?" I mused.

Eventually when there was a lull in the conversation, Father asked me what my needs were and what could He do to help. Whatever I wanted, my Father spared nothing when it came to my needs. He always thought of everything. He abundantly blessed even my family and

The Halls of Faith

friends. That night we feasted and drank in celebration into the wee hours. It was fabulous. Eventually, I fell asleep.

When I awoke, I was standing in the hallway with Emmanuel. Emmanuel looked at me with a twinkle in His eye and waved His arm towards the hallway. "Did you have a nice sleep?"

"Marvelous," I replied. "Was I dreaming?" I asked?

"Not at all," Emmanuel exclaimed. "It was as real as you and I standing here right now. Isn't the Father awesome?" I nodded in wonderment. I looked at my hand and noticed a diamond encrusted ring set in solid gold. It was a signet ring and bore God the Father's name on it. "This is really cool," I said with wonder." I pulled off the ring to look at it up close, and saw writing on the inside. It said,

"To my favorite son. Love, Dad."

I sat down staggering at the recollection of what I thought I had dreamed; now realizing it was reality.

"I was His favorite?" I could hardly fathom the thought.

> *I looked at my hand and noticed a diamond encrusted ring set in solid gold. It was a signet ring and bore God the Father's name on it*

"Hold that ring dear," Emmanuel said passionately. "Never take it off. That is a ring of authority. That is one of the identifying marks that you are our Fathers Son." Emmanuel extended his hand and showed me His. They were a matching pair. "You have the same authority that I have with the Father." Emmanuel beamed as He gave me a big hug and spoke with great pride, "You and I are one in Spirit. Come hold my hand for a moment. We need to bring the finished work of the cross on this important moment of time with our Father and yours."

I reached for Emmanuel's hand and immediately found myself transported back to that time when I was standing before an angry

The Halls of Faith

father—my dad. Suddenly, I felt Emmanuel's hand holding mine and reaching for my earthly father's hand. As the connection was made, suddenly I saw my earthly father in a new light. The pain immediately vanished, and all I could see and feel was the Father's love. I could feel how the Father loved me, and I could feel how the Father loved my dad. A great compassion came over me as I felt the hurts and pain that he had as a father. I felt the father wound that my father had from his father and family, a deep pain which had been such a disappointment to him and transferred to me melt away as I experienced Father Daddies love.

My father had been kicked out of his home when he was sixteen years of age and had ended up getting into trouble which ended up with him spending some numerous times in jail and in prison. He spent his whole life struggling with insecurity and rejection and that had spilled over onto me. Tears began to well up in my eyes, and as the dam burst, a mind-blowing cleansing began to take place. When I was finally able to compose myself, I turned to Emmanuel.

"Why am I able to see my Heavenly Father in this new way?" I inquired.

Emmanuel responded with tenderness in His heart, "You are passionately pursing relationship with the Father. I have healed the father wound in your heart. If you seek the Father, you will find Him. He loves to reveal himself for who He is. He loves for you to always experience His love. You have had a revelation of truth, and the lie of rejection has been exposed and dealt with. Father God is so happy when you see truth and embrace it. It makes Him happiest to see you free."

I nodded in agreement while Emmanuel turned his attention to the ambience of the hallway. We stood where the doorway had been before when we entered into the presence of Father God. I gasped with astonishment as I saw that what used to be a door before was now an unrestricted opening. The door had literally disappeared.

The Halls of Faith

"I have unrestricted access into the presence of Father and can enter anytime and for any reason?" I gasped with an unabashed astonishment!

"You are a son and sons have total access," Emmanuel responded with great pride in His voice.

Emmanuel proceeded to walk down the hallway bubbling away like a little boy who had just got a shiny new red wagon and was warming up to all the possibilities. He had introduced me to the Father and had helped set misconceptions right. Now we were walking down the new halls of faith.

"This will be very exciting for you," Emmanuel beamed. "This former hall of shame has now become a hall of faith. As you travel these halls, take time to ponder the writings and pictures on the wall. They will help to strengthen you when you are tempted to be discouraged or disillusioned. I am giving you a thought. When you look into your past, I want you to look only at the things that build your faith. Do not think about regrets or past failures. These are all under the blood. See I have painted all the walls."

"If you have confessed them as sin and repented, they are forgotten and gone as far as the east is from the west. If I don't remember them why should you?"

Emmanuel gave me an enthusiastic squeeze, as He continued with deep emotion, "Think on things that are pure and lovely. Look for good reports and memories to encourage you. I want you to search out anything that you see that you can be grateful or thankful for. I urge you to think about these things. That is why this hall of faith is so vital to your health. Speak it out loud so that you and others can hear it. This is an important part of having a healthy home."

Joyously, I began to amble down the hallways looking at pictures and reading quotes. The pictures were those of people who had influenced

The Halls of Faith

my life to greater faith and love. It told stories of how they did it. As I read about the influential people in my life, an anointing mantle come upon me. It was like a transfer was happening. I began to read some of the quotes on the wall and scripture verses that had impacted my life. Just reading some of the verses and stories gave me new strength. The first scripture verse said as follows:

> *"Seeing as we have been surrounded with such a cloud of witnesses let us lay aside every weight and the sin that does so easily beset us and let us run with patience the race that is set before us.*

(Hebrews 12:1) KJV

"These are the men and women of faith in the Bible", I said with awe. These are examples for me. I am to draw strength from their lives. My eyes were now opened. My mind drifted to people I had grown up with who had touched my life. I now was seeing the good that people had done without the bad experiences and offenses canceling them out. It was heartwarming. Compassion and love welled up in my heart.

> *Emmanuel only had eyes for me and they were filled with His amazing love*

I came to a section of scripture verses in the hallway that caught my attention. These verses spoke of who I really was.

Eagerly, I began to read that because I had put my faith and belief in Jesus Christ, He had declared me not guilty of sin (Romans 3:24). I read that there was no condemnation because Jesus lived in me (Romans 8:1), and that I was set free from the law of sin and death (Romans 8:2). Joy filled my heart as these wonderful promises of God settled by faith in my heart.

The Halls of Faith

I continued to soak in other passages of scriptures that declared me pure and holy in Christ (1 Corinthians 1:30); I was a new person in Christ, and I was brand new on the inside; the old life was gone. A new life had begun. (2 Corinthians 5:17)

Wasn't that the truth? I had given my life to Christ. Christ had given me this fantastic new house (heart), but because I did not know these beloved promises I believed devlin's lies and had allowed Fat Man to make a mess of my heart. I had moved all my old furniture back in and had taken the furniture that God had originally given me out because I thought I knew a better way. Sounds like I was back to that quiet rebellion and pride. I knew better and I was going to do it my way. My stuff was more comfortable you know. At least that is how I thought at the time.

But now, I was so excited because I was finally beginning to comprehend who I really was in my new life in Christ. I was taking back what was rightfully mine. I got more and more excited as I read that I was God's masterpiece (Ephesians 2:10); I was holy and without fault (Ephesians 1:4); my sins were taken away and I was forgiven (Ephesians 1:7).

I stepped back for a moment to let this really sink in. These were wonderful promises. Why had I not been in God's Word to learn these things? A holy anger rose up within me as I began to think of what else I wasn't being told. I must study this Word day and night so I can't be deceived. I wanted every right and privilege that belonged to me as an adopted son (Ephesians 1:5-6). I touched several plaques on the wall and movies came to life of different people in my life who had poured their hearts and souls into me; teachers, Sunday school teachers, friends, family…it was wonderful.

Now that the halls of shame had been turned to the halls of Faith, I was even beginning to remember good stories with my parents and

The Halls of Faith

siblings that I could not remember before. Before, I was subconsciously consumed by the bad memories which had cancelled out the good memories. Now, they were slowly coming back. I was so uplifted. As I turned to leave the hallway, I saw several other verses of scripture that caught my attention. I saw a plaque on the wall that proclaimed that I was blessed with every spiritual blessing in the heavenly realms because I belong to Christ Jesus. "Is this for real?" I thought. "Every blessing in the heavenly realms is mine? I just claim it by faith?" I was about to find out how true that was.

When I got to the end of the hall, a gorgeous painting was on the wall. The frame was an ancient gold trim. The painting showed a picture of my father with His arms held out invitingly to me--his son. You could see the tenderness in His eyes. At the top were the words "A Father's Blessing", along with a favorite scripture verse:

> *"The Lord bless you and keep you, the Lord make His face to shine upon you and be gracious unto you. The Lord lifts His countenance upon you and grants you His peace.*
>
> (Numbers 6:24-26) NKJV

Underneath the picture was a short prayer from my father:

> *I pray, Son that the Lord would cause to grow your love for God, yourself and others.*
>
> *I pray that you be given the mind of Christ and that the Holy Spirit will teach you all things.*
>
> *I pray that everything your hands touch will be blessed.*
>
> *I pray that you will be filled with love, joy and peace and I pray that you will be filled with a confidence that only God can place within you.*

The Halls of Faith

There was a time when I could not have seen a picture of this without negative emotion. I would not have believed that my father could look at me in this way and say these things to me and mean it. But my perception had been changed.

Emmanuel placed His hand on my shoulder and squeezed gently. I could feel the deep emotion, as he said to me, "You are my beloved son in whom I am well pleased. I will put it within those who hear you speak, that your words will have life and meaning to those who hear."

I turned to face Emmanuel giving Him an impulsive, strong hug. For several minutes we stood in a tight embrace as I felt all that He said about me settle deep within my spirit.

Somehow, with my perception of Father God being straightened out he had also enabled me see my earthly father looking at me the same way. It made no sense but the pain was gone.

I was loved, I was accepted, and I was important to God. A whole bunch of bottles in the 'D', 'F', and 'U' section had just got dumped in the trash, and Faith, Hope and Love were the new replacements. Doubt became Faith; Fear became Faith, and Discouragement became Hope. I had a new focus.

"More," I said. "I want more of you; I just want more. It is real. It is all true." I looked deep in Emmanuel's face and caressed His cheek. My focus on principles and doing the right thing had changed to a passion of being in the presence of the right person. A deep peace settled deep within me. It was my relationship to Emmanuel and Comforter that was bringing order to the chaos. It was beautiful. I could hardly wait for what was coming next.

The Halls of Faith

Notes

11

THE 'WHINE' CELLAR

As we moved through the hallways, we paused at the top of the stairs. An excited gleam came into Emmanuel's eyes as He gave my shoulder a gentle squeeze and a pat. "We are going to my favorite room!" Emmanuel exclaimed enthusiastically while rubbing His hands together vigorously.

I gave Emmanuel a quick sideways glance as my mind churned in anxious wonderment. "What in the world was He talking about anyway?"

We descended cautiously down the circular staircase to the basement. My mind was going in a million directions as I tried to figure out where He was taking me.

"We are now in the bottom of your heart," Emmanuel said with growing excitement. "This is the place where the furnace, water heater, water treatment, and well…. the 'whine' cellar is." Rhema and Comforter had all stopped what they were doing in the library and had come to join us. A great excitement and anticipation had begun to radiate from their eyes as they headed straight for the 'whine' cellar. They were like bees to nectar.

A puzzled look crept over my face. "Most of the problems in my life were because of this room. I had been intentionally avoiding that area, and I was almost annoyed that they even knew about this place. I hadn't told them. How had they found out?

I stuttered, as I hesitantly said, "I, I, rea, reaall, really don't want to go in there."

Why would anyone be excited to go to the place where I grumbled, complained and whined about everything? In fact, I usually sent Jack, my butler, down to this place to get me bottles of "whine" when I needed them. Panic had begun to grip me in such a way that I was growing dizzy from shortness of breath. I began to step slowly backwards and away from the door.

Come now," Emmanuel said, gripping my arm with growing enthusiasm, "Your destiny lies in here." Emmanuel's eyes shone bright in the semi-darkness of the damp basement.

"Are you sure?" I replied hesitantly. My eyebrows furrowed in towards the middle of my forehead, almost touching each other. Up to now, that room has been part of my greatest problem.

"Have faith in me and do not doubt," Emmanuel chided gently, as He gave me a playful whack on the back. "It is here that you will find your purpose. It is here that you will find your destiny."

I relaxed slightly letting out a quiet sigh. "Maybe He was right," I mumbled, in a barely audible voice.

Comforter placed His arms around my shoulder giving me a gentle hug while pinching my cheek. "It really will be alright," He said supportively. "Be strong! We will be right here beside you all the way."

The 'Whine' Cellar

Squaring my shoulders and lifting my chin up, I looked hesitantly at the old cellar door. My feet felt like bricks and the door looked overwhelming but, in obedience, I chose to trust Emmanuel's words (although, I did 'whine' a little bit). 'Whine' or not, He hadn't let me down yet, at least not from what I could see.

Taking several deep breaths, I stepped gingerly towards the door with my faithful trio tight right by my side.

I reached for the iron clasp latch and pushed down hard on the lever while putting my whole weight into its beefiness. I pushed open the old oak door, amidst obvious creeks and groans, and suddenly remembered why I always sent Jack down here to get my 'whine' bottles.

The exterior door was shaped like an old wine barrel and had cast iron strips across its front and outer trimmings... Emmanuel stepped simultaneously into the room and flicked on the light to reveal a gloomy, nasty cellar. It was dank and musty. I shivered involuntarily as I observed a dense fog permeating the entire room making it virtuously impossible to see anything. Emmanuel flicked on another switch which activated an exhaust fan. Moments later, the wet fog had mostly disappeared.

I pushed aside the spider webs that seemed to be everywhere and wiped the sticky residue on the back of my pants sneezing three times so loudly that I thought I was going to get a headache. Emmanuel flicked on his flashlight to get a closer look at the gloomy nasty cellar and began checking every crook and cranny. I shuddered again from the cool draft that found its way through this depressing cellar that seemed to crawl eerily down the back of my shirt.

All three sides of the 'whine' cellar contained racks and racks of wine bottles from every year going back to 1960. Many were covered in a thick residue of ancient dust but there seemed to be more bottles than not that were fairly new and exhibited only slight moisture on its exterior...

The Dwelling Place

On the fourth wall was the oak door where we had entered. The inside of the door was plain with no title or markings on it save a doorknob. A fog machine was in the corner billowing out fog that seemed to be firmly attached to the floor. It appeared that grumbling and whining had everything to do with this fog machine. The more grumbling and complaining that went on, the more fog would billow from the machine.

Obviously, I understood that it was my grumbling and complaining that fed this room. I immediately drew the parallel that this fog machine was linked to the thick fog I had seen in the church auditorium, which now seemed like eons ago. I didn't need Rhema to give me revelation on this one; it was quite obvious. Whining, complaining, and grumbling were sister cousins to a form of godliness.

A smug look briefly flitted across my face as I remembered how religious I could look complaining and grumbling. I think the term I had used was 'concerned Christian'.

> *Whatever you speak, either positively or negatively, will either bless you or curse you*

Thousands of bottles filled the shelves and were of all shapes, sizes and colors. Observing the years on the bottles gave me an indication that many of these bottles went back to the early 1960's.

"These bottles of wine do not get better with age," Comforter said, with a wry look. In fact, the further you go back and drink from the experiences of your past, the more you will get drunk in the flesh. These bottles represent all your whining, complaining and grumbling. All these years, you have come to me in a whiny, demanding and complaining spirit. This is why so many of your prayers have remained unanswered. If you regard a practice of sin and unforgiveness, God cannot hear your prayers to answer them. Several verses wafted through my mind as Comforter said this:

"If I regard iniquity in my heart the Lord will not hear me."

The 'Whine' Cellar

(Psalm 66:18) KJV

"But if you do not forgive, neither will your Father in heaven forgive your trespasses."

(Mark 11:26) KJV

"These bottles of 'whine' have been stored up in the bottom of your heart and have made you drunk in the flesh." Emmanuel said with a keen observation as He continued to shine his light over each of the bottles.

Now, it didn't escape my attention that there was a heat run and a cold air return feeding this room. The result of this was that this fog of grumbling and complaining had clouded my heart by bringing discord and confusion to me and those around me. The cold air return was sucking in the air from this room, including the fog, and distributing it through the furnace to be spread throughout the whole house.

Comforter held up one of the older bottles, shaking it a little in the light as He squinted His eyes while closely inspecting it. "Hmmm!" Comforter replied cautiously. "Looks like you have a nasty one swimming in here."

"Nasty what?" I interjected as I grabbed the bottle and took a hard look for myself. From the murky darkness of the bottle I could barely make out the outline of some foul spirit swimming around in circles. The spirit swam to the side where I was looking, and tried to take a bite out of me with its razor sharp teeth. It banged into the side of the bottle, then turned and kept swimming around in circles. It was just waiting for the time when someone would uncork the bottle and drink its poisonous liquid.

"Are you serious?" I bellowed as I jumped back while fumbling with the bottle and almost dropping it. "I did this with my complaining and grumbling?

The Dwelling Place

Comforter touched my arm and said, "as a man thinketh in His heart so he tends to speak from how he thinks.' (Proverbs 23:7)

"You have looked through your natural eyes with what you could <u>see</u> all your life. You have focused on what you could taste, touch, see, feel and hear, and you have defiled your heart with what you have <u>spoken and seen</u> in the natural. Whatever you speak, either positively or negatively, will either bless you or curse you," Comforter exhorted me. "You have been drinking from your experiences and it continues to defile you. You didn't drink from a grateful and thankful heart, but from one that thinks that life owes you. What you sow you tend to reap; but that is about to change for the better. That is why we are here. We created you and know exactly how your heart should function properly and efficiently. We are not here to expose you to put you down but to help you see where you have put yourself down and listened to the wrong voices. This is what has hurt you. The good thing is that it is never too late, as long as you are breathing. We are the architects of your heart—this house. If you follow our instructions, you will experience the life that we intended for you to have. Yes... we want you to live!"

> *If you follow our instructions, you will begin to experience the life that we have destined for you to live.*

As I was pondering what Comforter was telling me, I jumped up, startled by a great commotion behind me. I turned around to see that a holy anger had come over Emmanuel. He had begun to overturn the wine racks and smash the wine bottles. He picked up the fog machine and shattered it against the wall. Then He stomped on it until it ceased wheezing out that wretched fog.

I looked on in great amazement. Up to this point, I had only seen Emmanuel looking joyful or sad. He was usually pretty mellow. This was most certainly a totally new experience.

The 'Whine' Cellar

"What are you doing?" I cried out in fear.

I looked on in horror as the bottles broke to hear shrieks filling the air as little whiny devlins were released from their bottles. Some had been bottled up for forty years and were quite pickled in 'whine.'

`As they were released, they started to bellow out and complain and 'whine profusely.' They sounded like those screamer fire crackers.

They had barely got a word or scream out edgewise, when I heard,

"Be silent! You must leave, now!"

Emmanuel spoke authoritatively, "And I have been given the keys to this room and authority to set up My war room here.

"Be gone!"

I heard a loud whoooosh, and then all was quiet

12

THE WORSHIP CENTER

My willingness and repentance had given Emmanuel unabashed authority. Emmanuel turned to me with a holy fire in His eyes and a fierce determination on His face.

"From now on this is to be a house of prayer and worship.

Do nothing through grumbling and complaining but let your requests be known to God.

(Philippians 4:6) The Message

"This room is to become a garment of praise for a spirit of heaviness and a temple of worship," Emmanuel said, pausing to catch His breath (Isaiah 61:3). "It is from this room that I will teach you how to enter My Presence correctly. It is from here that you will learn to abandon yourself in worship--lose yourself in worship of me and be caught up in the spirit. I will teach you how to war in the spirit realm (the heavens). You will learn how to capture my heart through prayer and worship. This room will now be the *Wine Vat of My Presence*.

The Dwelling Place

Emmanuel had gone from anger to joy in like a nano-second. I think that what He was telling me got Himself so excited, that He was now twirling and dancing a jig in front of me.

Lifting His hands, He began to praise and sing clapping His hands together.

> **I Lift to You**
> **Pure and Holy praise**
> **From a heart**
> **That's filled with you**
>
> **As I burst forth**
> **With praise**
> **Your glory fills my face**
> **I will worship you**
> **All of my days**
>
> ©2007 To worship You
> Words and Music by John M. Davidson

"Come join me," Emmanuel burst out with a new verse of praise, while simultaneously linking arms with me and dancing a jig. He was quite excited about this new development of events unfolding before us.

"You are going to find out how your prayers will be answered. People will be healed and set free from the areas of their hearts that have been captured for so long. You are about to see remarkable breakthroughs," Emmanuel replied. "I see healing, I see healing. Whoooop Da!"

Puzzled, I looked at the Trinity Three and asked, "What is so different now?"

Emmanuel looked at me with both exuberance and surprise. He had the look of a little boy getting his first bike. Looking at me with a huge grin

The Worship Center

on His face He said, "You don't know!!! You have always guarded this room and kept it locked up. As a result, your emotions were bottled up and your heart was full of whining, complaining, doubt and unbelief. The atmosphere that surrounded your life was usually negative. You even sent a part of yourself, Jack, to go to the 'whine' cellar to get bottles of 'whine' for you. You probably didn't even know exactly how bad it was down here."

"But when you said, 'whatever it takes', and began to obey Me without question, repenting for everything that I brought before you, that gave Me the key to unlock this door. Now, you are pursuing intimacy with Me. You long for My presence more than anything and have spent long times soaking with Me. You are facing the fears of your heart. You are facing the fear in the deepest place and laying it all before Me.

"If your words were so powerful that a demon was deposited to wait until it was uncorked to create devastation in your life or someone else's, think what will happen when your praises and songs of My love are bottled and then released. Imagine the power of My love that will set people free.

"That attitude has given Me the authority to have access and control to the bottom of your heart. You are at the place where you have nothing to lose, because whatever I ask for, you are willing to give. You are about to see the greatest miracle."

Emmanuel motioned excitedly for me to come and stand directly in front of Him face to face. Comforter and Rhema stood behind me, one on each side ((I think to catch me if I fell). Imagine being slain in the spirit and being caught by Comforter and Rhema! What a hoot! Despite my vivid imagination, I felt my body starting to shake. Anticipation of something miraculous tantalized my senses.

"Open your mouth and stick out your tongue," Emmanuel said. Emmanuel reached inside His tunic and seemed to reach deep inside His

The Dwelling Place

own heart. As his hand came out of His tunic, He held in His hand a piece of His own heart. He reached up and put the piece of His heart up to my mouth and said, "Take, and eat this in remembrance of Me. This symbolizes all of My heart (body) that is given for you. This tongue is now dedicated to the Lord."

He then moved His gown to reveal a gash in His side. Placing a cup at the bottom of the wound, some blood trickled into the cup. Handing it to me Emmanuel said, "Drink! Drink all of it in remembrance of Me. This is a symbol of My blood that was shed for you. All of this is possible because of My blood." Emmanuel waved his hand indicating the remarkable change that had transformed my heart.

"Because you have chosen to live by faith in Me without doubting, I have given you this most precious gift. I have given you a new heart and a heart of flesh. I have given you My heart. This tongue is now a tongue of righteousness, a spring of living water. Not only will springs of living water flow from your belly, but they will also flow from your lips.

> *When you began to obey me without question, repenting for everything that I brought before you that gave me the key to unlock this door*

"With this tongue you will bring blessing; you will heal the sick and cast out demons; you will speak My words, and set the captives free. You will give Me all the glory for it is My heart within you that has given you the life that set you free.

"Go into the entire World and preach the good news to all people. Know that I am with you always even to the ends of the World. Let My love flow from My presence within you."

Because I was in a spirit realm all of this seemed very normal and expected. I knew this was symbolic but I also knew it was very real.

The Worship Center

I fell on my face in worship. A new compassion welled up within me. I had been half-hearted for most of my life, but I was watching my life become beauty from ashes. What had been destroyed by the canker worm was now being miraculously transformed before my eyes. "Whatever you want me to say; whatever you want me to do," I said as I broke before the Lord. A new confidence started to brew and percolate within me. The fires were burning.

"Let's get this room cleaned up," Emmanuel said. "I can hardly wait to restock this wine cellar with new wine. This is going to be a wine vat of my Presence."

I noticed that whenever I gave permission for the Trinity Three to do something, they did not hesitate for one minute, but got right to work.

Quickly, Emmanuel, Rhema, and Comforter swept and cleaned the room. Emmanuel began to paint the room with His special red paint that turned white when it dried. The paint was no sooner dried than there was a knock on the door.

The first deliveryman had boxes and boxes of new racks for the wine to fit on. The company that made the racks was from *Thankfulness and Gratefulness, LLC*. Just touching the racks, I found myself becoming more thankful and grateful. I turned to Emmanuel and gave him a big bear hug. I was so happy!

Quickly, we began to assemble them along the three walls. We bantered back and forth about things that we were both thankful and grateful for over a period of over an hour.

"Leave this corner open," Emmanuel said with an impish grin. I have a special treat for this area.

"Tell me," I said, trying to hold my excitement back. I felt like a little kid getting his first toy.

The Dwelling Place

"In good time; in good time," Emmanuel said with a very large smile.

We had no sooner finished assembling the racks when the second deliveryman arrived. He had cases and cases of new wine stacked up on a cart.

"Delivery from Heaven!" the man exclaimed. I ran out into the hall to help bring the cart in. There were boxes lined up all the way down the hall. Ripping off the top of the box, I began to grab bottles of wine. Emmanuel, Comforter and Rhema were dancing for joy behind me.

We were in the wine vat of His Presence and we were about to have a party and get drunk. I grabbed the first bottle and read the label *Joy Juice*; another read *Abandonment*, and another, *Worship in the Spirit*. Other bottles read as follows: P*raise, Creation worship, Character of God worship, Adoration, and Exultation*.

> You can get a drink any time you want," Comforter said as he placed seals on the bottles with His name on them

"You can get a drink any time you want," Comforter said elatedly as He placed seals on the bottles with His name on them. Rhema was also putting stickers of revelation on each bottle.

"I will give you revelations as you worship," Rhema said with a hearty laugh. "This will make your worship come alive and intense. It will sharpen your love for the Trinity Three." Rhema held up one bottle reading its contents, "Oooohhh! This one gets three stickers. This one is going to get you." Although I didn't hear Rhema audibly, His thoughts crossed my thinking as He finished marking each bottle and then placed it on the shelf.

"When you drink my praise, you worship me," Emmanuel whispered quietly in my ear as He wrapped His arms around me giving me a strong bear hug.

The Worship Center

"Revelation, knowledge and words of wisdom are now in each of these wine bottles. I want you to drink often and a lot. All you have to do is ask. In fact, I command you to be drunk with the Spirit.

I looked at Emmanuel and said with a lilt in my voice, "You don't have to tell me twice!"

"Come expectant, come ready and be willing to let my Spirit consume you. Let my Spirit permeate every pore of your being. Let my Spirit saturate every crack, crevice, and room of your house. This is the essence of a Spirit of worship and praise." By this time, Emmanuel was already on his second glass and was by now getting a little tipsy.

I reached for one box and read the words, *Angel wine*, in large print. "What is angel wine? I asked, inquisitively to Emmanuel.

"Oh! That is the double blessing wine," Emmanuel said, with a twinkle in his eye. "Open it up and see for yourself."

I began tearing off the top of the box and pulled out four bottles of wine; two in each hand. Dumbfounded, I held up one of the bottles close and peered intently inside. There was a little angel inside.

"This is the real deal," Emmanuel said. "When you drink this wine of praise, this angel is released to sing the most beautiful song of praise with you. He sings in harmony with your song of praise to the Father. Pretty neat huh?"

"Do these angels have names?" I asked.

"Oh yes, this one is Grateful; this other one is Thankful; this one is Appreciative and that one over there is Reverence."

I placed the angel wine on the racks and shook my head in wonderment. This really was messing with my theology. My thoughts were interrupted by the following words:

The Dwelling Place

"Worship is about being; it is about being still before God; it is letting Him know that it is all about Him. You don't need to ask for anything or demand anything," Emmanuel stated intently.

I looked appreciatively at Emmanuel as He stated in a very quiet reverent tone, "I just want to be in my Fathers presence and love Him for being Father God." Emmanuel handed me a full bottle of new wine and said, "Let's drink!" I looked at the bottle and read in bold print…Reverence—a full bodied red wine.

So, we drank together and enjoyed each other's presence. I drank in Emmanuel's love, grace and mercy.

Rhema began to reveal some deeper level truths that it was not about working and striving, telling God what to do or demanding His services, but in absolute surrender and devotion—prostrate at His feet drinking in His beauty. I was learning to be still and know that He is God.

> *I jumped up and down with passion as if trying to press in to more of His presence*

I couldn't get enough, I couldn't stay away. I just wanted to stay close by His side forever. My heart's desire began to be one of, "How can I be more in your presence today? How can I experience you more than anything else that I encounter today? Fill my vision Father. I want to be more aware of your presence than anything else." These thoughts filtered through my mind and I began to truly worship. Tears of joy streamed down my face as I abandoned myself to worshipping the King of the universe. My body vibrated and moved with excitement; I could not contain myself. I jumped up and down with passion trying to press in to more of His Presence.

Oh! The purity of the moment! It was just Jesus and I. I was in love with my Savior and I didn't care who knew. It was all about Him in me and Him flowing through me.

The Worship Center

Rhema began to minister words of revelation to my heart.

"Fix your thoughts on what is true and honorable and right. Think about things that are pure and lovely and admirable. Think about things that are excellent and worthy of praise."

(Phil. 4:8) The Message

"Everything else seemed so petty," I thought, as I began to worship, I began imagining things that were honorable and right. I began thinking of things that were excellent of praise, pure, lovely and admirable. I found God's compassion welling up within me. It was wonderful! It was so beautiful.

I suddenly felt what sounded like a rumbling noise outside. I ran upstairs for a moment to look outside the window. Somehow, all my neighbors' houses had moved closer to mine and I liked it. Haahhhmmm. I began to wonder whether they had moved closer to me, or did I just move closer to them? It was a mystery worth exploring. What I did know was this; I felt a new love brooding deep within for those who lived around me and for anyone I would come in contact with. It was truly exhilarating! It was paradoxically intoxicating! Something was happening from the bottom of my heart and it was working its way up and out!

> *Rhema began to reveal that it was not about working and striving, telling God what to do or demanding His services but in absolute surrender and devotion— prostrate at His feet drinking in His beauty. I couldn't get enough, I couldn't stay away. I just wanted to stay close by His Side*

"We have a world to win. If only they could see what I see!" I cried out impulsively.

"They will," Emmanuel said as He reached the top of the stairs and turned the corner just in time to catch me looking out my window at the neighbor's houses. "They will."

13

THE TROPHY ROOM

I hadn't noticed until now, but it suddenly dawned on me that whenever Emmanuel entered, cleaned and then refilled a room and then left, a strange thing happened; the door disappeared! What was that all about? The bedroom, throne room, kitchen, hallways, living room, pantry, basement, and now the newly named wine vat worship center had no doors…they had no doors…. NO DOORS!!! It was absolutely miraculous! It was freedomlicious!!! Emmanuel had even closed some doors that I should have never even opened in the first place to the enemy.

"There must be no secrets and no delays," Emmanuel said emphatically. I want total and complete access to any room, at any time, and for whatever reason. Do you still feel the same way? Are you still Ok with that?"

I nodded without any hesitation. It was mind-blowing to me how quickly I was getting used to this straightforwardness of Emmanuel.

The Dwelling Place

Whatever He said He meant and there was never any mind games. He was just genuine.

This room had become my favorite room in just the short while I was here. You could taste the joy and laughter in the air. It was so sweet to the taste. Ah! The worship and praise center—what a delight!! I swallowed quickly as the saliva juices squirted hard in my mouth at the thought of drinking in deep of the Lord.

Emmanuel had just returned to the wine vat to join me for some more wine. A feeling of satisfaction settled within me, and I burst forth into a new song of worship and praise. I looked up at the ceiling and was shocked yet wonderfully delighted to see a cloud of fire covering the whole ceiling. It was a searing white-hot fire. I turned to look at Emmanuel in quiet expectation, although I felt no fear and was totally at peace in my heart. It was astonishing that I could see this blazing fire layering the entire upper area, and yet I felt warm dew falling on me that was so refreshing and deliciously sweet. I paused to give another lingering gaze at the face of Emmanuel.

"You are seeing the Holiness of God, His grace and mercy all at the same time," Emmanuel responded reverently and graciously as He turned and caught my mesmerized look. He laughed a hearty laugh and said eloquently; "There is so much of the character and presence of God you have yet to learn. This will truly be the greatest adventure of your life."

I looked upward as a flame of fire separated itself, folded and floated its way down in our direction. Suddenly, it vaporized into a mist and fell like a cool breezy spray on our faces. Emmanuel's face was a glistening glow of joy as He continued his passionate promise to me.

"The doors of your heart are being removed, which gives me the ability to easily move from one room to another at a moment's notice. It is the mystery of Godliness. I now live in your heart, which enables you to

The Trophy Room

see and move just as easily with me, for we will always be together as one."

Emmanuel moved towards a door with no markings on it. It was in the corner and kind of out of the way.

"What room is this?" He inquired.

"Oh, that one goes to the garage," I replied blandly as I tried to downplay my response. "I keep all my most important prized possessions in there…"

I caught myself off guard as I realized what I had just done. I had just let one of my secret thoughts slip out of the bag.

Emmanuel nodded His head up and down almost imperceptivity, as He saw the disconcerting look registering on my face. He knew the struggle I was having and He was feeling my pain. I thought I had given it all, but Emmanuel was apparently not done. He had found another room in my heart where I was squirreling things away that I wanted for myself. He was a consuming fire. All I had to do was look up and see it in His eyes. There was a purpose and determination that had begun to manifest itself in those deep blue eyes that dared anyone to challenge Him. He was cleaning house and He was not going to stop. It was all or nothing.

> Just being in Emmanuel's presence had made everything that had seemed so important to me now seem so unimportant

At first a slow anger began to well up within me. "Is He going to take everything?" I seethed within myself. This is not fair! How rude!"

Emmanuel looked at me expectantly, but quietly. There was a quiet sense of patient, yet positive excitement in His eyes. If I was ready, He was ready. The steely blue look had all but disappeared. And a soft kindness had replaced the look. Slowly, I raised my eyes to the point

The Dwelling Place

where I was looking into His eyes; I slowly began to simmer down. There really was no pressure here, except on me. It was truly my choice. I shook my head in deep wonder.

In the past, I had been so used to being controlled and forced to serve God that I often focused on that as my excuse to do things my own way. That was not the case here. There was no defense to rest on. No excuse to defend. It appeared that Emmanuel was aggressively willing to clean house as long as I was one hundred and ten percent behind the program. If I wasn't ready or willing then Emmanuel would completely stop and wait. That was certainly what it looked like. There was not even a hint of manipulation or control. The only thing I could see that would compel me was His absolute love for me. I was stunned. Again, I could see His goodness trumping over my anger.

Finally I took a deep breath and said, "Whatever it takes, my Lord, whatever it takes. I'm ready."

Emmanuel gave me one last look to make sure it was my choice, held my gaze in quiet expectation, and then opened the door, entering the garage.

Surveying the entire area, Emmanuel noticed that it was a rather large three-stall place with a storage room. You would think I was rich; it had so many possessions in it.

"This looks more like a trophy room," Emmanuel observed astutely. A deep conviction and revelation came over me as my eyes scanned the room with Him. What at first looked like a beautiful room filled with all sorts of gadgets and trinkets, suddenly meant nothing to me. A scripture from Philippians jolted my thinking:

> *"But whatever was to my profit I now consider loss for the sake of Christ. What is more, I consider everything a loss compared to the surpassing greatness of knowing Christ Jesus my Lord, for whose*

The Trophy Room

sake I have lost all things. I consider them rubbish that I may gain Christ."

(Philippians 3:7-8) NIV

For a moment I winced painfully. Everything that used to be so important to me now seemed so unimportant after being in Emmanuel's Presence. I felt totally vulnerable yet I knew what I had to do.

"I want you more than I want this," I said with a deep resolve. "I want to know you. Everything else is worthless. Take these idols from my heart. Take these trophies that are on the shelves and walls."

Five minutes ago, I was secretly hiding these things for my own personal pleasure. Before, my thought process went something like this; "In case you don't know; you better have a nest egg; it is only smart. You need to save for your retirement."

Suddenly, all these wise and smart sayings took on a rather hollow sound. These were just my excuses for being selfish. These were just my excuses to cover my own insecurity and fear. I did not trust that Emmanuel could meet all my needs. Now, Emmanuel's unassuming compassion was melting my heart.

"Use them for your glory or destroy them." I cried out as I fell to my knees. I could hardly believe I was saying this, and yet I meant it. It didn't make logical sense.

From a guy who used to covet his seven gold cards, positions of leadership, credit lines and such this was earth shattering.

Too much had been revealed to me, though, and the cost of partial surrender was too much to bear.

If I was going to be a Christian, it had to be all or nothing. This was not about being a Christians for Christian's sake or about principle for that

The Dwelling Place

matter. It was about the Man. It was these three Men who were laying their lives down for me. I began to heave with great convulsions. I cried and cried.

For so long I had coveted all this junk. As I counted the cost, my heart felt great anguish. I had so much invested in this stuff, yet the pain was too great and the peace and joy was too real that I was experiencing with my new found friends and it pulled me hard in their direction.

Finally, after much agonizing and crying, I relented. A new sense of freedom and peace began to flood the garage with a new fragrance of a fresh scented perfume. From now on, I would heaven and the kingdom of God my treasure.

The Trinity Three began to walk around the trophy room/garage with a new freedom, and began to put their seal on the things they wanted to keep and seals on the things that had to be thrown out and burned; from cars, trucks, boats, jet skis, campers; down to cell phones, iPods, cameras, tools, lawn mowers, snow blowers and every other little thing.

"From now on," Emmanuel said, "If someone has need of something, and you have it here, let them use it. Do not be concerned if it comes back to you, comes back at all or comes back damaged. Do not let it bother you. Freely share of all that you have for it is now ours. This is our heart and all your possessions belong to us. Do it all in our name. Do not worry about protecting our belongings. Your heart is more important to us than the possession. It is more blessed to give than to receive."

Apprehension began to fill my heart. There were a couple of things that I secretly wanted to hang on too. I had said I would give it all but when Emmanuel thanked me for giving it all to Him and claimed it as his; that somehow sounded different. I had some things that I didn't allow anyone to touch. They were mine you know, for sentimental reasons. As I was thinking about these thoughts, I noticed that all activity in the garage had stopped. I looked over to Emmanuel and Comforter. I

The Trophy Room

noticed that they had just stopped and sat down. They were waiting for my decision.

"What!!!!" I said. "Are you reading my mind?"

"We can wait and come back in another six months," Emmanuel said with a thin smile. "It's your choice you know if you decide you want to hold onto things, it's up to you. There is no pressure here. Personally, we don't need your stuff. This is not for Our benefit. This is about the transparency of your heart. It's about you putting to death your selfish nature and living in the freedom of love that We give. Are you willing to give it all and trust Us that we have your best interest at heart and that We will take care of you, even if you lose it all?"

Rhema was writing profusely and a verse suddenly registered in my mind:

> "Those who love their life in this world will lose it. Those who despise their life in this world will keep it for eternal life."
>
> (John 12:15) NLT

> *I was beginning to realize that a self absorbed love in what I wanted to do would result in eternal loss.*

I squirmed as this verse burned itself deep into my mind. I looked over at Rhema who was writing slowly on His notepad. I watched as Emmanuel leaned back in an old easy chair that was stored in the garage. He hit the lever on the side and slid down deep into His chair, kicking His feet up into the air and interlocking His fingers behind His head.

Emmanuel closed His eyes as if preparing to take a nap. I pursed my lips and squinted. I had already lost decades of my life putting Emmanuel off and hurting Comforter. I had built up my nest egg and hoarded things all my life. How many times had I virtually lost it all? How many more times was I going to have to go through this?

The Dwelling Place

I had said they could be Lord of everything, and now I was changing my mind. "Hmmmm! Why do things have to be so difficult?" I thought. I was beginning to realize that a self absorbed love in what I wanted to do would result in eternal loss.

"Everything about my life must be an expression of love out towards others. It was in thinking of the needs of others first." I whispered this with a barely audible voice as the revelation settled deep within my soul. I groaned so deeply that I felt my possessions rattle in the garage.

As I watched intently, Rhema was jotting down a few notes on His notepad and doodling. As I pondered this dilemma, it dawned on me that if I chose to stop now and wait and hang onto my stuff, I opened the door for Fat Man to come back into my life with his cohorts to gain access to the newly clean and furnished areas of my heart. The Bible said that if I cleaned my house out and didn't fill and guard it with something new from God, the enemy would come back seven times worse. I really did not like that option. I was not about to revive Fat Man!

Taking a deep breath, and putting the smelling salts back in my pocket, a steely look came back into my eyes as I blurted out, "I choose life. I choose to be filled with your presence. I want Your love to flow from me. None of this means anything compared to what you are doing. Take it all!"

Emmanuel and Comforter stood up and put their work gloves back on grinning from ear to ear.

Emmanuel smiled profusely as He said, "Alright! Good. That's what I'm talking about. When you give me your heart—all of it, you also give me everything that flows from it and everything stored up in it. That includes your trophies and your most treasured possessions. I love it! You are beginning to understand. This is good! This is very good! I am so proud of you!"

The Trophy Room

I beamed as the encouraging words of Emmanuel settled within like a tasty stew after a hard day's work.

Emmanuel continued by saying, "You are beginning to trust us. We know your heart is aching right now from this decision, yet you are choosing to give it all to us. This is what we are looking for. This is what we mean by absolute surrender. You are counting the cost and you are feeling the weight of this loss. You will be surprised how good you are going to feel about this decision. It is in dying to your desires where you truly begin to live. The pain of living wrong will subside as the choice of doing what is right is walked out."

I nodded my head slowly as I heard, "Alright, here is what I want you to do," Emmanuel said enthusiastically. Be carefully attentive to the orphans and widows, the poor and the down and outers. These are worthy of a double portion. You minister to me when you help these precious souls in my name."(James 1:27). Use your possessions to bless them. Do this since they cannot return anything back to you." Emmanuel stopped to catch His breath and continued to look around.

The Trinity Three noticed an old grandfather clock in the storage room. It was very precious to me, and I treasured it greatly. Emmanuel, Rhema and Comforter walked straight up to it and began putting their seals and stamps on it.

"Time has been an idol to you for a long time, but now you must redeem the time because the days are evil," Comforter instructed me.

"Look for ways to make time count for eternity. Begin to think in terms of building treasure in Heaven and have fun doing it. If you're laughing a lot and enjoying life, you're probably on the right track. Look for something new to enjoy each day. Take time to rest. Be infectious and spread an atmosphere of joy to those you meet. (Ephesians 5:16) Be careful to not lose track of the time and forget about us, because the time is short and the days are evil (Romans 13:11). Spending vast quantities of

The Dwelling Place

time soaking in my Presence and waiting quietly with us before the Father is always encouraged. Spread the good news of the gospel to those you meet throughout your day."

"Yes, time had been an idol to me," I reflected, running my hands across the mahogany frame of the clock. My time was my time, you know. But now I see that even my time belongs to the Lord.

I focused back on what Comforter was saying, "Be careful of the World's media. It is a time stealer."

Comforter grunted as he tried to lift a chest that was about three feet long by two feet wide and about eighteen inches high that He discovered in the storage room. It contained about fifteen hundred verses that I had memorized as a child.

> *Selfishness and greed do not make possessions sweeter to own. It's in holding everything as a gift to give away that makes them sweeter*

There was also a journal where I had made some notations, and some testimonies about treasure hunting. "This storage room is the wrong place for this," Emmanuel stated firmly. "We will bring this up to the library for processing. Keep this journal by you at all times and write anything that has blessed or inspired you. This journal will be a great strength and comfort to you as you go through life. It is to be the testimonies of my healing, restoring and redeeming love that will inspire your faith."

I looked around the new room. A sense of relief flooded over me. Every item of value to the Trinity Three was now catalogued and had a seal from both Comforter and Rhema. I had given up my rights to ownership of any of my possessions. All my trophies were in the garbage. I picked up several of the trophies from the trash and read the inscriptions; 'greed' and 'Pride in one's possessions'.

The Trophy Room

"Hmmph! Not all things are tangible," I thought. "This is the right and holy thing to do." As I tossed the shiny trophies back in the garbage, I said to myself, "They are all rubbish!" Falling on my knees, I leaned forward prostrating myself on the ground and cried out, "I now own nothing, but what you entrust me to have." Reaching my hands out, I turned my palms out and open and with much conviction said, "Everything I hold or handle will be in an open hand."

Rhema was scratching out with a great flourish one of my songs that was being reiterated in my head as He wrote on His notepad. With deep conviction, I sang out with great passion:

> **If you love this World you lose**
> **If the World has a hold on you**
> **If the things you hold dear**
> **Hold your life in deepest fear**
> **And your life has lost meaning and hope**
>
>
> **Then take it to the Cross**
> **Consider all as lost**
> **All my houses and lands**
> **All my dreams and all my plans**
> **What I think, what I say, what I do**
> **Belong to you.**
>
> ©2007 Choose Today
> Words and Music by John M Davidson

Emmanuel looked at me with infinite love and compassion while saying, "I have such greater treasures than this that are yours for eternity. We will talk about that later though in great length. What excites me most is your heart. You are beginning to believe that I am more than enough. You are beginning to believe that I am more than any of these things. You are letting go of the temporal things so you can enjoy the greater things."

Emmanuel broadly waved his hand at all the 'things' in my garage. "Now that you have given them all to me, you will actually enjoy them more. Selfishness and greed do not make possessions sweeter to own. It's in holding everything as a gift to give away. You can't out give me."

Looking me intently in the eye, Emmanuel gently whispered, "I am so proud of you and delighted in helping you to discover who we intended you to be."

Emmanuel began stroking His chin and a faraway look came into His eyes. He turned to me and said, "Right now, though, we need to give some thorough attention to the water system. Your water source coming in from the outside has contaminants in it which can corrode and gum up anything it comes in contact with. We need to set up a state of the art water treatment system!

But first, how about you and I having ourselves another drink? Let's see what other surprises the delivery man brought to the Wine Vat and Worship Center…and stop frowning, you're looking too serious. It's time to laugh and enjoy ourselves!"

The Trophy Room

Notes

14

THE WATER TREATMENT SYSTEM

"Every exterior door and window must be checked and the water supply must be treated," Rhema wrote with a deep urgency. Unless Emmanuel touches each door and window and treats the water treatment system nothing is safe.

A verse became very clear in my thoughts as Rhema wrote passionately on His notepad,

> "Above all else, guard your heart, for it affects everything you do."
>
> (Proverbs 4:23) NLT

Emmanuel had finished checking all the windows and doors and proceeded to walked back downstairs to where the water treatment system should go... It looked like there had been a water treatment system there in the past, but a single pipe now joined the two connections.

The Dwelling Place

"Let's take a look at what we have here," Emmanuel said as he began pointing out the maze of waterlines starting with its entry into the house.

"This is where the water line enters your heart (house). Over here is the water heater, and as you look at the ceiling over here, there is a network of hot and cold water lines. Depending on their design of use, they can be used for either utility or drinking purpose.

"For utility purpose, we need to protect the water heater, the pipes and faucets. We also want to protect all the appliances, like the washing machine, dishwasher, shower heads and toilets."

"This house has had no protection for quite a while," Emmanuel said with deep concern as He finished doing a thorough inspection. Someone removed the system I originally installed and is trying to live without the proper protection.

Emmanuel lifted his eyes to me and with a quizzical look said, "Let me guess...Worldly Wendy?

I didn't dare tell Him that Freddy fleash was there at that time complaining about the water. He liked that carbonated flavored water. It gave him that biting taste. I gave Emmanuel a quirky, goofy smile knowing I had been discovered.

> *The water itself cannot be impure, but impurities can be in the water*

Emmanuel bent down on his haunches and turned to watch as Rhema pulled out a kit and began testing the quality of the water as it came into the house.

Revelation began to flood my mind, as I started to understand, that my eyes, ears, taste, touch and smell are exposed to worldly Wendy, Freddie fleash and damien devlin daily. As the River of Life flows into my

The Water Treatment System

life, my five senses have the ability to pull in TDS's that can camouflage themselves in the water."

"What is a TDS?" I asked out loud not even sure who I was asking the question to, but definitely curious for an answer. The revelation was so real that was flooding my mind that I wasn't even sure someone was talking to me.

"That is a *Total Dissolved Solid*. It is any mineral that can dissolve itself into the water," Rhema wrote intuitively on His pad. "Devlin will try to camouflage things as spiritual or even acceptable to find a way to flow into your heart. There are some things you will let in because of rebellion or pride; then there are some things that sneak in through ignorance. Of course there are some things that are just plain bad that can enter in."

It was at this point that Comforter interjected and said, "The water itself cannot be impure, but impurities can be in the water. If there are impurities in the water, then hardness will corrupt anything it touches. For example, if you have hard water (dirt in the water) in a natural setting, you will fill up the bottom of your water heater with lime and calcium. This will corrode and coat the heating element, thus taking it 30% longer to regenerate.

All water coming into your heart must be filtered through the cross

"If you let hardness into your life, then it will take more effort and teaching for Me to reach you. Your potential will be diminished and time will be lost. If you wash your clothes with hard or dirty water, it will take eight times more of the Word to get your clothes clean because the soap (Word) mixing with the hard water will create scum. They will cancel each other out.

"Letting hardness or impurities from Worldly Wendy mix in with the River of Life, will give others a distorted picture of the Lord Jesus. It also will create double mindedness in your life. You will become ineffective. It will actually choke the Word out.

I was reminded of a parable that Jesus had said about a farmer who planted seed and weeds had grown up and choked out the Word. This sounded very similar to that situation.

"Aren't You worried that people will see the TDS's and get the wrong impression of You? Won't people associate the TDS's with your character?" I spoke passionately being deeply troubled by what I was hearing.

Emmanuel laughed a hearty laugh while giving my shoulder a gentle push. "You forget that I am the Son of God. I am totally secure in myself and know who I am. I can take your sin on me and never get tainted with it. In fac., I already have. The great thing is that when you become a child of God, I give you that same power.

"The River of Life must be pure as it enters your heart," Emmanuel said fervently, "and pure as it leaves your heart to minister to others. Only I can make certain that this will happen. To solve this problem, I am going to install a water treatment system here,"

. "While we were talking, the deliveryman from KPS showed up with a long box. Emmanuel tore the cardboard off and presented a *Spiritual Water Treatment system*. It was shaped like a cross. The intake was on one side of the cross, and the outtake was on the other side of the cross. The whole cross-looking water treatment system was saturated with a red substance.

I was intrigued to see how this would work. I also started having a nagging feeling that I had seen this water treatment system twenty years ago when I had first got my new house but somehow over time I got the impression it wasn't that important.

The Water Treatment System

Emmanuel grabbed a couple of pipe wrenches, and started hooking everything up. "All water coming into your heart and home must be filtered through the cross," Emmanuel said with a grunt as He tightened the threads down on one side. "The cross is saturated with My blood. All water that comes out the other end will be pure living water. This system will not need to regenerate every so many gallons of use like a system in the natural world would, because My blood washes away all sin as far as the east is from the west. You will be able to add soap (Word), where needed with this living water and will find it will give you health, life, clean skin, and pure clean clothes. Your dishes will sparkle and everything you wash with it will glisten. Use this water of Life for everything."

"The big difference you will see is that because you are living in total obedience with all sin confessed, the Living Water flowing through you will not be cancelled out like it did in the past and create a spiritual scum. People will be able to see Me without all the hardness of Freddie fleash in the way. In fact, in time as you live in my love you are going to find a huge difference in Freddie fleash. He has been following the wrong master for so long that he doesn't know who his real master is. You will see a new discipline and devotion in him soon. As your spirit continues to get clearer vision, you will re train him. Your flesh is neither good nor evil. It will eventually always follow the heart's desire.

"Anyway," Emmanuel said turning back to the matters of the present, "the Word of God will actually grow and multiply as you apply it to my Living Water. You will experience great fullness and fruitfulness."

"It's that easy," Emmanuel said with a wide grin. "You die daily to your selfish desires and let the love of God flow through you."

The Dwelling Place

"Wash the dust of worldly Wendy off yourself daily. Don't let anything of this world build up in you. Just being in the world and being exposed to things you see, hear, smell, touch and taste needs the washing of the Word. Keep a clean house. Take lots of body showers. Make it your goal to be clean and pure. Make it your passion to live holy even as I have declared you to be holy".

Emmanuel looked me square in the eyes and with an intensity I had not seen to this point said, "Living Holy does not make you Holy, but you live Holy because you are already declared to be Holy. If you use only the pure Living Water and my Word (soap), and remove your old man (hardness), you will discover that everything will grow to its full potential of use. Living Holy will help you to see your identity clearly. Wash all your clothes in treated water. Don't forget to drink eight glasses of living water every day."

> *Living holy does not make you holy but you live holy because you are already declared to be holy*

"That is a lot of water," I exclaimed.

"Well, that's because you need a lot of the Word. If you hide my Word (Living Water) in your heart you will not sin against me or yourself," Emmanuel said encouragingly. (Ps.119:11)

"If you drink lots of water day and night you will prosper and have good success," (Josh 1:8) Comforter instructed.

"If you hide God's Word in your heart you will get lots of revelation," Rhema wrote with a flourish on His notepad.

I was so grateful to my three amazing companions. They were so patient and taught me in detail everything I needed to know.

Our discourse was interrupted as I heard Emmanuel say with a deep sigh, "I could use a break,"

The Water Treatment System

"Me too!" I piped up while looking over at Comforter and Rhema who both jumped up and nodded in unison.

"Imagine that," I thought. "Emmanuel, Comforter and Rhema needed a break!" I pondered for a moment on the difference between Worldly Wendy's philosophy that you "deserve a break" and Emmanuel's simple "Let's take a break because it is a necessary thing to do.

Our hearts leapt for joy as we headed back to the wine vat of His Presence. It was time to get drunk. Arm in arm we sang songs of joy and praise to the Father. He was so worthy to be worshipped. Comforter and Rhema were clapping and high fiving. Getting drunk meant we would be "in the Spirit".

Emmanuel ran ahead and picked up a bottle of 'Joy Juice' and 'Adoration'.

Comforter picked up the bottle from Emmanuel and held it up in the air while looking at the date on the label. It was 33AD.

> *Living Holy will help you to see your identity clearly*

"This was a good year. Let's celebrate Emmanuel's Resurrection," Comforter said joyously. He sat down at the table and poured each of us a glass. It was time to relax and reminisce. It was time to get smashed in the Holy Spirit. It was great to be a Christian! Worship had begun again, and it was not even noon yet!

As we sat there getting drunk in the Spirit, Emmanuel said with a quiet exuberance to me, "Did you notice the new addition to the Worship and Praise Center?"

Shaking my head, I turned to look behind me. Squealing with delight, I started jumping up and down. While we were in the trophy room, someone had come and installed a Jacuzzi. I turned to see a man rounding the corner dressed in purple with a purple base ball hat. "What can Purple do for you?" I heard him chime as he gave a big grin. "I love Kingdom Postal Service," I said shaking my head

You brought me a Jacuzzi!" I sang back, as he rounded the corner with his tool box and disappeared from sight.

I heard an echo from the KPS man echo down the hallway. "Enjoy!"

"This Jacuzzi is a very important part of your worship," Emmanuel said with a growing enthusiasm. He proceeded to clap His hands with joy. "It is here that you will learn to spend from a few minutes to a few hours soaking in the Presence of the Lord."

"Soaking?" I said inquisitively.

"Yes, soaking," Emmanuel said with a lilt in His voice. "Now that We have pure Living Water that has been filtered through your amazing water treatment system, I want you to sit in the Living Water that fills this Jacuzzi and just listen. Listen and be in God's presence. At first it will be only for a few minutes until you get used to the hot water. You may find it hard to concentrate and be still at first, but over time, I want you to spend more and more time soaking. Your walk with the Father is to be more about being than doing. It is about being in the Presence of God and just listening. I provided you with this amazing soaking music to listen to. I have anointed it," Comforter said confidently, "to be an oil and wine to your spirit."

"Would you teach me how?" I asked. "I mean to do this 'soaking thing'?"

Comforter and Emmanuel laughed a joyous laugh. "It would be our pleasure." Minutes later we were all in the Jacuzzi soaking in the Presence of the Father. My head was filled with Godly thoughts and dreams as Comforter ministered to me. Spiritual thoughts and scripture

The Water Treatment System

were drawn up from the pool of my subconscious, as I rested in the Presence of God. Emmanuel put a cd on and we soaked in its worship.

It was one of the first songs that the Holy Spirit had birthed in me when I was pursing the presence of God for forty days.

More of You
More of You
O Lord I want more of You (2 xs)

Saturate me
Soak me again
Your Spirit stirring
Deep within
Take my whole life
Your presence fill
Teach me Your ways
I will be still

©2006 More of You
Words and Music by John M. Davidson

I dozed off into a deep sleep but even while I slept, I found myself being refreshed and ministered to. Ha! There was no condemnation. There was no shame. I had fallen asleep worshipping the Father.

It was sooooo awesome! Emmanuel and Comforter leaned back in the Jacuzzi and breathed in the steam as it wafted off the water. Sweat streamed off our faces as the heat of God's Holiness surrounded us.

I awoke for a moment to gaze over at Emmanuel and Comforter. I noticed a deep satisfied smile cross their faces as they rested in the Father's love. Emmanuel had two cucumber slices over His eyes and His head was tilted back with His mouth wide open. He let out a little snort

The Dwelling Place

as He too had settled into a deep sleep. Every once in a while you would hear Him mumble in His sleep, "More of You Father, More of You."

"Amazing!" I thought. "I had this all wrong."

Does anything offend these guys? They were so easy to be with! It seems like the key was to worship the Father together. It was resting in each other's presence enjoying each other and being in harmony with each other. If you fall asleep doing it, that's OK too. "Hmmmmm!"

I remember Jesus asking Peter in the Garden of Gethsemane if he would stay awake and pray for awhile. Rhema showed me that there were different times and seasons. That time was an urgent time to press in. This was different. This was a season to rest; this was a season to soak.

I found this to be so interesting and fascinating. I was actually feeling no shame or condemnation. I dreamed of the Fathers love as I dozed off into a deep sleep of peace and rest.

After a lengthy refreshing time of worship or should I say, 'worsleep', I awoke to Emmanuel bringing me a pure, clear, cold glass of water.

. "This is the best water you will ever drink," Emmanuel said with a satisfied sigh. "I got this from the kitchen sink. It's the first glass of purified water from the new system. That Water Treatment System makes the water so crystal pure, even the ice cubes are like glass!"

I held the glass up to the window. It was true. You could clearly see the trees outside without any distortion. This had to be really pure water because I could not even see the ice cubes. I slowly drank the whole glass, savoring its restorative attributes..

Wow! It really was so satisfying and refreshing! Revelation flooded my mind as the Living Water satisfied my thirst. I burst out in adoration and praise again.

The Water Treatment System

"Thank You, Emmanuel, that really quenched my thirst," I said enthusiastically.

"You're welcome", Emmanuel responded with a welcoming laugh, as I handed Him the glass back. "There is always more where that came from."

"What do you call that kind of water?" I said inquisitively.

"Oh, we call that *Waterade*," Emmanuel quipped.

"That's funny!" I said. "That's real funny." I laughed so hard my sides hurt.

I dried myself off and changed clothes. I was having a bit of a hard time walking as we headed back to the library. I was feeling just a little bit tipsy. Soaking for an hour had made me so relaxed, I felt weak at the knees.

We were getting ready to climb the stairs when Emmanuel noticed the furnace off to the left. Stepping away from the stairs He walked over to the furnace and began to make a thorough inspection.

Taking a handkerchief out of His pocket, Emmanuel began to rub an area where there was a name plate. It was totally covered in grime and dirt. Getting down on His hands and knees He took a flashlight out of His pocket and began to rub His cheek as a slow frown began to form...

15

THE FURNACE

"Aaahhh! I see you only have an 80% furnace here; let me upgrade that," Emmanuel replied confidently as He pulled the cover off the main unit and began looking at the schematics on the cover. "Let's upgrade you to a 100% capacity. I have a new brand name that will replace this old furnace," Emmanuel stated with keen observation. "It is perfectly suited for this house and will completely solve your heating and cooling problems."

I heard a clump on the steps. Already a couple of workers from KPS were coming down the stairs carrying a big box. In it was a brand new furnace.

"This is remarkable!" I said with a profound sense of wonder. "I didn't even ask and you answered."

"Oh, but you did ask," Emmanuel said.

"I did?" was my response as I frowned slightly.

The Dwelling Place

"You already had told me to put good things in your heart and you gave me full permission," Emmanuel responded fervently as He gave me a broad smile. Eagerly, I looked over the Workers shoulders as they pulled the brand spanking new furnace out of the box, set it upright on the floor and started tearing out the old.

Emmanuel began to chuckle, as He pointed to the label on the old furnace. "You had that old WD furnace in here."

"I had a WD furnace in my house?" I asked feeling quite dumbfounded. "What is a WD furnace?"

"You have a worldly desire furnace," Emmanuel explained patiently. "Let me ask you something. Did you find this furnace to be unpredictable and that it made you hot or cold in the flesh?" Without waiting for me to answer, Emmanuel continued, "Would I be guessing right to say that it put off an atmosphere in your heart that catered to the old man and his cohorts? This furnace used to cause you all kinds of problems didn't it?"

I gave Emmanuel a startled look. "Well yeah, it sure did," I said shaking my head profusely. "It was almost like my emotions were out of control. I was up and down and could not get good airflow when I needed it. I felt like a yo-yo. This furnace sometimes made me hot in the flesh. I got really angry, lustful, bitter and worried. I was easily offended, and got dry and itchy skin. When I turned the A/C on, I got cold and distant; I was emotionally disconnected. I found that I was wrapping blankets around myself and isolating myself from others; it was awful. It was almost like the air that I breathed encouraged me to cater to my sinful nature within me. I thought that was normal. Was that why I was having a hard time putting to death the fat man?"

I was sure Rhema was getting writer's cramp. He was writing the Words that Emmanuel was saying to me in revelation form so I could easily understand. It was as if the light had been turned on, and I saw the atmosphere of my heart for what it really was. It really was a worldly

The Furnace

desire atmosphere. This furnace in my heart was actually affecting the air I breathed, and it produced a worldly atmosphere. It suddenly dawned on me that the WD air flowing through the air ducts was the FOG.

"Oh my!" I gasped. This furnace was distributing a form of godliness throughout my heart. A worldly desire furnace could do that? I paced the floor for a moment as I tried to figure this all out.

"Who talked you into installing this furnace in your house? This house came standard with a GD furnace, Emmanuel said with a quizzical look on His face.

I thought hard for a moment until I remembered a conversation I had years ago with worldly Wendy. "Now I remember," I said as jumped up from my chair. I raised my index finger in the air as my mouth was caught in an open motion. "Uhhhhhh, worldly Wendy told me about this furnace and said it was the best type to put in. I never thought twice about it. It seemed like the right thing to do at the time."

"As you can see," Emmanuel said firmly. "Listening to the wrong voices can get you into a lot of trouble."

"Tell me about this new furnace," I said anxiously, feeling a bit uncomfortable at being duped. Obviously I had been deceived into installing the wrong heating and cooling system. Hope began to rise up within me with a new intensity. "I had been running the wrong furnace all this time but now ..." My thoughts were interrupted by...

"This is the new GD furnace," Emmanuel replied, with great vigor. It truly is the best furnace on the market. Emmanuel was running His fingers lightly over the top of the furnace, as He smiled with great admiration.

"What does GD stand for?" I asked inquisitively, snapping back to the reality of the moment.

The Dwelling Place

Emmanuel lifted His hand off the furnace, stopped and looked me evenly in the eye. He placed His hands on either side of my shoulders, gripping them tightly, and said fervently, "This furnace stands for *Godly Desire*. I am putting a *Godly Desire* in your heart, but you need something to trigger it.

"I can help with that," Comforter said as he strode confidently into the room. Comforter reached into the box and pulled out an item that looked like a watch. "I am putting this remarkable thermostat in your hands," Comforter responded excitedly. "There is no end in either direction for this thermostat. You can either turn it up for greater fiery desire for the things of God, or you can turn it down for cool and refreshing times. There, see the A/C button there?" Emmanuel placed my finger on the dial so I could become accustomed to it. "This thermostat is state of the art. There is a switch here to turn it to hot or cold. If you desire more of God, turn the thermostat up; yield to it; meditate on the directions. The stronger *Godly Desire* flows through your heart, the more easily things will function properly in your heart and home. This furnace was tailor made for this house."

Emmanuel smiled excitedly as His eyes moved between Comforters and mine as he sensed my excitement.

I jolted upright as I began to comprehend the significance of this magnificent machine.

"When you sense that things are cool outside your heart, and worldly Wendy is pressing in on you, you will naturally want to turn *Godly Desire* up for more heat. When you sense the heat of persecution, pressures and stress, turn the thermostat to cool for those healing, refreshing times. This is the air you breathe; this is the atmosphere. Let your heart be saturated with the air of *Godly Desire*," Comforter instructed. "This thermostat is state of the art. A company called 'Self Control' makes it. It is actually one of My companies. You probably know

The Furnace

the umbrella corporation. It is called 'Fruit of the Spirit'." I laughed as I caught the connection.

I held the thermostat in my hands in wonder and examined it thoroughly. It really did look more like a wrist watch than a thermostat which I was accustomed to seeing attached to the wall.

"Put it on," Emmanuel said eagerly. "This thermostat is designed to wear like a watch. You will want to keep it on at all times so you have easy access to change the temperature and humidity levels as they need to be adjusted."

I put the wristwatch thermostat on my hand and continued examining it.

"Oh! And it is voice activated. All you have to do is say, 'I need more *Godly Desire*'."

"I need more *Godly Desire*," I spoke calmly and clearly as I held my wrist up near my mouth. I heard a whirling noise and a fan start up, and Viola! The furnace started blowing Godly Desire through the duct works. I raised my hands in mock surrender.

"This is so easy," I stated while shaking my head at this incredible discovery. I loved the idea that I could ask for more. All I needed to do was ask for Godly Desire to kick in, and by simply asking, the air of God's presence would fill my heart. The infrastructure was installed. I was ecstatic! I would be able to have coolness in the summer months and heat in the winter months. No matter what the season and I had the feeling that I might often experience several seasons in one day, I was covered no matter what.

"So, how do I get *Godly Desire* again?" I asked in almost a teasing way.

The Dwelling Place

Emmanuel and Comforter both laughed a hearty laugh. Ever patient, they explained it calmly again

"You already have it within you and it is connected to each room of your heart. The furnace I just installed is *Godly Desire*. All you have to do is ask, and the thermostat on your arm will remotely fire up the furnace for more heat, or cool it for refreshing times of rest and strengthening.

"Now be careful," Emmanuel exhorted. "If you lust after Worldly Wendy or give your love to her, you will inadvertently reinstall that old WD furnace back. That's what happened last time and you got tricked into installing a rouge furnace."

"Yeah!" Comforter said cautiously, "If you run after the world your thermostat will go invisible. It will simply disappear."

"That's right," Emmanuel said. "If you love the world self control goes out the window."

The last thing I wanted to do is make it harder for me to follow after my three friends. I shook my head with a fierce determined look. There was no way I was going to let that happens again

"Now, back to this new GD furnace," Emmanuel explained meticulously. "All you have to do is ask. You have heat runs and cold air returns. I give *Godly Desire* to saturate the air of your heart, and I have given you the ability to reciprocate, and flow that *Godly Desire* back to me through your prayers, love and devotion. Remember, your identity is not in this furnace or its hot or cold air ducts. You are not your furnace," Emmanuel stressed several times to me. But this furnace will help you to express your identity and it will make it easier for you to have relationship with Us...

Emmanuel handed me the thermostat and as I put it on my wrist, felt a self-respect growing in me. Courage began to manifest itself. I began

The Furnace

to understand that the Christian life was not about me becoming a zero or a nobody. Certainly I could not draw one tiny little thing from fat man. Why would I want to? He was dead! In my new man though, just like Adam in the Garden of Eden, I had great responsibility. Emmanuel and Comforter were giving me great responsibility for my spiritual destiny.

All my life I had been told I was nothing; I'd been told there was "nutton in Dutton". Dutton was the town I grew up in. I had felt spiritually powerless. It had to be all Jesus, I was told, and yet still nothing happened. I tried to let Him do it all, but did not see significant results. I was living my life through performance and duty, not by an intimate relationship with my Creator and Father. I was waiting for God to do everything, and I just sat back and did nothing, and guess what? Nothing happened.

But here I am, a new creation with a new heart that is basically clean, and Emmanuel has placed His desire in my heart and given me the responsibility to control its highs and lows. Self-control was a fruit of the spirit, and I would have the ability to control 'me'. I was empowered to do what is right. I saw that to believe anything else would be a lie. Is this what it meant, "I can do all things through Christ who strengthens me?" I had been waiting so long for Emmanuel and Comforter, with the Fathers help, to do things in me, and here I am being told, you have my Word, you have Comforter, you have a new heart and spirit and you have a body which can now listen to your spirit; now go and do it.

I continued to meditate on that concept that *Godly Desire* was my responsibility to moderate. "Wow! Was that really possible? Emmanuel and Comforter gave me *Godly Desire* and left me to manage and operate it by self-control. What a gift!"

Slowly, other concepts that had developed in my life began to make sense, like the pantry. It was my responsibility to give the right ingredients to Conscience. I was to choose what was stored up in my life.

The Dwelling Place

Good things come from God and life gives me good things and bad things, and obviously devlin is trying to give me bad things. I must choose. I must be humble and teachable and listen to the right voices.

It was at this point that I had a conflicting thought.

"What about Jack?" I muttered to myself.

Suddenly, I felt a bit confused. Jack was my security guard, so to speak, that protected me. He made most of the decisions that helped keep me safe. He was the one who made me feel important and significant. He's the one who fetched the 'whine' bottles.

I had known Jack almost my whole life, and he was the one who controlled things and kept things safe. He was the one who made a lot of the decisions for me.

> *Emmanuel gave me Godly Desire and left me to manage and operate it; by self-control*

Although I knew Jack, he had not been totally visible until now. He was the one I turned to when I needed help the most. "What about Jack?" I sputtered. "How did He fit into all of this? Now I am being told that I must make choices."

"You can ask me about Jack," Emmanuel said gently, interrupting my conflicting thoughts. Up until this moment, Jack had been almost like a shadow in the background. When a wound or hurt was imminent, he was always out there like a wall to protect me. He pulled the curtains shut when pain looked into the window of my heart. He did what seemed best to protect me from the wounds and hurts I had experienced in my life. I had always wondered about Jack. He was like a shadow, always present, but not consciously. He was my life; a part of me that I had created and yet, it seemed that things were changing.

The Furnace

It wasn't like we talked consciously to each other or even answered each other. He was a part of my mind that had been developed as a young child to protect me. I was now starting to listen and rely more on Emmanuel and was finding Him more reliable and true. He could be trusted for the right outcome. But oh, it was those times of hurt and pain that seemed to cause a sharp right angle turn. I would turn away from trusting Emmanuel's love and it would be as if I jumped right back to depending on Jack again.

It was hard to make sense of this. There were times when I was living in joy and in the presence of Emmanuel, and then, out of the blue, I would respond from that quiet rebellion and go back to my sinful patterns of behavior. It was as if a part of me was acting contrary to what I now believed. I often felt even double minded. What was that all about?

> *It seemed as if I had responded out of the blue from that quiet rebellion and went back to my sinful patterns of behavior*

I turned to Emmanuel in exasperation and said, "What does this mean? How does Jack fit into all of this?"

Looking deep into my anguished eyes, Emmanuel lovingly said, "Jack is a part of you. You made him up to help protect yourself when you were five years old. Remember that Christmas Eve night when you were four going on five that you and I have visited so many times? You were so hurt about not getting those Christmas presents because you were told that you were bad. You were made to watch and could not play with your brothers when they got their presents. This was your way of coping with that hurt and the pain. You did not know that I was there protecting you and caring for you. When you were hurt so bad and felt that deep rejection from your parents-- you put up a wall. That wall was actually Jack, who you created to protect yourself from being hurt so deeply.

The Dwelling Place

"But, Jack looks and feels so real; I need Him," I wailed.

Tears were splashing angrily down my face. I pounded my fists on Emmanuel's chest as the pain inside racked my body. Emmanuel drew me close and held me gently as He stroked my hair softly. I felt the firm heartbeat of God my Father pounding strongly in measured beats against my ear as I buried my head deeper into His chest...

"I know," Comforter cooed gently, as He came along side us and placed a loving hand on my arm. "Jack has done a good job for you in your eyes all these years, but the outcome was never meant for your core identity to be satisfied by yourself or a creation that you made to protect you. Only Emmanuel can do that!

Emmanuel picked up from where Comforter had left off and continued,

"Jack was always there and always faithful, but you created him to replace me. Jack can never love you unconditionally; he can never give you peace and rest. Only I can do that. He can only protect you from being hurt by creating distance and then often his decisions are not what are truly best for you. They actually cause you more pain. Can you see that?"

> *The outcome was never meant for your core identity to be satisfied by yourself or a creation that you made to protect you. Only Emmanuel can do that*

Rhema was writing furiously as Emmanuel continued to speak soothingly to me. My breathing was hot and heavy. Panic was welling up in my throat. Could I totally give up Jack for Jesus?

"Has the outcome ever been totally peaceful and satisfying with Jack, or has he mostly catered to your whims and wishes?" Emmanuel said in a very calming way to me.

The Furnace

I thought deeply about this for a moment. There were some good times, but mostly I seemed to be in a deeper mess…. hahmmmm! Resolution began to stir within me. I had spent enough time with Emmanuel to see the solution. Jack had to go. I had said 'whatever it takes'. Pain struck my heart. The connection between Jack and I was so strong.

"Can I say goodbye to Jack?" I asked Emmanuel softly. "Will he be alone and hurt?"

"Every person, even the ones you create is always treated with honor and respect," Emmanuel stated with a calm reassurance. "He can come to My feet and find peace and rest."

I quickly motioned to Jack to come near us. Jack appeared from the shadows of a side door.

"I heard everything," Jack said, with sadness in his eyes and a crackling sound in his voice. "I don't want to leave. What will I do?" Jack asked meekly. "I need to keep busy. I have things to do. I need to help you."

My heart prompted me to sadness as I observed a great struggle reflecting in Jacks eyes.

Rhema was again writing as if on a mission. Almost immediately, thoughts began to flood through my mind that I was to take notice of the tattoos, jewelry and glasses that Jack wore, for they had tremendous significance, but to shelf it away until later. Now was not the time. Jack wore a pair of black glasses with lens that had a rose colored hue. When he talked, you could see a tongue stud that was silver and it looked like a pearl pierced through the middle of his tongue. In his ears were hearing aids and he had emerald studded earrings. On each of his fingers were tattoos that looked like black dots (one for each finger). He also had a silver nose ring.

The Dwelling Place

Sadness filled my eyes as I lifted my eyes to catch his. "Jack, you have been a good friend. You really did try every way you could to help me; but it is time for me to move on. Only Jesus can truly fill the spot that you have been helping me with."

I reached out to touch Jack and gave him a gentle squeeze. "I just did not see it until now." I said with measured breath. "Thank you for everything. You must go to the feet of Jesus. There you will find peace and rest," I looked at Jack with a firmness and resolution in my eyes.

Emmanuel looked at Jack and said, "If I can give you peace and rest, would you like that?" Jack looked almost relieved.

"I would like that," Jack sighed with relief. "I long for peace and rest. I'm tired of feeling that I am living life over and over like a repeating tape recorder with no end."

The words had hardly escaped his mouth and he was gone. I fell on my knees to the floor crying profusely and weeping. Great globs of green and black goo came gushing up from deep within me and splattered on the floor. I heaved and coughed and felt like I was gagging for what seemed like forever, and then it suddenly stopped. I looked over to the door, holding my stomach and stared at the place that Jack had left while rocking back and forth on my knees; it was closed.

I sat there on the floor gazing at the door where Jack had just gone through and watched Comforter bring a basin of warm water, some wash clothes and towels, and began to help me clean up the green goo. Comforter began humming a love song that I had written for my wife while staying with friends down in Belize, South America over a Christmas Break.

> **You are the love of my life**
> **All I have and all I am (are yours)**
> **No matter what comes my way**
> **We'll do it hand in hand**

The Furnace

**Our love will last forever
It will stand. It will stand.**

2007©Our Love is forever
Words and Music by John Davidson

While Rhema was writing, it suddenly dawned on me that Comforter was singing this to me as His lover. This was directly from His heart to mine. I felt the bonds between my wife and myself and the trinity three suddenly tightens up in a tightly wrapped cord. While He continued to minister to me, Emmanuel walked over to the door and touched it. He lightly traced the outside edge of the door on all four sides with His finger.

"It is finished," Emmanuel said quietly. Taking out his paintbrush, He began to paint the door with His special red paint. The door turned from red to white almost immediately. A moment later, it began to fade and then disappeared totally from sight. The door was gone and all that was left was the wall!

I looked on in amazement. Jack was gone; the door for Jack to come back was closed. Emmanuel had painted it with His special red paint and now even the door had disappeared. All that remained was Emmanuel and I.

> Do you believe that I am more than enough?" Emmanuel said softly?

"Do you believe that I am more than enough?" Emmanuel said softly.

A new soundness and freshness began to strengthen my mind. My thought processes were suddenly clearer and quicker. It did not seem conflicted. Wow! I felt free. It was as if my mind had integrated itself together.

"How many tens of millions of people had done what I had done to protect themselves?" I wondered with no little uncertainty. My thoughts swirled with this incredible revelation of myself. To cope with the pain in

The Dwelling Place

their heart the only way they knew how even as I did was by creating someone or something to protect themselves? How much longer could I have gone before I would have gone too far? How close had I come to the edge? Some people have gone so far with their creations that they eventually went insane. I was so grateful this had not gone to that extent.

My thoughts came back to the matter at hand. I began to feel a great freedom and suddenly realized that I still held the remote thermostat in my hands. Putting my finger on the dial, I turned it up for more *Godly Desire*. I heard a click in the furnace and the burners kicked on. I smiled to myself as I felt Emmanuel's approving smile. Emmanuel reached over and squeezed my shoulder. "I guess I'll take that as a yes! You know what this means now, don't you?"

"What?" I replied, turning to face Emmanuel.

"With Jack gone, you have to replace him with someone else; someone you trust."

With *Godly Desire* now blowing directly in my face, I laughed and said with eager delight, "That's easy; I replace him with You!"

"I knew you would," Emmanuel replied laughing easily with a deep, hearty laugh. "I just wanted you to hear yourself say it. You no longer need to fear the door. I have sealed it with my blood."

I embraced Emmanuel deeply and hugged Him as if I would never let Him go. I felt so secure in His arms.

"You are so completely satisfying," I blurted out. "I am so at peace in Your arms."

Emmanuel responded by giving me a long and satisfying bear hug in return. As I rested in Emmanuel's embrace, Emmanuel whispered softly yet tenderly in my ear. "Son, I have not given you a spirit of fear, but of love, power and a sound mind."

The Furnace

The workers had just finishing installing the furnace and had finished all the necessary testing. After giving us a thumbs-up, we climbed the stairs and headed for the library. Having Emmanuel in my heart and giving Him full access to do or change things as He wished was a mind-boggling experience. I was shaking my head wondering why I had ever thought that I could do a better job on my own. Why I ever thought that those yahoo knuckleheads and Fat Man had even one best thread of interest that was good for me was now beyond my wildest imagination.

Emmanuel had a satisfied look on his face and I knew it was because a key function necessary to my well being had been integrated into my heart and house.

Emmanuel turned his head back towards me and said, "I will leave a couple of glasses of cold water sitting on the table near the library door. Watch out for those invisible ice cubes." Emmanuel's eyes twinkled as He gave me a warm nod. You will need all the strength I can give you to process that room."

"What a guy!" I thought. "He always seems to know my needs before I ask."

Emmanuel had this unique ability to make me feel that I was on the same level as Him. We were becoming knit together as best friends. I felt so honored by Him. It hadn't dawned on me yet that I had stopped calling Him Master.

16

THE OLD LIBRARY

As I walked down the hallways of faith, I gathered strength from the scriptures on the walls. Already *Godly Desire* was filling my senses and motivating me as I walked through the hallways and into the living room. The atmosphere was becoming more and more conducive to following after God. My mind felt so clear and the ringing in my ears had stopped. I breathed in deeply, savoring every moment. All things were so new. I could not seem to drink in enough of this new beauty.

Emmanuel joined me by doing the same. We paused for a moment to reflect on the great things that Father God was doing in and through me. Taking in a deep gulp of air we both held it in until our eyes and cheeks began to bulge. Suddenly, we both burst out laughing as we could hold it no longer. We gave each other knowing looks and high fives.

I glanced around the room and observed that the rooms seemed to be more spacious and brighter than previously noted. I noticed that most of the rooms were clean but empty. The walls sparkled with the fresh white paint that had been applied. It was so invigorating. I wondered

The Dwelling Place

when or how the furniture, plants, carpet, and pictures for the walls would arrive...especially the living room; it was always the main room that people saw and enjoyed the most. I had a sense that it would not be long before these rooms would look cozy and comfortable. I turned to Emmanuel and made a passing comment about replacing what was in the rooms with something else.

Emmanuel gave me an affectionate smile and replied, "It will be sooner than you think and more wonderful than you could ever imagine."

I was trying to think what was so different about the living room. It suddenly dawned on me. The maze of brick walls that had subdivided the living room was completely gone. The stonework was also gone and the walls were freshly painted.

I shook my head in wonderment as Emmanuel and I sauntered through the living room on our way to the library. The living room now had the feel of being fresh, uncluttered, and spacious.

> Every action and reaction, comes back to your thought processes

We eventually came to a door off the living room hallway. I grabbed my glass of water from the end table and took a deep drink. I was so thirsty that I spilled the water, and it trickled off my chin creating a water spot on my shirt. Breathing a sigh of contentment, I brushed the water spot and followed Emmanuel as He opened the door and we both stepped in.

The room had pine bookshelves on two walls opposite each other. The wall opposite the door was all windows. In front of the window was a large desk with a beautiful leather chair. The bookshelves were built from the top of the ceiling to bottom of the floor. It was obviously some kind of office or library.

A beautiful pine ladder on rollers allowed a person to move the ladder back and forth to reach books that were hard to reach on the top

The Old Library

shelves. I reached out to touch the ladder and gave it a gentle shove. The ladder moved effortlessly along its rollers making a low whirling noise. The shelves were not open like the kind where you could see the spines on the books, as in a typical library. They were divided up into sections with stained glass doors on them. The stained glass was etched with all sorts of religious pictures. I turned with a perplexed look to Emmanuel and inquired about the significance of this room.

"Everything in this room has to do with how you think. Every action and reaction comes back to your thought processes. All these books represent your belief systems," Emmanuel said. "When you were born you didn't have much of a belief system about what would make you happy, sad or indifferent. This room was practically empty at that time. Over time though, you have developed beliefs and attitudes and thought structures about life through interaction with family, friends, acquaintances, the environment, the Bible, and so forth as you have grown up.

"Some of your belief systems are built on Biblical ideals and some are built on Worldly Wendy and Freddie fleshly ideals. There is a whole section of books that Jack wrote here also. Even with Jack gone, we will still have to contend with the belief system he has written into your heart."

"Who is Jill? Do I know this author?" I asked while picking up a well-worn book off the shelf and leafing casually through its pages. "There seems to be a whole section of books by her."

I ran my finger along the spines of the books and wondered about their age. They looked quite worn.

Rhema scribbled a note on His pad and revelation hit me. "Jill is the counterpart to Jack and another part of you that you have created. Be patient; you are almost ready to confront her." I turned my attention

The Dwelling Place

back to the structure of the shelves. I so admired the elegant doors and stained glass that hid all the books.

"The doors and stained glass pictures are indicative of a religious spirit that surrounds your belief system," Emmanuel said cutting through my thinking like a knife... "It all looks beautiful and holy to the untrained eye. You grew up in a religious home, but you did not embrace things from a willing heart. Today, we will begin to sort that all out."

I frowned at the interjection. I was just beginning to admire these beautiful and spiritual looking stained glass windows. "How do we do that?" I asked pensively.

"Well, Comforter and Rhema are going to teach and reveal all things to you. The pine book shelves have just as much significance as the books on the shelves. I need to go meet the delivery person. With what is happening in this room in the next few hours, I believe the living room is going to be filled with fine furniture. I am really excited to show you what I have for you. I have given this a lot of thought," Emmanuel said, as He rubbed His hands together with gleeful expectation.

"Hmmm!" I said to myself, "I wonder what that means? It would be nice to have the living room complete. That's it isn't it!"

Emmanuel placed a hand over His mouth to cover an obvious grin and with a twinkle in his eye went whistling out the door. As I watched him leave, the door disappeared! "No doors!" I mused in amazement.

I took a deep breath and turned to Comforter and Rhema. It was time to get down to business. "I'm ready," I said as I breathed nervously.

Comforter turned to look at me with a kind, steady gaze, gave my arm a gentle pat, and then turned and took an old book off the shelf and laid it on the desk. Rhema had already opened a beautiful leather bound book on the desk top. It was the master key and everything on the

The Old Library

shelves must line up to what was in this ancient book. They began matching up belief systems from my library to what was in the old worn book. After an hour of cross referencing and writing things down, Comforter gave me a grave look and said, "I have an immediate assignment for you. We were looking for positive beliefs but all we have found so far is nine hundred wrong belief systems that you have."

"What?" I said dumbfounded. "What do you mean there are nine hundred wrong belief systems?" I felt a little uncomfortable that they found so many things in such a short time that I wrongly believed.

"If you don't change these wrong belief systems, you will find yourself continually double minded and your heart breached by Fat Man and his cohorts. Those guys are real sneaky and they are real perturbed right now. They are looking for any way they can to get back into this house and take possession. It is also your choice whether you leave Jack at Jesus' feet, or invite him back. The choice is yours."

> You can have the cleanest house, but if you hold on to these belief systems that don't line up with the living Word they will destroy you

Comforter continued to tell me that by building the right thoughts inside me and making them a part of this library, I build firewalls that the enemy can't get through.

"Firewalls", I thought. "It's just like in a computer. You need to have a good protection system in place or viruses will invade and destroy. "It seems that I had already been invaded with viruses and Trojan horses so to speak," I murmured as I pursed my lips together thoughtfully. "It's no wonder I felt confused, sluggish and ineffective."

"The right thoughts and actions come from this master key that we are comparing your belief systems too. In this book are the very words of God.

The Dwelling Place

This master key as I was about to find out was in fact was absolute to these three guys. It was the plumb line and it was amazing how serious they took this book.

Take these twenty-one verses on God's promises from this Bible and memorize them completely," Comforter said with conviction. "I don't want you just to memorize them, but meditate on them day and night. We will then teach you how to implement them. Just these twenty-one verses combined with Rhema's revelation, will cancel out eight hundred of these wrong belief systems. In fact, not only will it cancel them out, but it will actually be like a knife cutting right through to the heart of the matter, and will divide it out from soul and spirit. It will take a while and you will have to put in practice what you meditate on, but the results will be that you will have good success.

"Meditating on these verses has to be in the context of developing intimacy with the Trinity Three," Comforter said. "You must displace orphan thinking and replace it with son-ship thinking; we are here to help make that happen in you. We will add more verses later, but this will be a great start for you. If you just memorize these verses though, without developing intimacy with us, you only build more stained glass windows. You cannot look at this as simply an assignment. You cannot see this as simply a chore to do. These are the very words of Life from Emmanuel. Do all in context of relationship with him. If We find it invaluable to compare your beliefs to this book, then you need to find it just as important to memorize and meditate on these verses from this book to put it in your life.

"Cancel any distractions that Worldly Wendy is cabling and inter netting into your heart," Comforter stated emphatically. "You must stop the flow of these wrong belief systems.

The Old Library

"You can have the cleanest house, but if you hold on to these belief systems that don't line up with the Living Word, they will destroy you. You will face a situation and will revert back to what you believe; wrongly, I might add, and it will open a doorway for the enemy to walk right back in. We must change what you believe!

"Turn around," Comforter said. "Now stand up straight." Taking a steel rod, He miraculously fused it into my back. "You now have a spiritual backbone. This will help you discipline yourself for the task ahead."

"Twenty-one verses would take care of 90% of my wrong belief systems," I mumbled under my breath. The fact that it was exactly twenty-one verses did not escape me. Reaching the age of twenty-one was symbolic with becoming a man. I needed to put away childish behavior and childish thinking. I couldn't believe it took me this long to realize this.

> Meditating on these verses has to be in the context of developing intimacy with the trinity three

"Ooops! I can't believe I just said 'can't'! Man, I better get these verses down, and fast. I got to stop saying 'can't'."

Rhema handed me a scroll with His seal on it. "This will be necessary. My seal will open up these words to your heart and give you a totally new meaning. Stay near to us as you complete this assignment. This is not an assignment of intellect, but an assignment of the Spirit.

I took the scroll, broke the seal and began to read the scriptures that Rhema had written down.

As I read the Words of God, they began to leap off the page at me and give new meaning. I was desperate to get these words deep in my heart. My belief system depended on it. I began to devour the Word that had been revealed to me.

The Dwelling Place

"You must love the Lord your God with all your heart, all your soul, and all your mind... and your neighbor as yourself."

(Mathew 22:37) NLT

This first verse gave me the impression that it was the most important verse of all. The word 'all' seemed to be jumping out at me pretty strong. Revelation flooded my mind as I began to see that it really was all or nothing. I could not afford to make the same mistake again that I started to make in the trophy room. God was a loving God and a faith God. I could not come at this half-heartedly. I continued to read:

"And I am convinced that nothing can ever separate us from His love. Death can't, and life can't. Our fears for today, our worries about tomorrow, and even the powers of hell can't keep God's love away. Whether we are high above the sky or in the deepest ocean, nothing in all creation will ever be able to separate us from the love of God that is revealed in Christ Jesus our Lord."

(Romans 8:38-39) NLT

As I read this verse, I began to reminisce though this incredible journey. With Rhema writing profusely, downloads came fast and furious as I compared this written Word with my new experience.

Emmanuel, Rhema and Comforter seemed to have one main focus. That focus was to pour into me an amazing amount of patient love so I could experience the freedom of being all God originally intended me to be. To know that nothing could ever separate me from this beautiful relationship brought tears to my eyes. I felt a settling take place within me. It was done. It was finished. It was like water and an orange. Comforter and Emmanuel are symbolic of the water and I am symbolic of the orange. When you combine the two, you get orange juice. I am a unique flavor all my own for the world to taste. You can no longer separate the two. I am forever mingled and attached to God's love. It

The Old Library

has become a part of me, enhanced and completed who I am. Also, there is no other orange juice that tastes just like me.

I continued to pull out another set of verses and would find these verses to become life verses.

> *"And may you have the power to understand, as all God's people should, how wide, how long, how high, and how deep his love really is.*
>
> *May you experience the love of Christ, though it is so great you will never fully understand it? Then you will be filled with the fullness of life and power that comes from God".*

(Ephesians 3:18-19) NLT

Meditating on these first three sets of verse, produced revelations of God's love and how they were tied to painful memories in my past. One of the most powerful of these memories was in going back to that time when I was four years old on Christmas Eve. I was meeting with a friend of mine,

> *You don't have to strive for my love. I have more than enough for the both of you*

an elder in our church with whom we got together fairly regularly for two years. During one of these times, we spent several hours asking Jesus to take us to painful memories, and then reveal Himself in those memories to bring healing, forgiveness and freedom. Almost a dozen times, Jesus brought me back to that memory of Christmas Eve and the loss of presents, each from a different angle, but the first time was the most powerful.

I saw myself reliving this experience and being all alone in the corner watching my brothers playing with their Christmas presents. I had been told that I could not have any presents for Christmas because I was bad.

The Dwelling Place

I saw my brother playing with his Lionel train set and Jimmy with his car dash. All of a sudden, it was as clear as anything I could ever see; in my sadness of being alienated from experiencing Christmas and getting no earthly presents, I saw Jesus and He was holding presents in both arms.

His smile was radiant. He looked at me with adoring eyes and said, "John, I brought you some presents. May I play with you?"

I stood motionless, overwhelmed by Jesus' words. His large warm smile was so disarming and contagious, and the eagerness in His eyes melted my aching heart. Suddenly, with a mixed expression of joy and pain, I burst out crying and ran into His arms.

"Where have you been," I sobbed. "I have been so all alone." I buried my face in Jesus' chest and cried uncontrollably.

Jesus carefully set down the presents and hugged me tighter while groaning as He said, "I was always here. I have never left you nor have I forsaken you." Jesus stroked my hair, as He whispered gently. "You just never knew where to look until now. It's alright, though, you have found me now." Jesus spoke with a reassuring tone as He continued to stroke my hair.

After comforting for awhile, Jesus responded with renewed enthusiasm, "Look what I got for you!" He handed me one of the presents, and with great excitement watched as I began ripping off the paper. With a great cry of delight, my eyes opened wide as saucers as I saw a shiny new car dash. This was no ordinary car dash though. Compared to what Jimmy had, this was like comparing a Yugo to a Cadillac.

"This is for me?" I cried out with joy, as I stood overwhelmed by such generosity and love.

The Old Library

"I brought you only the best, my precious son!" Jesus beamed with admiration in His eyes.

"But what about all the bad things I've done," I cried hanging my head in shame. "I don't deserve to have Christmas or any Christmas presents."

"Oooohhh," Jesus said stroking my head with tenderness reserved only for the closest of family. "Johnny, you're an amazing kid. I love you so much and I believe in you. You don't need to be jealous of Jimmy. You don't have to strive for My love either. I have more than enough for the both of you.

"No matter what you do or say, nothing can separate you from my love. My heart is to draw you closer to myself. It is never to push you away. I love being with you. I love hearing you laugh and seeing you play. I love looking at your face, of seeing the nuances in your facial expressions and the subtleties of your voice. It is so beautiful to me. Everything about you is beautiful. I love doing all these things with you. Nothing gives me greater joy than spending time with you...OK? I love looking into your hazel brown eyes. These are eyes I created that reveal the depth of your soul. I love looking deep within you. I have been looking forward to this moment for a long time!"

Jesus turned His head sideways and down as He finished saying this so He could look me squarely in my eyes. I still hung my head slightly out of fear that I would be spanked or disciplined in some way. I still felt apprehensive and unsure of what He was saying, but the beginning sparks of trust and hope were igniting and had begun to birth themselves deep within. My mind swirled in anguish as I felt hope rise and fall in those agonizing seconds. What if Jesus was kidding with me and this was some kind of cruel joke? What if He was going to leave and take these presents away?

The Dwelling Place

Reading my thoughts Jesus, put His index finger in a curled position and placed it under my chin. He then gently lifted my face up so He could gaze into my tear stricken eyes and said, "You don't need to be afraid, My dear son, ever again. I will always be here for you and will never withhold My love from you. You can always trust me".

Straightening Himself up, Jesus' countenance changed from a quiet demeanor to a man of action. "Ok! Let's play then!" Jesus responded with a deep belly laugh. He clapped His hands together, and after a moment He laid His hand on the other present tapping His finger seeing if I would get the hint.

> I will always be here for you and will never withhold my love from you. You can always trust me

"Hey! What's in the other package?" I asked, jumping up and down while reaching for the huge present. By now all apprehension was gone.

"Well, let's see," Jesus said with a broad grin. We began to tear open the large box which held a complete Lionel train set.

I stared at it in awe because it was the deluxe version. With a squeal of delight, I joined Jesus as we began to assemble tracks on the sheet of plywood and attach everything together. All night long we played together until we had completed a wide array of tunnels, bridges and train yards. It actually took three sheets of plywood to hold everything together. It looked like a picture out of the Ozark Mountains. It was complete with trees, fields, a real stream of water that flowed under the bridge and everything. I never laughed so hard or enjoyed someone's company so much.

We talked and talked as if we had been friends forever. Suddenly, the vision was gone and I was left sobbing. Even though the vision was over, I did not feel alone. I had a revelation of God's love in a place of my earliest memory outside the womb. I had experienced God's love; a love I

The Old Library

felt I didn't deserve, but yet it was poured out freely on me. This memory that had held so much pain was now filled with such joy, love and good memories. Love like a healing oil poured through all the cracks bringing life and healing.

The remarkable thing was the dream didn't isolate my mom, dad, Jimmy or Rick, but rather put things in a new light. I wasn't jealous anymore, and I wasn't angry and bitter. In fact, I seemed to have a deeper understanding and compassion in their own struggle to discover God's love. They had struggles just like me. They were in their own journey of discovery. The pain was gone, and in its place was compassion. All I had needed was a revelation of God's love, and then to experience it and have it fill all my vision. I felt an eagerness bubble from within that they would experience what I had and to touch this unconditional love; the warmth of Jesus' eyes and His healing touch. I opened my hand to see in it a folded up piece of paper. I unfolded it and read:

> "You can come back to this memory any time you want. I will always be there for you."
>
> Love Jesus

I had seen 1 John 2:15 from the negative side in the past.

> "Love not the world neither the things in the world. If anyone loves the world the love of the Father is not in him." KJV

Here I was living in the dark looking at the light, rather than living in the light dispelling the darkness. Before this vision, I would try to not love the world or lust after things or power. If I did, I felt ashamed and isolated and felt that God's love was not in me. So, I would work hard not

The Dwelling Place

to lust, pursue after things, TV, movies, etc. I would make vows to not look at anything evil. It was either all do's, do's, do's, or it is all don't, don't, don'ts. Do read your Bible, do pray, and do go to church; do, do, and do. My focus was on the dos and don'ts

. Certainly there is value in faithfulness, self control and character. But in my focus, I was missing it and I found it impossible to sustain this focus long term. It became an up and down roller coaster ride of willing myself to be 'holy'. It was hard and not fun and I had to grit myself to do it. I found I was asking myself, "Is this the way it is supposed to be?"

I found myself getting angry because I couldn't sustain the Christian life and would end up being critical and judgmental towards others for not measuring up.

Jesus said that He is the Life and that He came to give Life more abundantly. Should it be this hard? There had to be another reality.

The awesome thing was that there was another reality. I saw it in this revelation of Jesus' love to me. It was in the reality of seeing Ephesians 3:18-19. If I got the power to understand (the revelation) as to how deep and wide, how long and tall God's love was so that it filled my whole vision, and then walk His love out by experiencing His love in everything I do, then I would be filled with all the fullness and power that is in Christ Jesus. The result is that I would not sin.

It is in pursuing passionately after His love. It is not focusing on my sin or trying hard not to do it. It is in focusing in on His love. It is in living in His Presence and enjoying Him.

I never remember Jesus once telling me I was wrong or that He wouldn't play with me until I said I was sorry. It was the outpouring of His goodness and love that brought me to repentance. I was so overwhelmed by His love and mercy; I couldn't help but be sorry for what I had done. This was especially true after feeling His amazing love. Slowly

The Old Library

I began to incorporate and meditate on these verses. I was so amazed at what I was learning. Lies that I had believed all my life were now being exposed for the smear veneer that had clouded my eyes. If this is a revelation of His love, what else am I missing? I began to read and meditate more.

> *"And these signs will accompany those who believe. In my name they will drive out demons, they will speak in new tongues...they will place their hands on sick people and they will get well.*
>
> (Mark 16:18) KJV
>
> *"I tell you the truth, anyone who has faith in me will do what I am doing. And I will do anything you ask in my name, so that the Son may bring glory to the Father. You may ask anything in my name and I will do it."*
>
> (John 14:12-14) NIV
>
> *"The truth is, you can go directly to the Father and ask him, and he will grant your request because you use my name."*
>
> (John 16:23) NLT
>
> *"Have faith in God. Jesus answered. I tell you the truth. If anyone says to this mountain, Go, throw you into the sea, and does not doubt in his heart, but believes that what he says will happen. It will be done for him. Therefore, I tell you, whatever you ask for in prayer, believe that you have received it, and it will be yours."*
>
> (Mark 11:22-24) NIV
>
> *"But when he asks he must believe and not doubt, because he who doubts is like a wave of the sea blown and tossed by the*

The Dwelling Place

wind. That man should not think he would receive anything from the Lord. He is a double minded man, unstable in all he does."

(James 1:6) NIV

"For no matter how many promises God has made, they are "Yes" in Christ."

(2 Corinthians 1:20) NIV

"What this means is that those who become Christians become new persons. They are not the same anymore, for the old life is gone. A new life has begun!"

(2 Corinthians 5:17) NLT

"And I will give you a new heart with new and right desires, and I will put a new spirit in you. I will take out your stony heart of sin and give you a new, obedient heart."

(Ezekiel 36:26) NLT

"I have been crucified with Christ, it is no longer I who live, but Christ lives in me and the life which I now live in the flesh, I live by faith in the Son of God who loved me and gave Himself for me."

(Galatians 2:20) NKJV

"In Him and through faith in Him, we may approach God with freedom and confidence."

(Ephesians 3:12) NIV

"...You are to say to that offense, be you plucked up by the root and be planted in the sea and you shall have already obeyed me."

(Luke 17:6) KJV greek expanded

The Old Library

The more I meditated on these verses, the clearer it became. Emmanuel had given me a set of core verses that spoke to the foundation of my thinking and living. It was about seeing everything through faith, hope and love, but especially love.

Love was to fill my whole vision and be the sum of my experience. This love relationship with my Creator would foster faith and hope. It was starting to make sense in my mind. Now, how do I get it incorporated into my heart so it becomes a part of my experience?

I was so close. I was only one foot away from experiencing God's fullness and power. It was the distance between my ears to my heart. I was about to find out that I was even a lot closer than I thought.

Notes

PART II

FULLNESS OF GODLINESS

17

FULLNESS REVEALED

After reading through these verses and seeing how they had just affected my life in these last few moments, I resolved to get serious about making these verses a part of me. Clearing a corner on the desk, I began the task of putting these verses into a usable form so I could memorize them. I put them on 3 x 5 cards, laminated them and kept them in my pocket.

I thought, meditated, worshiped and talked to Emmanuel and Comforter as they taught me the meaning of these verses. I included these verses and incorporated them into my daily life until they became a part of me. Because I was meditating on them so much, I came across things in my everyday life that paralleled what I was meditating on. It was through this that I found fresh revelation and application to my daily life.

As I pondered these things and meditated on them, I began to realize that we had already begun the move from the first part of the message; <u>a form of godliness</u> to a <u>power of godliness.</u>

The Dwelling Place

We were now transitioning to fullness. My heart began to race and an excitement began to rise up within me. Already, I could see Rhema writing furiously on His notepad. It was amazing that when He wrote on that notepad, a few minutes later, I had new revelation. He wrote, and I experienced. My mind would get illuminated!! I could see in my mind's eye what He was trying to tell me.

Everything about being a child of God came back to faith and love. It was to be a faith in God, love for God and love for others. I was discovering that faith in God was not about trying harder, but rather spending more and more time in my Daddy's Presence and getting to know Him better. He wanted me to experience Him through every activity and situation in my ordinary day. The more I knew Him and experienced Him, the more I experienced faith in God. Relationship created intimacy which created faith. To know Him is to love Him, and to love Him is to trust Him. It is easy to have faith in someone you trust.

I was getting the picture that He must increase and I must decrease. The meaning of this decreasing thing though, was changing. It was about partnering up. I felt important to Emmanuel. It was not about less of me, but it was about more of Him. These guys kept getting me to realize more of myself, and for a long time that really threw me for a loop.

> *Salvation was designed for me to have eternal relationship with my Father*

The difference, though, was that it was not a focus on self, but liberating me to all that God had designed me to be. I was the best of who I was when I was in their Presence. The part of me that was selfish minded, self absorbed, or lived in self worship, that is what had to decrease. In fact it had to die. The part of me that loved God and others from a pure heart, that part was to partner with God and increase. That was the part of me that God had made and declared a *new creation*. I actually thought more of me as I discovered my real identity. I had responsibility and it felt good; I was

Fullness Revealed

including Emmanuel in everything. I found my 'being' flowed from my love of being in relationship with them. My decreasing was becoming more of realizing that it was more about Him in me. I became more of me as I realized more of Him in me. This type of thinking required more expression of gratefulness and thankfulness than ever before.

Why? Because I was learning to discern correctly between the two and sometimes the selfish me would want to take credit for the new me.

The sudden increase in knowledge and understanding of my authority and the awesomeness of being a new creation caused me to realize that it was Him that was working, and was continuing to work within me everything that I was and ever hoped to be.

For so long I had been looking at things from my perception. Now that I was looking at things from the heart of God, it was like a new revelation. As my heart became single minded and focused on Him, His thoughts and desires began to become the dominating force in my heart. New meaning came from this Psalm:

> "Delight yourself in the Lord and he will give you the desires of your heart."
>
> (Psalm 37:4) KJV

Whatever is cleaned out of my house must be exchanged for something else

I had known my desires, but what were His desires? As I pondered this thought it was already becoming clearer to me. As He cleaned out the rooms of my heart and as I let the Trinity Three have total access to every room of my heart, His desires and my desires were becoming one. I began to love His desires for only He had my best interests at heart. Whatever His heart was for me, it would be perfect. I was experiencing a strong desire to do His will. This desire came from deep within me, but it was a deep desire to please Him. I was experiencing a deep fulfillment and peace within. The Rhema Word began to stir stronger

The Dwelling Place

Rhema's revelation to me was that I must believe that Jesus is the answer to every thought, action and deed in my life. Salvation comes from Him. I had confessed my sins and asked Jesus to come into my heart and be my Lord and Savior. Now that He is my Lord and Savior, my heart's desires are that I would love Him with all my heart, soul, and mind (whatever it takes) and love everyone around me just as much as I would love myself. This love would flow from His intimate Presence brooding within. I just released what was within me.

I had begun to believe that when I touched someone, the presence of God flowed from me into them. Just my walking into a room would change the atmosphere, because I carried this precious treasure within me. Salvation was not just a pinpoint prayer of repentance, but also a salvation that had a beginning; never an ending. I had missed the value of the gifts and revelations from God because I restricted the Fathers intimate involvement in my life. The water treatment system, the GD furnace, the mahogany book shelves was all available at salvations birth but I had ignored it. But now I was beginning to see that salvation was designed for me to have eternal relationship with my Father. It was salvation of being freed from lies and established in truth.

> God never takes something away but that he gives something better in its place

Another impression that Rhema was hammering home, is that the Word of God has every answer and solution for my life. I must trust His Word completely. His Word is the solution to everything I face and do. Comforter would teach me everything I need to know. I could trust Him completely.

The last thing given to me was to believe that every promise in the Word of God is for me, and I must believe and claim every one of them by faith. All of this revelation began to flood my mind and heart with anointing oil, and I began to get very excited.

Fullness Revealed

My heart began to well up with an abundant joy. I began to believe that I could trust and have total faith in Jesus. His death was real and His resurrection from the dead was a sure thing.

"My purpose is to give life in all its fullness."

(John 10:10) NLT

This was the source of fullness in my life; the life of Jesus Christ. I began to worship and say, "Thank you for saving me and giving me this wonderful life where I can have a deep and satisfying relationship with you." I raised my hands high towards heaven lost in exquisite worship. Whatever is cleaned out of my house must be exchanged for something else. If I choose to remove hate, it must be replaced with God's love. If I chose to remove stealing, it must be replaced with giving; remove worry and replace it with praise and thanksgiving; remove doubt, replace with faith; remove anger, replace with meekness; sickness with healing, and a garment of praise for a spirit of heaviness

"Amazing!" I thought. God never takes something away, but that He always gives something better for us to put in its place. I need to learn God's promises so I can begin to apply them with Comforter's help.

I saw, again, that I was partnering with God to implement them. I grabbed the list of promises that Comforter and Rhema had given me. This was no longer a chore. I wanted to memorize and meditate on these promises. I began to see that they were life for me. Fullness of joy flooded my heart. A great peace enveloped me. My purpose and destiny were becoming clearer and clearer.

I had gone from thinking like a brass incense censer, to living like a golden incense censer. Not only was I a priest unto the Lord, but I was also a pure and holy vessel. I was not living and ministering from the outer courts, but I was living in the Holy of Holies of God's Presence. I was a vessel completely yielded. I had become a golden incense censer

The Dwelling Place

burning with the Holy Ghost. I had chosen to be obedient to whatever it took, and through Jesus blood, I had been made pure and holy.

As I sought after the heart of God and His desires, my prayer life exploded. I just wanted Him. He put His incense on the coals and then put a coal on my lips and I began to pray His heart for the world. The power of Godliness was exploding within me. My concept and thoughts of God were drastically changing. His power at work in me was increasing the width and length, the height and depth of His love. The more His love became real in my very experience, my own capacity to love exploded. I was filled to all fullness, overflowing and energized. It was all according to His power that worked within me. To Him is all the glory through Jesus Christ. I could hardly wait for what was next!

Fullness Revealed

Notes

18

THE CLOSET

A quantity of plain cardboard boxes from the *KPS Delivery Co* had just been delivered. Emmanuel called me from the library for a minute to help Him carry some boxes of clothes into the bedroom.

Curiosity assaulted my senses as to why I was being brought back to the bedroom while memorizing and meditating on the promises of God. I was beginning to learn that nothing was done without a purpose or plan with Emmanuel.

"This should be interesting," I reasoned intuitively.

"I did some online shopping while you were in the library," Emmanuel beamed at me enthusiastically. He pointed excitedly towards several boxes that were stacked in a neat pile on the floor.

"Astonishing!" I thought, "I wasn't even aware that Emmanuel knew about eBay."

The Dwelling Place

Emmanuel let out a belly laugh and roared profusely behind me. "I didn't buy these clothes from eBay. These are heavenly clothes. I had my trustworthy angel bring them to me."

I peered curiously out the window to see a purple panel truck pulling away from the curb. On the side in gold lettering were the words, Kingdom Postal Service. Under that was the motto. *What Can Purple Do For You*?

"KPS," I mouthed the words in a low whisper. "Ain't that the cat's meow!"

In the driver's seat was the same angel I had seen in the beginning of this vision. I had almost forgotten about him. Ever since the Trinity Three had arrived, he had been silent and seemingly absent.

"I haven't seen the angel for awhile," I spoke as if to myself.

"He always defers to us when we arrive, but he is here as well as a myriad of other angels; I keep him real busy," Emmanuel replied with a small grunt, lifting two of the boxes and carrying them down the hall towards the bedroom. "I had Him adjust your contact lens while you were sleeping so that you would focus on the necessary. There is so much in this realm to experience that it would blow your mind to the point where you would not even be able to function correctly if we showed you everything."

"Will I ever be able to see it all?" I asked Emmanuel longingly, looking intently into His eyes.

Emmanuel stopped for a moment and set the boxes on a chair in the hall. He turned to face me directly as He put His hands on both shoulders. Without hesitation, He affectionately replied, "I am not holding things from you; I am holding them for you. Intimacy precedes revelation. It is My love that holds and sustains you. The more of My love that you carry

The Closet

consistently within you, the more of the secret places will be revealed to you. I can hardly wait for the time when you are able to see, touch, taste, smell and feel My glory on a consistent basis. Nothing would make me more excited than to show you all my glory. All in due time though."

I squeezed Emmanuel's arms in a response of deep appreciation.

Emmanuel broke contact and motioned excitedly for me to follow Him into the bedroom. Emmanuel grabbed the couple of boxes He had been carrying, and I followed suit as I scampered behind carrying several boxes of clothes myself.

Setting them on the bed, I tore the top off one of the boxes and began pulling out an absolutely gorgeous garment. I felt like a five year old at Christmas time. It was actually an undergarment, but it was designed to cover me from the bottom of my feet to the top of my head. It was exquisitely tailored made and its simplicity was breathtaking as it radiated a purest light with its absolute beauty. I stood there breathless and in wonderment.

> *I am not holding things from you; I am holding them for you. Intimacy precedes revelation*

Emmanuel said excitedly, "Try it on, come on, hurry! It's made just for you!"

I looked away for a moment from the box of clothes to glance in the mirror at what I was currently wearing. I looked at myself from head to toe, and reflected on the fact that these were the clothes that I had been wearing my whole life. These clothes and my current under garments were the 'in brand' that had allured and captivated me from an early age. I mean all my friends had the same brand. We bought them all from the same cool store in the mall and we were pretty much proud of our clothes.

The Dwelling Place

Growing curious, I unbuttoned the shirt I was wearing and pulled it off. I peered at the nametag on the collar to read its inscription.

"Just as I thought," I said out loud, "*Filthy Rags.*" A hint of a smile spread across my face. Yep! The brand name on my collar read just as I had remembered. I had loved that brand name for a long time. It kind of made me feel deliciously dirty on the inside when I had put these clothes on. I turned from the mirror and looked inside my closet at the rows and rows of clothes hanging on the hangers. They were different colors and styles, but all of them were from the same company. I really was addicted to these *Filthy Rags.* It hadn't dawned on me until now, but I was remembering back to when worldly Wendy had encouraged me to wear these clothes. She said all the kids were wearing them. It was cool and hip. I remember thinking I didn't want to be different and stand out like some dork.

I reflected down memory lane for a moment to remember how it used to be funny to make crude jokes about it. Now, I felt this prickly feeling crawling down my neck, and I just wanted to shed them as fast as possible.... and burn them. Yes, burn them all! I wanted to burn everything; what I was wearing and everything that was in the closet.

The smile disappeared off my face as I wiped the back of my hand over my mouth and a steely glint crept into my eyes. Rhema was writing like a detective gone mad who had solved a crime, and it was all becoming crystal clear. I began to see it all in pictures. These clothes were now seen for what they really were:

"*Rough garments to deceive.*"

"*And violent*" (Mal. 2:16)

"*They had been spotted by the Flesh.*" (Jude 1:23)

"*And moth eaten*" (Jas. 5:2)

The Closet

I paused for a moment. That really explained my 'holy' jeans. And I thought they came from the factory looking like that. Wasn't that just like worldly Wendy to convince me that moth eaten jeans were cool to wear? They really were filthy rags and I no longer wanted to associate with them.

I began ripping off all my designer clothes that had previously fascinated me and made me feel so cool. After undressing, I stood naked before Emmanuel; well, almost naked. I was still wearing my moth eaten underwear. A man has to keep some pride, you know. A deep conviction and confession tumbled from my lips.

"I give up my filthy rags for this beautiful garment." Now that I had seen the truth, I could have nothing less. "Tell me, what kind of garment is this?" I breathed excitedly as I ran my hand gently over its magnificent surface.

> It is God's love that holds and sustains you. The more of His love that you carry consistently within you, the more of the secret places will be revealed to you

"It is a garment of humility," Emmanuel replied softly as He too lightly ran His fingers over its surface. You could see a deep delight and love for the beauty of this garment radiate from Emmanuel's face. "It is designed to form fit your personality and character. In fact it will enhance it. When you wear this garment, it will help you to remember that your identity is in Christ and not in your own effort. This is a garment of humility." Emmanuel's face shimmered with deep emotion, as He inspected every inch of this garment. He really did love humility.

"Take a quick shower and try this on!" Emmanuel said with a burst of enthusiasm. "You will be delighted with the results. Oh, and ditch the moth eaten underwear." I looked in the mirror one last time as I headed to the shower. Yeah, they really were moth eaten. Pretty much all that was left was the elastic band and a small amount of cloth. As I looked in

The Dwelling Place

the mirror, I had a thought. "Was this how new inventions started? I snapped the elastic band and mentally pondered what I might call it. Hmmm! Maybe I would call it a "S" string.

"Well, it hardly mattered now," I said, shaking my head at the thought. "I didn't look that good in it anyway. I had something far more amazing to wear now."

Emmanuel was jumping up and down like a little kid as I scampered off excitedly to the body shower to wash myself in the Living Water. Wow! Even the bathroom had the smell now of humility. I turned on the multiple shower heads on and stepped in. Comforter called out from the other room, "I put a little surprise in the water for you!" I looked at my arms and hands as the hot water cascaded off my glistening skin. Everything seemed to be normal. I looked all around the shower again and at myself for several minutes trying to figure out what He was talking about. I continued to lather myself from head to toe with the Word.

> *There was a sense of knowing that everything in my life that I was or would ever do was directly or indirectly the result of God's working in and through my life.*

Suddenly, I felt a warm, tingling sensation all over my body as tongues of fire began to erupt all over me. A new boldness filled me. I was being baptized by fire. "Shaba Shundi!!" I cried out. Something had just erupted from deep within my spirit like a volcano and I began to laugh like crazy. I held my stomach for dear life as deep waves of joy swept over me. Oh boy, I could tell this was going to hurt A new wave of holy laughter gripped me and I felt the corners of my mouth touch the back side of my head as new waves of joy and laughter overwhelmed me.

The next thing I remember, I was lying on the shower floor basking in the rains of God's Presence and Power. I was singing at the top of my lungs in a mixture of song and words. Eventually, I recovered enough to get up and out of the shower.

The Closet

After drying off, I reached for this magnificent garment I had just been given, and quickly put it on. Emmanuel entered the bathroom touching me gently on the shoulder and said, "Never take this off. This undergarment is to be your companion day and night."

I fell on my face before Emmanuel and said, "I am your humble servant, to do your will." The next twenty minutes were spent worshipping the Lord...in humility.

Lifting myself off the tile floor, I washed my face trying to rub out a grout line that had marked my face, while being glued to the floor for so long. I felt so strangely different. It was like a quiet confidence. There were now things I believed about myself. I felt whole and complete, but not more confident about myself than I ought to think. There was a sense of knowing that everything in my life that I was or would ever do was directly or indirectly the result of God's working in and through my life.

> *All you have to do is put it on, wear it and share it*

Emmanuel gave me a pleased look while extending His hand to give me a high five and said enthusiastically, "Let's look at some of the other magnificent clothes I have for you. Don't worry about the grout line look though. It kind of suits you." Emmanuel punched my arm and ducked, as I tossed the wash cloth at Him. After gaining our composure, we walked back into the bedroom to look at some more clothes.

I marveled at the beautiful garment that I pulled out next. I thought the first one was exquisite, but this one was just as amazing. The tag on the collar read 'compassion'. I pulled another one out that read 'kindness', and another 'gentleness', and then 'joy, patience, goodness and self control'. I looked at the box that they were delivered in. It was stamped with a large umbrella. It was the insignia for a corporation that oversaw the production of the shirts.

The Dwelling Place

I laughed as I read the name. It was 'Fruit of the Spirit'. I had heard of Fruit of the Loom, but this went way beyond...well, way beyond. The humor and creativity of Emmanuel and the Father brought such joy. What a blessing! I shouldn't have been surprised. Look at a giraffe and a hippopotamus; now that's creativity. I held up the shirts to the light and admired them. These shirts were all beautiful pastel shirts of the finest cloth; they were all tailor made to fit me, and were all the colors of the rainbow. "Ha! Just like God's promises!" I said shaking my head in wonderment.

"All these new clothes are for me?" I gasped!

"They are all for you," Emmanuel said, grinning from ear to ear. "The neat thing is that you can wear all these shirts at one time and it will appear as if you are wearing one shirt. As you have need for one shirt to display itself, you can just think it, and it will reveal itself. In fact, the shirt will display the fruit that you need to show as you step out to minister to people; it is that easy. This is a miracle that I have created in heaven for you. If you think it by faith, it will be available to you. It is my gift to you. All you have to do is put it on, wear it and share it."

"Wowzer dowzer!" I thought. "It will seem that I am wearing just one outfit, but whatever I need, I can call it out by faith and that piece of clothing will manifest itself to that situation, people, or group I am with. This is a definite creative technology in clothing,"

"Not just call it out, but act it out," I said with a low whistle. "It is as you act it out, it will reveal itself. I've heard it said that you fake it until you make it, but I don't think this is it."

Emmanuel laughed as he clapped His hands. "It's kind of hard to fake what is real inside of you. Hey, Look at this!" Emmanuel held up a shirt and pointed out the label for me to see. I've labeled it 'Spirit Design'." I marveled again as I held up the *Spirit Design* collection. It was so exciting and comforting that these clothes were designed and made by

The Closet

a heavenly corporation with unlimited funds; and the umbrella corporation over all this was *Fruit of the Spirit*.

Emmanuel smiled warmly and said, "This isn't new technology. This has been around from eternity past. This clothing line started coming off the textile looms of Heaven the day I was resurrected and sent Comforter back to earth." Emmanuel laughed again, clapping His hands. It seemed that He was having way too much fun.

"Thank you so much," I responded heartily. "I am so grateful. This is absolutely remarkable," I said. "Is there anything else I need?" I inquired as I sang the last couple words.

Emmanuel placed his hands on my head and said, "I am anointing you with strength and dignity. Every piece of clothing you need to wear will be marked by the power of my strength and my dignity.

"You are not quite complete with your clothing though," Comforter chimed in.

> *If you think it by faith, it will be available to you*

"You don't need to get me anything more," I protested. "This is more than enough. You've done too much already. I have everything I need!" I raised my hand with my palm extended out to Emmanuel and Comforter.

Emmanuel and Comforter both gave me a long and penetrating gaze. I immediately realized my error in trying to teach the teacher. And what was I thinking? I had given them the 'hand'!

Realizing the pride and self-sufficiency of my heart I responded meekly, "What else do I need?" I looked sheepishly at the two as I felt the blood drain from my face.

The Dwelling Place

Emmanuel paused while I slipped out of the moth eaten underwear I had so deftly just slipped back on and put the garment of humility back on that I had so quickly taken off.

"This is the outer suit that completes everything else that you are wearing," Emmanuel said, opening one of the last boxes to reveal a shimmering outfit. It was a suit shaped like a bulletproof vest that was hanging in its entire splendor on a golden hanger. I touched it, and found it soft to the touch. It was the most beautiful material I had ever felt. It was weightless and as smooth as silk.

"What is this?" I exclaimed with exuberance. I looked in wonder at the glistening outfit.

"This will cover all your vital organs and most importantly your heart," Emmanuel exclaimed with deep conviction. This was tailor made exclusively for you. It is a coat of righteousness. You are to wear this vest at all times. This is the outer garment. It is soft and supple, but no weapon of the enemy can penetrate it. We have code-named it 'the investment'.

"The Investment?" I said, with a slight scowl on my forehead. "Why is it named the 'investment'?"

"Well, you got to break the word up to get it." Emmanuel said as He began to explain with a twinkle in His eyes as to what He meant by breaking up the word.

"You take the first part of the word, 'in' because it is the 'in' thing. In the kingdom realm it will always be the 'in' thing. Actually, it is the only thing. 'Vest', because it is a vest and 'ment' because that is what it cost me. It cost me a mint. You know, I gave my life so you could have this. It will protect you and give you unfettered access to Father."

The Closet

Slipping on this shimmering garment, I paused to reflect on Emmanuel's humor. It was kind of dry, but I liked it. It made Him more real. I shook my head as I thought about the corny thing that Emmanuel had just said, and then put my whole attention on what I had just put on. I felt a series of emotions rise up within me: boldness, acceptance, justice, strength and dignity. A fire began to ignite within my heart and a fierce glow came to my eyes. A new sense of purpose and destiny vibrated within my chest. Something about this vest had stirred up amazing feelings within me.

"I am loved by God. I can now walk right into the throne room with boldness," I said with deep conviction and boldness. These words resonated from deep within me as I looked in the mirror and adjusted the garment while fastening the buttons. Confidence began to transform my countenance.

"Yes!" Emmanuel exclaimed with radiance. "Now, you can go into the throne room of grace and stand before the Father with full confidence. My vest of righteousness is the outward expression of what I have already done in you, and it gives you full access to Father's house and His Presence.

I have cleared customs and this is your passport," Emmanuel said with authority. Emmanuel began bouncing up and down on the balls of His feet. He could get so passionate about things.

Holding the purple passport in my hands, I thumbed through the pages. The letters on the passport illuminated with an incandescent light as I grazed my hand across its surface. These were the papers that went with the vest. It was a Kingdom passport and it had my name and picture on the inside cover. On the second page were words in bold print.

NO RESTRICTIONS – FULL ACCESS GRANTED

"What does this mean?" I asked eagerly.

The Dwelling Place

"It means you can go with my blessing to any country in the world and preach the gospel." I looked dumbfounded at Emmanuel and asked,

"It's my choice?"

"It's your choice," Emmanuel replied cordially. "I haven't groomed you to be a mindless robot groveling as to what my Will is. My Will is the whole world. Where do you want to go?" Emmanuel looked tenderly into my eyes, waiting for my response.

"The Philippines," I said vigorously. "Then make your preparations and go. You have my blessing."

"Wow," I said, "Just like that. He trusts me to make the choice of what is the desire of my heart."

I remembered as a kid growing up that I was so scared that God would make me go be a missionary to some place that I would totally hate. I visualized myself in some jungle running away from snakes and eating grubs and worms as I preached in some dialect that took me ten years to learn.

Respect and honor grew at a rapid rate within me as I turned to Emmanuel. Suddenly, it didn't seem so corny what Emmanuel had said. This truly was an investment. It was Emmanuel's investment in me, and I would always treasure this vest.

"What else do I need?" I asked impulsively. An eagerness was gripping me and II was getting more and more excited with each new piece of clothing that Emmanuel gave me, and also with each new release of trust that He endowed on me.

Emmanuel handed me a belt and a pair of shoes. I reached out for the belt and shoes, and held one in each hand inspecting every inch of their design and shape. There was nothing about them that looked special, but the fact that Emmanuel had placed them in my hands, told

The Closet

me there had to be some great significance. Sitting down I began to slip on the shoes and then thread the belt through the loops in my pants. Jumping up, a new eagerness began to well up within me.

"I am ready to tell the good news and my testimony to whomever, wherever and whenever," I said with great enthusiasm.

"Wow," I said. "Where did that emotion and resolve come from?" I blurted out. "I must be about the Kingdom business," I said earnestly. "I can hardly wait." Understanding began to formulate within my spirit. Putting on this belt and these shoes had released something within me. It had put a desire of direction within that compelled me to a purpose.

"These are the shoes of readiness," Emmanuel instructed fervently. "You have told me 'whatever it takes, whenever it takes'. Well, now is the time. These shoes give you eagerness and boldness. This belt will give you discernment, wisdom and understanding to proclaim what Comforter puts into you as light. He will give you the discernment to make the transfer from one realm to the other. You see through a glass dimly, but this belt will make the change so you will be enabled to see as I see and hear as I hear. Then you will be able to talk what you see."

"I am ready," I sang out zealously!

"Not so fast," Emmanuel said cautiously.

Emmanuel handed me a hat that was large and form fitting. It actually covered all my hair and had a chinstrap on it. "This is a hat of salvation," Emmanuel declared emphatically.

I put it on wondering why a piece of clothing that represented salvation covered my head and not my heart. "Salvation must be critical to protecting my mind," I reasoned.

"You are to never, ever to take this helmet off," Emmanuel said intensely; His eyes were penetrating to the very depths of my soul. "By

The Dwelling Place

putting this on, you signify and acknowledge that I am the way, the truth and the life. I am the only one who can restore relationship with the Father. I am the one who saves and keeps saving. I am the only mediator between the Father and yourself. Salvation will be a daily experience and a faithful friend to you until you die. I saved you from your sins and restored relationship with our Father, and I keep saving you unto myself. There are so many wonderful ways that I save you daily. You will learn these as we journey together," Emmanuel said with deep emotion;

I knew from His intensity that this had to be very, very important.

It is a helmet, because only you can take it off. Only you can apostate yourself from the truth. Only you can choose to practice sin and grieve the Father. Only you can choose to live in bitterness and refuse to forgive others. Only you can refuse to know me. Now that I have given you this helmet, keep it on and let it transform you mind. Let me save you daily. Stay close by my side, for I can never leave you or forsake you.

After experiencing strong emotions that enveloped me with waves of His love, Emmanuel then preceded to hand me a book. As I held it in my right hand and angled it back and forth, I noticed how it changed from a book to a sword.

"This is my Word," Emmanuel said decisively. "This book will be an offensive weapon to you. Learn it from cover to cover. Be diligent and learn how to be skillful in its use. The enemy has had thousands of years to study this weapon and pervert it. You have had only a few minutes in comparison. But fear not, I have overcome worldly Wendy, Freddie fleash, and devlin, (including all his henchmen). I am far greater in you because I live in you and have totally and completely equipped you for whatever you will face out here. Be strong and very courageous. For I am with you wherever you go."

Emmanuel had an intense sober look on His face as He exhorted me.

The Closet

I stood mesmerized by what was happening. Emmanuel extended His hand to me as if he was giving me something.

I did not see anything at all in His hand and looked at Emanuel blankly.

"I am giving this to you," Emmanuel said. "Take it. I am giving you the ability to believe my promises."

"I don't see anything," I said in a confused voice. "What am I supposed to do?"

"Believe my Word. Reach out your hand and take what I am giving you," Emmanuel said again.

"But, I don't see anything," I said with exasperation.

"You must believe and trust me," Emmanuel said resolutely.

> *You must believe my promises and step out on what you can't see. When you do, then you will see what you don't see*

I finally reached out my hand to grab what He was giving to me...even though I did not see anything. As I did the unseen became the seen, and I found myself holding on to a massive shield. It was the Shield of Faith. I looked in wonderment at this gorgeous shield in my hand. On the front of the shield was a crest that was personal to me and my family. On the shield was the Davidson Crest. On the crest was a picture of me with my head on Jesus chest. My wife was close under my right arm with her head on my chest and Mark and Rachael was arm in arm on the opposite side of Jesus with His arm around both of them. My left hand was clutched behind Jesus shoulders and neck and in my right hand was a sword which I held horizontally across the front of my family. Across the bottom where the words;

A *heart of worship and a world to save*.

The Dwelling Place

"This is how it will be," Emmanuel said. "You must believe my promises and step out on what you can't see. When you do, then you will see what you don't see. Then you will be able to do what you were called to do.

Now, what did I just do?" Emmanuel asked pointedly.

"You just gave me faith," I replied.

"No I didn't. I gave you eyes to see and ears to hear and I have given you my promises. I gave you a command and you trusted me and obeyed. I have given you the ability to have faith. I give everyone a measure of faith at salvation, a mustard seed of faith so to speak. But there are levels of faith and faith comes by hearing and hearing by the Word of God. (Romans 10:17)

"Every good and perfect gift comes from above from the father of lights, but I have designed you so that faith will come and build in you as you read my promises and meditate on them. They are all for the taking. As you step out and begin to live out my promises, faith will rise up within you. Faith will appear as a shield to you."

> *These clothes did not make me righteous but they enabled me to live the righteous life that I was already declared to be.*

"So faith comes by hearing and hearing by the Word of God," I said as the light began to come on.

"Yes," Emmanuel said ardently. "Faith is taking what you don't see as if you do see it."

Emmanuel stood in front of me, smiled and said, "Raise your sword and point it at me." Emmanuel placed both hands on the blade and said, "Now pull it back." As I did, the sword drew blood as its sharpness penetrated His skin.

"Oh!" I gasped. "I am so sorry. I did not mean to hurt you!"

The Closet

My gaze was riveted to Emmanuel's as He ignored my last comment and said, "This represents what I did at the Cross. You must realize that this Word is nothing without my blood. It is by the shedding of my blood. Without it there is no forgiveness of sin. I am the Word. I fulfilled the Word, and now all that I am I give to you. You are complete in me."

As Emmanuel stepped back, Comforter came up to me up and stood in front of me, holding His hands the same way as Emmanuel did. He said, "Pull on the blade. As I did it ripped through His hands. I did not apologize this time but waited. A rushing wind filled the air. The wind intensified until it was at hurricane strength. I expected to see blood, but instead I felt the wind. "You are born of the Spirit. You will follow me wherever I send you just as the wind goes where it pleases (John 3). I will teach you all things so that you will be just like your Lord. You will be perfectly taught by me. Listen for the still quiet voice. You will know it is me because I have been sent to be a witness within you." As Comforter spoke these things I found myself in the eye of the hurricane and it was completely still. I was seeing the extremes of His nature at the same time.

Almost immediately the wind stopped and Rhema approached me and grabbed the blade with both hands. As I pulled and it ripped through His hands, pure and holy light flowed from the cuts in His hands.

Understanding and knowledge, wisdom and discernment flooded my entire being. "Without revelation, you will not be able to understand the mysteries of God and the Word; you will not be able to experience my love," Rhema revealed into my heart; "Ask for a spirit of revelation and it will be given to you. Seek my presence and you will find it. Knock and revelation will be opened to you." I began to feel the call of destiny on my life. The Trinity Three were commissioning me. Emmanuel, Comforter and Rhema had opened up themselves, sharing their true essence. The Sword of the Spirit was the Word of God. Emmanuel was the Word of God and Rhema was the revelation of the Word of God.

The Dwelling Place

As I stood there fully clothed, the Trinity Three circled around me. As they laid hands on me, I heard a commission and a blessing.

In unison they said, "You are My son in whom I am well pleased." Suddenly, as if by a miracle, the different layers of the clothes became as one. I was wearing one suit of clothing, but distinctly maintaining its uniqueness. Everything was tailor fit. I truly felt like a new creation. (2 Corinthians 5:17) I was fully fit for service.

There was a deep sense of understanding, (thanks to Rhema's constant writing); that these clothes did not make me righteous, but they enabled me to live the righteous life that I was already declared to be. I was not my filthy rags but neither was I my righteous ward robe either. My identity was in being a son. Waves of love continued to wash over me like a flood. I fell to my knees and worshipped. The presence of God was around me, over me, and within me.

> *I was not leaking from broken worthlessness. I was overflowing from a marked vessel useful and valuable to God*

I had gone from living like a brass incense censer in the outer courts to being a golden incense censer living in the inner court of God's Presence. Not only was I a priest unto the Lord, but I was also a pure and holy vessel. A golden incense censor burning with the coals of the Holy Ghost. I had chosen to be obedient to whatever it took and through Jesus blood; I had been made pure and holy.

As I sought after the heart of God and His desires, I saw an exploding prayer life. I couldn't be stopped I would not be shut up. All I wanted to do was be with the Trinity Three. All I wanted to do was to talk with them and to listen to their heart for me. He put His incense on the coals, and I began to pray His heart for the world. Prayer was not something I did but someone I did it with. It was talking with my dear friends. I could not get enough.

The Closet

The power of Godliness was exploding within me. My concept and thoughts of God were drastically changing. His power at work was increasing my understanding and expression of the width and length, the height and depth of His love. The more His love became real to me; the more it began to not just surpass my knowledge of Him, but to become part of my very experience. I began to find my own capacities to love explode. I was filled to all fullness and overflowing. I was energized and I was full. In fact, I was overflowing, and it was all according to His power that worked within me. To Him is all the glory through Jesus Christ.

For so long I had seen myself as a cracked and broken vessel, but now I saw that it was the finger of God etching His testimonies in me. I was not leaking from broken worthlessness. I was overflowing from a marked vessel useful and valuable to God. The more people drank from my vessel, the more it flowed. The more I stepped out to touch people the Living Water would bubble and overflow. The incredible thing though, was no matter how much spilled or flowed out, no matter how much was drunk, I always remained full.

> *For so long I had seen myself as a cracked and broken vessel, but now I saw that it was the finger of God etching His testimonies in me*

Before when I prayed "Fill me up," it was because I saw myself empty and unable to retain His presence. Now when I prayed to "Fill me up," it was with recognition of abundance not lack. I was full so keep filling. I was the picture of a full vessel and another vessel adding more so that it overflowed. You could not touch me without getting wet. You could not stand near me without being affected by the "wet" Presence of God, in a practical way; I began to see my house as a home for whoever wanted to come in. My home was the demonstration of the goodness of God at work. I felt my heart opening up in love. Father's dwelling place was my heart, and it was from my heart and home that all who would desire would experience His love through me.

The Dwelling Place

As Comforter and Rhema prepared to go back to the library, Comforter placed an arm around my shoulder and spoke softly into my ear, "Reaffirm daily the armor that you wear. Do it with authority. Always be thankful and grateful for the authority and power given to you. Take nothing for granted. Remember that the wine racks that hold the wine of worship are from <u>Gratefulness and Thankfulness LLC.</u>

"Soon you will have people knocking on your door," Emmanuel spoke excitedly. "There is a polarity shift beginning to happen in and around your house. Just like people were drawn to me, they are going to start to be drawn to you. Be ready to have an answer for the hope that is within you."

Fathers' dwelling place was my heart and it was from my heart and home that all who would desire would experience His love through me.

Rhema and Comforter left at this point to go back to the library. A few minutes later, I was heading back towards the library myself feeling a great excitement within. "Nothing better than wearing a new set of clothes," I said with a satisfied sigh. "Especially these; they were exhilarating." I felt like a million bucks. My sense of self worth and joy was incredible, but more importantly, my understanding and experience of God's love was full and brimming within me. "What else could I need?" I asked myself. "I am so full and overflowing.

The Closet

Notes

19

THE LIVING ROOM

As I walked towards the library, I passed from the hall of faith into the living room. I gasped as I felt such a joy welling up within me. The room was filled with the most beautiful design structure. I saw an elegant card on the end table that read *Designs by Joy*. All the furniture, plants, lights and everything was from the *Joy Collection*. I jumped into a joy recliner, leaned back and started laughing out a loud belly laugh. I leaned over the side of the recliner and examined all the different types of buttons that created all different kinds of scenarios of bliss.

I turned one on of the knobs and began to feel pulsations of delight travel up and down my back. The vibrations were heavenly. As I snuggled deep into the recliner, I looked up to see a radiant brightness in the room. All around were lights of joyfulness. Just looking at the lights put a large smile on my face. One could feel the glory of God lighting up the room. The lights seemed to pulse and shimmer with a radiating satisfaction.

The Dwelling Place

My heart was filled with gratefulness and thankfulness to Emmanuel for this wonderful gift. He had done it. He had promised to fill the living room with wonderful furniture and decorations and, Wow! It was truly amazing. The joy within was so intense that I began to see rainbow swirls dancing before my eyes.

Not only was there a new design collection, but Emmanuel had added a beautiful fountain that flowed from deep within the wall. The water was crystal clear and reflected everything of joy in the room. Where the water originated from was beyond me, but it was truly breathtaking. Above the fountain was a spacious sky light that allowed the sun to shine in and give light and warmth to the room. I looked from the fountain and even the plants were crying out and singing praises to the King. They shimmered and gave off vibrations of grateful sounds.

I jumped out of the recliner to look at the pictures on the walls. They were pictures of smiling, happy people who had been touched by God's love. They were people who had been touched by my life. There were laughing faces and joyous quotations everywhere. It was wonderful!

Everything about the room was a picture of ecstatic ecstasy. Before this room had been called the living room, but now it truly was the "Living" room. It was alive with exultation and singing. This was truly a gift from the Lord. I lay down on the couch for a moment and heard the words, "When you sleep I will fill you with joy unspeakable. You will wake up refreshed and alive." A song began to well up within me.

> **O taste and see that the Lord is good**
> **O taste and see that the Lord is good**
> **Your love is like a bubbling brook**
> **Your love is like a bubbling brook**
> **You fill my heart with Joy, Joy, Joy, Joy,**
> **You fill my heart with Joy.**

The Living Room

©2010 God's Love
Words and Music by John M. Davidson

Just sitting there, I could sense that one who rested here would get a deep, refreshing sleep. I could hardly fathom how the couch was so soft yet firm. It was so delightfully comfortable. I propped myself up on one elbow and pulled one of the cushions off the sofa and read the tag to find out what the sofa couch was full of. "What kind of filling was in this couch that made it so soft and yet so firm?" I mused to myself while humming the tune.

I peered at the tag focusing on what was imprinted there. "Hah! Remarkable!" I cried out. The tag read 'glory'

"Glory, glory, glory!" I cried out. "No wonder it was so comfortable and yet so firm. It was full of glory. I could not help contain my laughter.

Rhema was laughing so hard He could hardly write on his notepad. Despite His difficulty, my spirit suddenly visualized it as I put it all together.

I declared it out loud, "This couch gives you a joy unspeakable and is full of glory." My heart was exploding within me. I began to change the tune and sing a little song that I had learned as a child:

> "I have the Joy, joy, joy, joy,
> Down in my heart, where?
> Down in my heart, Where?
> Down in my heart
> I have the joy, joy, joy, joy,
> Down in my heart
> Down in my heart to stay."

Rolling off the couch, I flopped on the floor and ran my hands across the surface of the carpet. I lay on my back for a minute and exaggerated

The Dwelling Place

the motions of making an angel, like I did as child in the winter snow. The carpet was silky smooth and yet had a heavenly touch. I lay there worshipping while enjoying the luxurious softness of the deep plush carpet.

"You fill my heart with joy, joy, joy, joy," I sang softly. Rhema continued to write, and I began to understand that this was a special fiber made from the finest wool of a sheep without spot or blemish. It had a special stain protection in it. How it worked was if you stayed in close relationship with the manufacturer, it would always stay clean. The carpet was treated with a special solution that went all the way through the fibers and kept it white as wool.

In fact, Rhema said that if Emmanuel added some of His special red paint to the Living Water, it changed it into a powerful detergent that could be used for shampooing the carpets. "That red paint that turns white when it dries is an amazing product," I exclaimed excitedly. "It's like an all purpose cleaner and paint".

"You never have to fear inviting people into your living room of joy," Emmanuel said, clapping His hands together in glee. "In fact, that is what I want you to do. Do not fear that they will mess up your living room and steal your joy. Remember, I have given you self control and you have the power within you to always keep this room in its present state. It is part of the package of being a new man in Christ. Joy trumps over fear. That is why there is a fountain here. It is designed to flow outward. As long as you choose to let my love and joy flow out to people, fear, doubt and unbelief cannot come in. Be an outward force to be reckoned with.

Most people need to see to believe, before they will believe to see. Most people need to see in action a living room such as yours that does not need to be influenced by its environment, people or things to experience joy and happiness. Live teachable and humble and saturate yourself in my love. Let it flow from your house with ease."

The Living Room

I was bubbling with joy and jumping up in the air while clicking my heels together as I left the living room to go to the library. I had never experienced anything like this before and I liked it. Reluctantly, I walked across the living room to go to the library. Comforter and Rhema were waiting for me in the library to discuss urgent business. I just wanted to stay here, though, and enjoy this atmosphere forever. It was so amazing.

I did one more angel on the carpet and jumped up sheepishly looking around. Just as I was about to turn the handle to the library door, I noticed a shadow fall across the living room wall. Something was growing outside the window of my heart and was placing an ominous shadow across my living room of joy. I took my hand off the doorknob, turned and walked over to the picture window. A deep frown settled on my face. I placed both my hands on my hips and pondered this new set of events.

NOTES

20

THE FENCE AND THE TREE

Out of nowhere, I noticed a green picket fence that seemed to be encircling my heart. At first it appeared afar off, but the more I looked at it, the more the fence seemed to be moving closer and closer. This was not your typical fence, though. It was a picket fence on top, but the middle part of the fence was shaped like a 'O'. Scattered all over the fence were multiple little 'o's of different shapes and sizes. Underneath that scenario were two little sticks planted firmly inside of two tiny little tennis shoes. On the tongue of the shoe written in a bold blue was the name 'sike'. It was the most famous name brand in this realm, and I could see why. Just looking at these shoes, fence and the words rolling off its tongue was very troubling and it was 'psyching' me out!

"What in the world is this phenomenon?" I asked with apprehensive caution. You could hear a cadence very faintly, like in the military-- "Right, right, right, right, right; Right, right, right, right, right!" The closer the fence came, the louder it got. As it got louder, I noticed a peculiar tree, growing outside my window, and this fence which seemed to be communicating with each other. The fence said, "Right, right, right, right," and the tree said, "Wrong." I looked again at the tennis shoes on

The Dwelling Place

the fence, while scratching my head with one hand and rubbing my chin with the other. Both of the shoes were right feet.

"That's odd!" I thought.

Again, the cadence pieced the air with a sharp shrill interrupting my thoughts as its military cadence rang out, "Right, right, right, right... The tree swayed as it said, "Wrong", and the fence continued to march closer.

Right in front of my picture window, I watched as this peculiar tree was growing up and out. I had never seen this species of tree before. Whatever it was it, was growing at an enormous rate and continued to cast longer and deeper shadows on my living room wall. As I stood there looking at it, I noticed that it had grown from two inches in circumference to about twelve inches, and it was continuing to grow at an extremely rapid rate. I had now been standing here at the picture window for about ten minutes and the tree was already fifty feet tall. As it grew, it continued to sway in cadence to the marching of the fence and communicate with it.

I took note that the neighbors had begun congregating under my tree, and they were busy pointing and whispering to each other. Some had become red faced and were starting to make staccato type gestures at each other. A few had grown quite rowdy and had even started yelling and pushing each other. One person was even poking another person in the chest with his finger. Some were pointing back at my house with animated gestures as if they were pleading a case. The cadence changed from Right, right, right, right, wrong," to "I'm right, you're wrong! I'm right, you're wrong!"

I could hear a clucking sound as many were shaking their heads and wagging their tongues as if in complete disbelief. "Can you believe it? Have you heard? Did you know? How rude! Oh, that was juicy!" I was catching bits and pieces of their conversation as they interacted

The Fence and the Tree

gregariously with each other. Tightness was building deep within my chest and I found myself growing more and more annoyed.

While I was watching, I heard little pops and bangs, and noticed similar trees starting to grow in various neighbors' yards also. Similar fences were popping up here and there and it appeared as if the neighbor's houses started moving further and further away from each other.

"Nooooo! That couldn't be, could it? How would that even be possible?" I cried out in horror. The more they talked, the more pops and bangs could be heard and a literal forest was growing in the community. I looked to see that a cloud had developed from all this commotion and was slowly blocking out the sun.

As I stood mesmerized by this event unfolding before me, Comforter and Rhema stepped out of the Library, engrossed in a deep conversation. Seeing me at the picture window in the living room, Comforter and Rhema walked over towards me while simultaneously giving me hand motions as if they were trying to get my attention that they urgently needed to see me.

"We were just looking for you," they said directly and urgently. "We need to see you in the library right away."

As they walked quickly over to me, Comforter said with a knowing smile, "Oh I see you have a fence crowding your house and a sycamine tree growing outside your window." I watched with growing consternation and anxiety at the rapidly unfolding turmoil happening outside.

"Seems like a cavalier attitude," I thought, as I grew more and more peeved. I felt a movement under my feet and almost fell over. A loud crackling noise followed. Bam! Bam! Bam, crackle pop!

The Dwelling Place

"What was that?" I cried out, reaching out for my coffee table to steady myself. Now I was getting really angry and scared. A deep shudder and sound like a heavy sigh rippled through the house. "The floor just moved!" I yelled out in desperate fear. Rhema was writing furiously on His notepad.

"That fence is not just an ordinary fence and it is not there to protect you," Comforter said, raising His voice so I could hear over the deafening noise. "It is designed to shut others out from having access to your home. It is designed to isolate you from your neighbors and create division. That is an 'O' fence."

"An 'O' fence," I thought to myself. I forgot that I was peeved for the moment and feeling puzzled, frantically racked my brain to get some sort of understanding.

"Lord, give me the cause of all this," I cried out desperately.

Suddenly, fresh revelation began to flood my mind. Rhema had drawn a picture with one word written underneath. He definitely wanted to make sure I got this one right. That fence represented an 'o'ffense. Someone had just said or done something to me and I had taken offense. That was the word that He had written. That was the key. It was the word—*Offense*. Now, instead of me guarding my heart with God's Word; this fence was guarding my heart so that no one was able to get in.

"How could that be?" I thought, "I had been so full of joy." To make matters worse, people were congregating outside my house under my sycamine tree and were fast becoming offended also. They were getting all hot and bothered and were taking sides. Now, new trees and fences were sprouting and moving in their yards.

A jolt shook the living room. The joy that was there a few minutes ago was fast fading as upheaval seemed to erupt everywhere. The whole house gave a violent shudder and deep sighs echoed through the rooms.

The Fence and the Tree

Suddenly, a root from the tree outside the window began to emerge through the floor. The floor splintered and creaked as more roots wormed their way through. Somehow, it had penetrated the foundation of my heart and home and was now stealing the joy from my living room! It was entwining its way through the room and upsetting the furniture. It was stealing the joy from my heart!

I watched in horror as the pictures on the wall came crashing to the floor and shattered into a million pieces. A root had pierced through one of the cushions and was seeking to disrupt the stuffing. Within minutes, everything was in upheaval and the roots had over taken the room. Bits of glory were now floating in the air.

"What kind of tree is that?" I cried out in despair; "this 'sick' tree or whatever it is." A lack of forgiveness and bitterness was fast flooding my heart at the intrusion of this fast growing tree.

Rhema continued to scribble furiously on His notepad.

Comforter began to explain to me that when someone says something hurtful to you, or does something that goes against your expectations and you take offense at what that person says or does; it will steal your joy. As soon as you let a root of bitterness start, it will find its way into your heart. He also said that if you fail someone's expectations or they fail yours that is when this sycamine tree will grow.

"But everyone has many expectations of each other," I spoke out with deep concern. I was quickly realizing that this conversation was going to take a while.

"Exactly," Comforter quipped. "How you deal with your expectations and others will have a profound effect on your life and those around you."

The Dwelling Place

I looked on in consternation as more violent shakes tore at the house and stones came crashing out of nowhere and began to fill the fountain. My fountain of joy was fast becoming destroyed. Names were written in bold print on the stones and it was unmistakable. One of the stones read *stress* and another *worry*. *Bitterness, anger* and *unforgiveness* were others to name a few.

I quickly searched through the rubble to find my Bible dictionary that had been lying on the coffee table earlier. I needed to understand what kind of tree a sycamine tree was. This rapidly growing tree was giving me great concern and heart burn. I had never seen something grow so fast. I found the recliner of joy on top of the Bible dictionary which was buried under some rubble. After moving the recliner out of the way I picked up the book and began wiping off the dust and dirt.

I rapidly began shuffling through the pages and finally found the information I needed. *I found that a sycamine tree was a tree that grew in the Middle East. It fared best in dry climate with little or no water, grew fast and easily, yet was hard to remove. In fact, if you cut it down without removing its roots it would just grow back. It was usually planted at a place where two paths met. Its root system once set, was almost impossible to remove.

The root system tended to go deep and grew as big beneath the surface as it did above the ground. It created a lot of shade as its branches grew out wide. A little bitter fig grew on its branches and trunk. The tree was used for building coffins as it was a hard dense wood that was almost impervious to water and lasted a long time. In fact, the Pharaohs used it as coffins.

My book flew out of my hand, somersaulted across the room, and landed in a heap ten feet away as another jolt threw me sideways. The floor shifted again and shuddered viciously as I heard ominous creaks and groans. More wood splintered in the floor as another root wormed its way through. Jumping back, I yelped with surprise as a root climbed its

The Fence and the Tree

way up and over my shoe and snaked its way through one of the coffee tables.

More revelation began to barrage my mind. Someone had just said something to me and it had offended me. Someone had failed my expectations and I had taken offense. This offense was fast setting its root of bitterness deep into my heart. Just a small drop of bitterness, a small bitter fig, so to speak, a single thought had grown out of nothing, and it was seeking to worm its way deep into the foundation of my heart and disrupt my joy. It had taken almost nothing to grow, just a drop of water to cause it to sprout to this gigantulous size. It was just a thought, a spoken rebellious idea, a proud ambition, and voila! Look at the results. I had not immediately applied God's Word and taken this offense to Emmanuel, and it had begun to disrupt my neighbor's living rooms

"These trees, if not dealt with, eventually take over and breed death and sickness within you," Comforter explained. "Do you see the significance of these sycamine trees growing where two paths met? Look outside at the tree. It grows strategically where it has easy access for people to walk to it. This signifies that offenses happen when two people's paths cross and something is said that could cause a rise in one or both people.

Rhema drew a picture of a telephone. "Yeah, it's like picking up the telephone to call someone!"

I gasped. That is exactly what I had just done. Someone had failed my perception of an expectation that I had about them, and I was quick to jump on the telephone to give my friend an earful. "Did you know? Can you believe it?" I asked. "I can't believe that so and so said that...how rude!"

"What must I do," I cried out. Revelation flooded my mind as Rhema's Word settled deep within me.

The Dwelling Place

The answer was to be found in Luke 17:6. When offenses come, (and they will come) I am to say to that offense, "(offense), be you plucked up by the root and planted in the sea and you shall have already obeyed me.

"I don't get it," I blubbered. "How does that help?"

Tears were streaming down my face and my heart was caught up in a whirlpool of anguish as I looked up into Comforters eyes. Comforter looked me squarely in the eye and said, "Everyone has different expectations of each other and everyone is at a different level of maturity. When someone violates your expectations you have been given authority as a son or daughter to speak straight to that offense. You speak to the offense, not to your friend, coworker or casual acquaintance about the offense. Just as you clearly see this tree and fence, you clearly have authority to speak directly to that offense and command it to be planted firmly in the sea of forgetfulness and forgiveness. When you do that it will already have been done."

"That's all I have to do?" I said with deep agony. It seemed too simple.

"In the natural realm this may seem foolish, but in the kingdom realm this is how things work," Comforter instructed me.

Grabbing another chair to steady myself, I cried out to that offense as another shudder shook the room. "You root of bitterness; you have no authority to disrupt my heart. I pick you up by the root and plant you in the sea. You must obey me because I base this solely on God's word. It is done. You shall have already obeyed me."

I had hardly got the words out of my mouth when I saw the tree, roots and all pull up out of the ground and disappear over the horizon; a moment later I heard a loud splash.

The Fence and the Tree

I dropped down into a heap in the only chair not turned over. I still was breathing very erratically from all the excitement. "That was easy...that was easy...that was easy." I looked around the rubble perplexed while looking for the source of the sound. Moving a pillow, I found that a book had landed on my "Easy button" from Office Max. I stood there with my hands on my hips shaking my head.

"That was easy," I responded with a laugh as I set the easy button back on the end table.

Comforter grinned as He said, "Sometimes even the rocks and the trees ..." He gestured to my red 'easy button, "and other objects cry out.

"Why do you plant the sycamine tree in the sea rather than cast it?" I asked inquisitively, changing the subject slightly while still trying to catch my breath.

Again revelation flooded my mind as Rhema wrote on his notepad. "A sycamine tree cannot live in salt water. Salt water represents a place that I have created where you can send something so it will be totally forgotten. It is a sea of forgetfulness. If it is planted or rooted in the sea, it will die there; if it is cast in the sea, it can come floating back to shore and find its way back to your heart."

I began to nod my head with understanding. I looked out my living room window and noticed that the fence had just as quickly disappeared. I got on the phone and called back some of the people I had invited to my party and told them what I had done and asked their forgiveness. After I hung up, I noticed that a few of the houses were now inching their way back closer to mine and their trees and fences were flying through the air towards the ocean.

I had backtracked and talked to some of the offended parties and asked their forgiveness for my anger and bitterness but it was like taking a whole bag of feathers from a pillow and shaking it into the wind. It would be a difficult task to retrieve them all. The problem was that I couldn't remember everyone I had talked to, and in the meantime they had talked to other people and so forth. I nodded my head slowly and pressed my lips together. I could not live in regret, but there was definitely an important lesson I needed to learn and grow in response to this experience.

I turned my attention back to the matter at hand and reflected on this amazing sea. Yeah! Nothing can live in God's sea of forgetfulness that is planted there. That is why you visualize it as being firmly planted there. "Whoop, whoop, whoop!" I blurted out as I danced with joyful realization.

I looked out my window to see that everyone had left my yard and most had gone back to their own houses. I sadly looked at all the damage I had created. Some people still had their fences and sycamine trees planted in their yards and were holding on to that offense. They had taken up my offense and made it their own.

They were not ready to let go yet. Was I seeing that right or was someone even painting their fence…white? They were trying to whitewash things over. I knew it wasn't Emmanuel's paint because His went on red before it turned white. They thought that by just painting over the offenses, they could brush things under the carpet (so to speak). It was as if they were saying, "I am going to ignore this. If I do it will go away." The problem was that they all had sustained cuts and bruises that needed to be treated so they would heal.

Some of the other neighbors had moved to other people's yards to continue their discussion that they had begun in mine. I had learned a great lesson. People find it very easy to pick up an offense from someone else, and even if I take care of the root of bitterness and forgive the person that I felt had failed my expectations; others could go on and carry an offense for me for years and not even now that I had taken care of things.

The Fence and the Tree

Rhema continued to write on His notepad and new revelation flashed before me. This had been just one offense and one tree. I began to see that some people, and even I had at times, had let things grow to the point where you couldn't see the forest for the trees. There had been so many "o" fences and sycamine trees sprouting in my yard that it was thick like a forest. Multiple fences had crowded my heart with chains and locks to help keep people out. I saw the grave danger of letting any offense get rooted near my heart for it took very little time before it overran and infested the inside of my heart. Offenses are rooted in unbelief, fear and pride. It was a great little incubator for the wrong sort of folks! I didn't realize it, but Comforter and Rhema were preparing me to go back into the library.

"If devlin can steal your joy, he has won half the battle," Comforter instructed. "The devil has no authority, but he jabbers a lot hoping someone will listen. He uses Fat man to get someone to bite on his words and take them to heart. He will get you to think something is not fair or that someone failed you, and get you to take it personally, and then you have given him permission to steal your joy. Once he steals your joy, he can insert a spirit of heaviness. That heaviness will lead to disappointment, bitterness, hate and...oh, you wouldn't like the end results.

> *The devil has no authority but he jabbers a lot hoping someone will listen*

This was how devlin's henchmen had gotten so much control and had shut down people's hearts as I saw in the FOG. The FOG took on a visible form of godliness that was an eight foot deep cloud. It had totally permeated the sanctuary of the church where I had first met the angel. It was the result of offenses that had happened with each other and a lack of intimacy with Father.

I began to see that in these last few days I had gotten busy and had not had time to meditate on the Word. I began to see that things could

The Dwelling Place

spread so fast and create so much damage. Something that was a little speck to me and didn't matter at all, yet another person took it as a big deal and it filled their whole vision. Through thoughts, speculations and imaginations, devlin found a fortress in which he could dwell, making me ineffective. Messes could be created so fast which in turn could ruin my joy. I had spoken one harsh word to someone and all this turmoil had happened. I was feeling a little down.

For the next fifteen minutes Comforter gave me words of comfort and encouragement. They encouraged me as to what my authority as a royal son was. Rhema and Comforter then disappeared back into the library while I sat looking at the mess that had been created by my offense. The living room was totally trashed, and the furniture was dirty and overturned. Holes were punched through the carpet and it was deeply soiled. Everything was in complete upheaval. The fountain was still filled with stones of worry, anxiety and stress. I was feeling a little bit like a naughty boy who had just broken something and was in deep trouble when Emmanuel entered the room. "I'm so sorry I broke..."

> *And I saw my destiny from the future. It was the souls of men*

Emmanuel smiled, and held up his hand. "Shalom," Emmanuel said soothingly. "I am not here to scold you. Rhema and Comforter told me what happened. I'm here to help put things back in order. I'm here to help restore your joy.

I hear you took authority over the tree and the fence. Good for you! That's a huge victory! I also heard you ask for forgiveness. Excellent! I brought you a glass of cold water and some bread I just baked. Here, eat, drink and refresh yourself. This is good stuff. Here taste this bread. I call it the Bread of Life." As I ate the fresh hot bread from the oven, Emmanuel told me how proud He was of me and that I was a man after God's own heart. He wrapped His arms around me and held me tight. He

The Fence and the Tree

got excited as he whispered in my ear and told me how He had just been talking with the Father about me, and He wanted me to know that I was totally one hundred percent loved and accepted by my Father. In fact, they had just been discussing the plans and dreams they had for me. They were discussing my future and my destiny. Tears welled up in my eyes as I felt the warmth of the Father's love. No matter what I did it seemed Emmanuel always responded by bringing me a warmth of acceptance and love; no blame and no shame. Emmanuel acted like nothing bad had even happened.

"A house without doors," I pondered. That's how life was with Emmanuel and Comforter. They always hoped and believed in me, and their love was continually covering over my sins and short comings. Here I was feeling a little hungry and thirsty, and He brought the right Word in season and the drink I needed to revive me.

"You are a winner and an over comer and I believe in you," Emmanuel spoke tenderly, but with deep conviction. A new peace and contentment settled deep within my heart, Revelation filtered into my mind as a verse from the Psalms came into clarity:

"He restores my soul."

(Psalm 23:4) KJV

After finishing the bread and water, Emmanuel pulled out a bottle of wine and said with a twinkle in His eye, "Do you want to get drunk in the Spirit? This is an excellent wine. I call this one 'Joy unspeakable'."

I laughed eagerly while agreeing that I could use some joy unspeakable right now. I reached out for a glass as Emmanuel poured a generous quantity. Within minutes, Emmanuel and I were prostrate on the floor giving honor and glory to the Father. We looked like drunken sailors who acted like they were out of their minds, and yet my mind had never been clearer or my purpose stronger.

The Dwelling Place

We could not stop laughing; we were so full of joy. Before long, a new strength seemed to build from within and enveloped me. Warmth spread from my head to my toes. This was so different from my stained glass religious thinking that I usually felt that I must be prim and proper or God will poke me with a fork for putting my elbows on the table while eating.

There was no doubt, 'the joy of the Lord was my strength'. It hadn't dawned on me yet, but a transition was slowly happening in my heart. I was moving from 'Master' to 'Son' to 'Friend.'

I was becoming more comfortable with Father, Emmanuel and Comforter....and it seemed to be happening mostly on the floor with a bottle in my hand! There was such a mutual honor that had developed between us. I knew their hearts and they knew mine. I wanted to enjoy their company. I was eager to spend time with them and it was fun. I began to ponder the four sets of eyes. It suddenly dawned on me who the fourth set of eyes was that was on the sword. Father God was the fourth.

After a time of extended worship, I got up off the floor. Rubbing my eyes, I looked around the living room to see everything exactly in order as it was before. Even the fountain was clear and bubbling again, and the stones were gone. My heart cried out impulsively:

"In your presence is fullness of joy"

(Psalm 16:11) KJV

I beamed as I turned around and proceeded to walk towards the library. There was tremendous joy welling up within my being as I impulsively did a little jig; a little dance so to speak, as small giggles of ecstasy erupted from deep within me. I could not help but sigh with an unspeakable bliss. I had cast all my cares on Him and the results had turned out to be outstanding.

The Fence and the Tree

Rhema was glowing as He wrote enduring words of revelation on His notepad. As He wrote, a deep and satisfying peace began to settle like a warm quilted blanket around my spirit.

"Nothing broken, nothing missing," I spoke softly yet endearingly under my breath. "Health, prosperity and peace," That is what Emmanuel had spoken to me. It all made sense now. I sat down for a moment in the recliner of joy to observe all that had just happened to me. I leaned back and snuggled in the chair while exhaling a sigh of content.

"Shalom," I said reverently while rolling the word off my tongue while savoring it's essence like a choice rib eye steak. It was true that when Emmanuel spoke words over you, it would bring health, prosperity and peace. He brought life and in an exceedingly, abundant way.

"A word fitly spoken is like apples of gold in settings of silver."

(Proverbs 25:11) NKJV

"I like that," I said with a quiet satisfaction as I eased myself out of the chair and continued to make my way across the living room while savoring this verse in my heart that Rhema had just revealed to me. Emmanuel had such a way of saying the right thing at the right time.

"Isn't God good?" I breathed out slowly with deep satisfaction. I really enjoyed getting drunk in the spirit because there was no hangover and everything felt so good. I knew I had to be careful about putting my trust in my feelings but I was happy that there wasn't this icky residue feeling inside me. I breathed deeply again while relishing the contentment of feeling so full and content. I paused and looked back once more at the living room of joy. Emmanuel had left the room, but His presence could be seen and felt everywhere. With a wide smile, I turned the handle to the library and pushed opened the door.

Thanks to Dave Rosenberg of Living Savior Ministries for his research on the Sycamine tree/ forgiveness

21

THE NEW LIBRARY

As I walked into the library, I let out a cry. The whole library was in a shambles. Pages of books were ripped out and were lying on the floor.

"What a mess," My mind swirled with a back road of a million different directions intersecting and then shooting out into another million random directions. "These were all my belief systems and thought processes. Why were they all crumpled up and lying on the floor? What a trip!" I thought. "I could have such joy in one area and also have such a mess in another"

Comforter was in a deep conversation with….

"Where was Rhema? And who was Comforter talking too?"

The Dwelling Place

Comforter was furiously comparing my thoughts and beliefs to the big old leather bound book. It looked like only a few pages had passed the test and they were in the 'out' box on the desk.

"Did I really give them permission to do this?" I fumed. I must have been crazy as it looked worse than the beginning. The four foot deep pile of pages that was piled in a heap in the middle of the floor shuttered and shook.

I leaped backwards as a hand popped out from the middle of the pile with a piece of paper clutched firmly in its grasp.

"I found one!" It was Rhema, who had been totally buried by the large pile of unbelief's. "I found a good belief. Yeeeaaaah!" The whole thing looked absolutely ridiculous to me.

> *You need a righteous structure in your life.*

Why Rhema would be excited about the one belief, when there were thousands of beliefs that were wrong, was beyond me. Comforter huddled together with Rhema and read the right belief with great joy. "This is great!" Comforter burst out enthusiastically. Put it in the out box. Rhema dropped it in the out box with the few other right beliefs.

"We have 20 pages we can use out of this library!" Comforter blurted out excitedly.

"Twenty pages!" I burst out, laughing nervously. "There is a whole library of belief systems and thoughts here. There has got to be thirty to forty thousand pages here and hundreds of books and you are only about a twentieth of the way through. Are you saying my belief system and thought processes stink?"

"Well…. basically yes, but the good news is that we got twenty good pages of beliefs to build on; and these are foundational," Comforter said with great enthusiasm while shaking my shoulder with his left hand. "This is where we want to focus." My mouth dropped open as I started to whine. I wasn't thinking of the twenty; I was looking at the thirty thousand times fifty beliefs per page.

This was a big deal. How could this be? I nervously began to chew on one of my finger nails. "Ow!" I said with an annoyed jerk. I shook my hand as I looked at the sliver of nail I had just chewed off. I had chewed too far and blood had started to ooze from the tip of my fingernail.

"That is one revelation I didn't need. Where's the love?" I complained bitterly."

Comforter ignored my last comment and said urgently, "We can fix this, but you must let us work into you 2 Corinthians 10:3-5."

"What is 2 Corinthians 10:3-5," I asked tentatively. For a brief moment my lips squished together into a little pout. After seeing Comforters patient look, I began to soften a little as I realized that this was not their fault. It was mine and I needed to take some responsibility here.

"Well," Comforter exclaimed, as He started explaining to me in a loving and gentle way, "You live in this world as a human being in the flesh, but you must not live according to the flesh. A lot of these belief systems have created strongholds in your life. You have let Freddy fleash run around and do whatever he wants to do for one. He has had no discipline from you. Also, your thoughts, speculations, and imaginations that you have built up in your mind have made a great habitation for your enemy damien devlin. You must use weapons that are Godly, not carnal. You must cast down every high thing and argument that exalts itself against God, and bring every thought captive in obedience to God. You need a righteous structure in your life."

The Dwelling Place

"Every thought?" I muttered to myself. "That is a lot of thoughts. I don't know about all this. I can't seem to help myself or have the ability to say no."

"Yes!" Comforter said with deep excitement squeezing my shoulder even harder. "Listen to these words:

> "We are human, but we don't wage war with human plans and methods. We use God's mighty weapons, not mere worldly weapons, to knock down the Devil's strongholds With these weapons we break down every proud argument that keeps people from knowing God. With these weapons we conquer their rebellious ideas, and we teach them to obey Christ."

(2 Corinthians 10:3-5) NLT

"Yes, most of these thoughts and beliefs have to go," Comforter said, as He held up a paper He had ripped out of one of the books. "As a man thinks in his heart so is he," Comforter said with urgency. "And you can say no to your flesh, the world and the devil. What you believe will determine the kind of person you believe yourself to be. The way this house is trashed and destroyed is indicative of how you thought of yourself. You have lived your life based on your feelings, especially how Freddie flesh felt."

Take for example the sycamine tree and offenses we just witnessed," Comforter said. "The Word of God says:

> "Great peace has they who love thy law (Word of God) and nothing shall offend them."

(Psalm 119:165) KJV

"When God's Word and His Presence become the very part of you, you will find a lot of things that people say and do will not offend you the

The New Library

way it used to. Let's look at some of these belief systems that you have incorporated into your life."

"I thought that it is impossible that offenses will come," I said somewhat perplexed. I was thinking of the first verse in Luke 17.

"Very true," Comforter said. "You will always be in a process of going from glory to glory, but the more of God's Word that you build into your life the less you will find that you will be offended.

"Relationship with us will produce love and love covers a multitude of sins. Offenses will come, but you will find yourself less offended by the offense" I turned towards Comforter as he began to read my belief systems.

"Obey your thirst," Comforter read slowly. "Where did you get that one from?"

"I think I saw it on TV," I said.

"That's your problem right there," Comforter retorted.

"You deserve a break today." Rhema was reading another one. Rhema ripped it up into little pieces of confetti, shaking his head vehemently.

"And this one is pure nonsense, He who has the most toys wins!" Emmanuel said, as he walked into the room and scooped up a pile of papers from the floor to see what had been torn out. Emmanuel shuffled through papers reading other beliefs like, "You owe it to yourself; you have a right to…Wow, this one was almost a book's worth. You need to gratify to satisfy; the bigger the better; a little look won't kill you; you can't trust anyone; you can't do this, what's the use; why even try; no one loves me, no one cares; he's out to get me; one more time won't hurt." The list continued on and on and on of wrong beliefs.

The Dwelling Place

Emmanuel turned to me and said fiercely, "<u>Anything</u> that is not firmly based on the Word of God is a wrong belief system. It must line up with the old leather book."

My mind was swirling. I was really squirming under the scrutiny of my beliefs being examined in this intense light. As I was struggling with the immensity of the situation, the fax machine kicked on and started printing.

"Who is sending me a fax?" I said rather hesitantly.

Emmanuel interjected by saying, "By the confession of your mouth you are establishing new belief systems. Right now you doubt our ability to bring lasting change into your life," Emmanuel stopped taking for a moment as he picked up the completed fax and started reading several new belief systems.

Emmanuel shook His head giving a wry look as He read the ridiculous belief systems I had just formulated in my own strength. I had just confessed that I could not do this because it was too hard for me. Somehow, I was still envisioning seeing myself doing things through Fat man rather that my new man. I was identifying with Freddie flesh in his undisciplined, weakened condition. I was still tying my identity to this nasty old creature.

Emmanuel looked me lovingly in the eye and with loving encouragement said:

"You can do all things through Christ who strengthens you."

(Philippians 4:13).

The New Library

"Look at all the amazing changes I have done in your heart already. I have been by your side all this time and yet you still doubt me?"

I looked at Emmanuel with a blank stupid look like a deer in the headlights while watching all that was happening and revealing itself before me. I began to reason to myself, "I must meditate on God's Word day and night so I know His promises. I need to know the right belief system to have Comforter and Rhema build into my life."

I closed my eyes, crying out desperately as I fell flat on my face. How could I have been so foolish? I had spent so much time giving my attention to worldly Wendy; watching her philosophies, studying and listening to her, and had let myself become <u>distracted and captivated</u> by her allurements.

When God's Word and His presence become the very part of you, you will find a lot of things people say and do will not offend you the way it used to.

"I am just naturally developing Worldly Wendy and Freddie Fleash belief systems," I blurted out. "It's like I'm numb and dumb to the right things and alive to the wrong things."

Suddenly all the hours and hours of watching TV, internet, sports, and personal agendas all seemed like wood, hay and stubble. I began to understand that all the things I was pursuing to fill my mind and heart with were based on a wrong belief system. Precious time was being wasted filling my mind with interesting, probably not even sinful stuff, but worthless junk and it was causing me to develop wrong belief systems about what would make me happy. If nothing else, it was numbing me to being sensitive and open to what Comforter and Emmanuel was trying to say to me. All the things I was filling my mind with was encouraging and causing me to cater to how Fat Man thought and operated.

No wonder I felt so powerless to effect change or see change released through my life. Off to the side, Rhema was drawing with a flourish something on His notepad. A picture suddenly developed of me driving down the highway. I was eager and determined to get to my destination and looking sideways, I saw Emmanuel in the passenger seat. I heard this thumpity, thumpity, thump and the wheel jumped erratically in my hands. Ignoring it became impossible as I found myself drastically slowing down and swerving from side to side. It was very difficult to manage the car. Emmanuel looked over at me and said, "We have a flat tire; you need to pull over so we can fix it. This is not something you can ignore." Suddenly the picture ended and I was left wondering about this mini-vision.

"What does this mean?" I asked, while looking at Emmanuel for an answer to the story.

Emmanuel pulled up a chair and strattled it by sitting backwards while folding his arms across the back of the chair. Leaning forward while resting his chin on his hands He looked me direct in the eyes and said, "The flat tire represents wrong beliefs and lies that you have believed about yourself. Lies and wrong beliefs will slow you down and make life very difficult to navigate. These lies could even pull you right off the road of life and could result in a terrible accident. Flat tires cannot be ignored nor should you ignore wrong beliefs. There will be times you have to let me help you to fix your flat tire; to change it out for the truth. Sometimes you just need to stop and address issues. I am here to help you. Let me help you."

My thoughts were dancing around within my head as I reasoned out loud "If I don't know what God's thoughts and belief systems are for my life, there is a whole world out there controlled by an unseen force that has a detailed agenda to help direct my thoughts and belief systems for me.

"I cannot be fooled anymore," I said firmly. New resolve and determination flooded my heart. The Word of God and knowing its

The New Library

promises made more and more sense. Getting off the floor, I stood up and stretched, tightened my new belt tighter and said, "Let's begin. I'll do whatever it takes. There is no other choice. It's kill or be killed; I will no longer let the enemy kill, maim and destroy my life. My worship is not to be shared towards anyone but the Father. I must say no to Freddie fleash no matter how painful it will be."

Emmanuel and Comforter smiled in approval as they saw that their instruction was beginning to sink in. "There is one more very important truth you need to know," Comforter said as he handed me a very large sledgehammer and a pair of work gloves.

"What is this for," I asked?

"There is truth to damien devlin's influence, but let's not give him any credit for what he doesn't deserve. The reality is that most of what has happened here is a result of your own beliefs that you developed in your own strength. It is in living by what you feel rather than by the choice of self control that God has placed within you. It was through your vanity. Let me explain.

"Do you see all those book shelves? I want you to smash them all into tiny bits and throw them into a pile in the front yard to be burned." My mouth dropped open in shock as I looked at my beautiful pine shelves with stained glass windows. It was such a beautiful structure for holding all my belief systems.

"Wh, Wha, What do you mean?" I stammered.

"These bookshelves represent the structure that you have built to accommodate your belief systems. These shelves represent proud arguments and rebellious ideas (2 Corinthians 10:3-5). They are the mindset of your heart as you developed your belief system over the years based on pride and rebellion. These are not authentic furniture designed

The Dwelling Place

to go with this house. This was something you brought in. You did this with Fat Mans help

I looked at the pine shelves, and saw an inscription at the base of the shelves. It read 'fear, doubt, and unbelief'. The writing all around the outside and top had the inscription, 'structure in unrighteousness'. I looked back at Comforter with a puzzled look.

"Deep within you is this core belief that you must be in control. It is this belief that all that you affect are the result of your accomplishments. So you manipulate things, try to dominate and control what is around you to protect your core beliefs about what will satisfy you and make you happy. You develop your beliefs from your own mind's eye of what will benefit you. Your core beliefs are faulty and the underlying foundation is one of fear, doubt, and unbelief. Every belief that you have developed has been influenced and filtered by this foundation." Comforter stopped for a moment to gauge how I was receiving things. After he saw that I was receiving things well he continued. This is not self control.

> *You are still thinking from the wrong structure of thinking. A structure that I have not designed for you to live from*

"You are responding with selfish pride and rebellion and must have things your way, but yet you have responded out of fear, doubt and unbelief. It is a double edged sword that causes you to be double minded in all you do. It is also a perfect greenhouse for devlin to set up house and slowly gain control. Because self love is the core structure of your life, in order to accomplish your ends you will do whatever it takes by manipulating, dominating and controlling things to fulfill your selfish ambitions and desires. All of this is surrounded by a structure of unrighteousness. All your beliefs are saturated in the skin of a 'lie'.

"You may believe things that are true in many cases, but never the less they are encapsulated in lies. You hide behind stained glass doors

The New Library

that look very spiritual and holy, yet it is all designed to protect and insulate and make you look good to God, others and sadly yourself.

This whole structure is like a black hole sucking everything into it. This structure has actually created emptiness in your life that no one can fill. Anyone trying to help you gets sucked into this emptiness and nothingness. Because you put your trust and hope in things, people and power, you are destroying and being destroyed by the very things that you crave to satisfy you.

Comforter paused for a moment to let the immensity of what He was saying sink in.

"Look at all these cockroach type bugs and worms scurrying and slithering around these shelves, and in and out of these books." Comforter was holding on to a large magnifying glass and was peering through them at something moving on the library shelves. "Here! Take this magnifying glass and look closely at them. You have nasty cockroaches and worms crawling on your pine bookshelves."

"What! Cockroaches and worms?" I blurted out. I held up the magnifying glass and zeroed in on the bugs. Stepping back in horror I was startled at their appearance. They had the head of a man, but the body of a cockroach. The worms had nasty looking eyes; they were really ugly. They were chewing on my books and shelving units and then swallowing and regurgitating it back up.

The surface of the books and shelves at a closer examination was a smear of nasty vomit. It was truly hideous!

"So, this is what is feeding my heart and house," I surmised with a slow measured breath. These guys were eating me out of house and home. I could see that anyone physically or mentally touching my shelves would be contaminated and corrupted.

The Dwelling Place

I crumpled to my knees as the weight of this revelation hit me with a slow measured force. For a long time, I just sat and digested what I had just seen. I was trying to live the Christian life from the wrong mindset. Now even my beautiful pine bookshelves were revealed to be only a veneer of beauty. It was a structure in danger of eminent collapse. The shelves had been consumed from the inside out. Everything I had built was in the context of listening to fat man.

Emmanuel and Comforter placed a hand on each shoulder and let their presence saturate my being. A deep love oozed from my head all the way down to the soles of my feet. Even with what I was seeing, awe overwhelmed my heart and I knew that I was totally loved and accepted. They were just here to help me realize the best of who they had made me to be. They were here to help set me free from the lies that had been destroying me. That meant some stuff had to go to let the good stuff come in. I was beginning to see that even though my righteousness was declared to be filthy rags or in my case filthy library shelves, I somehow saw that these guys were not identifying or tying my identity with these shelves. It was just a glimmer of understanding, at this point, but it gave me hope.

I honestly could not have taken such a disclosure without feeling totally loved and accepted by my trio of friends. It's hard to let go of your old stuff. Thank God for revelation because it was bringing everything into focus. A slow burning anger began to seethe within me. I had allowed myself to be deceived. The lie was becoming exposed. I began to feel resolve building up within me. Looking up, I gazed into Comforters eyes as he said,

"If you memorize and meditate on these twenty-one verses that I gave to you earlier," Comforter exhorted "and put them on this structure of shelves, you will become like the Pharisees of the Bible; religious and full of truth but void of life, love, and God's presence being alive in your life. You can no longer live from the premise of these shelves.

The New Library

"You have been saved from all of this unrighteous structure. You no longer need to live from this mindset. It is all based in a lie. You need to tear down these old shelves and have new ones built," Comforter stated. "You need a new set of shelves with no doors or stained glass. Your belief system is to be an open book to all. It needs to be built on the right premise."

"If these are the wrong shelves then, what are to be the right shelves, and what structure are they to be made of?" I asked inquisitively yet feeling frustrated at the same time.

"I want to build your new shelving system based on doctrine, reproofs and correction," Comforter said.

"You want me to build a new shelving system based on what?" I said somewhat bemused. Somehow this did not sound like much fun.

"Yes, doctrine, reproofs, and correction," Comforter said, with an even greater conviction. "I know that this sounds like I am asking you to drink prune juice but it's not like that at all."

Rhema began to write notes on His note pad. Revelation began to slowly filter into my mind as I started to understand that I must be a person who would be willing to receive instruction. I must be able to accept a "righteous structure" into my life. It must be the main component of the shelves that I build. It would be a place where the new beliefs of God's Word would have a safe greenhouse and environment to grow. It had to be a place the enemy could not penetrate. It had to be the right thought structure. It had to be an instruction in righteousness. I had to live from the right attitudes.

If I chose to live my life within a structure of doctrine, rebuke and correction that would mean that I would absolutely surrender my life to be willing to be taught the truth. I was setting myself up for any situation. Whether it was a person, event, circumstance, or the Word of God, I

The Dwelling Place

would choose to be teachable and humble; I needed God and others in my life. It was in realizing that God and others were responsible for the person I am discovering myself to be.

Freedom began to flood my soul at the prospect of this. Damien devlin could not inhabit and build a stronghold from this environment. He could only build a stronghold from a structure of shelves that would hold proud arguments, rebellious ideas, or unbelief.

"This is why God resists the proud but gives grace to the humble," I thought to myself. My new man could sustain this structure. It was perfectly designed for him.

Emmanuel turned, placing a comforting hand on my hand. "You have been paying a mortgage on this house for twenty years that has already been paid. You have been harassed and threatened into foreclosure on a house that devlin has no authority over. Aren't you glad you gave that signed document to fat man, devlin, Freddie fleash and worldly Wendy? You are beginning to understand that we hold the paper on this house and we've given you total authority over it. It is your choice to accept our love and our help but it is not something we will try to manipulate or exercise control over for you. Our purpose for you is not to control you but to help you see that you have been empowered to self control yourself. It will be painful at first to say no to your flesh when it wants to fall into self pity, lust, anger, or pride, but eventually you will see the peaceable fruits of righteousness."

I fell prostrate before Emmanuel. "I love you so much. I am not only willing, but eager to do your will, O Lord. I understand now. My battle is not with what I can see. There is a definite world system out there that is for real, and if I don't know what I stand for I will be destroyed. I will end up falling for anything.

Like David in the Psalms, I began to cry out:

The New Library

"Search me O God and know my heart, try me and know my thoughts and see if there is any wicked way in me and lead me in the way everlasting."

(Psalm 139:23) KJV

I had this new house (heart), but was still carrying around the old library shelves. It was like moving into this new house with all of your old furniture. That is what I had done. God had given me this new house and I had moved all my old junk, thinking patterns and wrong attitudes into this new house.

I began to understand how some people got saved and received total deliverance in some areas. They had gotten a revelation and they had not moved that piece of furniture or junk into their new house. Some people actually got it right from the beginning and walked into their destiny immediately in a certain area. I, however, had not done that in most areas.

As I lay there weeping before Emmanuel, a new song began to well up from deep within me. Emmanuel and Comforter's words were penetrating to my deepest core, and I saw that it was my pride and rebellion that were holding me back. I thought I had made such great strides but I had only moved from open rebellion to a quiet rebellion. Now I was slowly beginning to see that it was His love that made all the difference. I began to sing:

> **God make a fresh start in me**
> **Put a fresh wind in my sails**
> **Create a clean heart in me**
> **From the inside out**
> **For I long for you**
> **Make me pure within**
> **God create a clean heart in me**
> **That I might see your face**

The Dwelling Place

Stir within my soul
Reach down deep don't let go
For I need you Your my hope
Hold me tight
Don't let go

©2007 Fresh Start
Words and Music by John M Davidson

A deep peace began to settle deep within my soul. After a few moments, I turned up the heat on the thermostat. I realized that I needed more *Godly Desire*. I was choosing to operate out of self control. I wanted to clearly see Emmanuel's face. Oh, I know I was seeing Him. I was talking to Him. But I wanted more. I wanted to see Him operate from the inside out and experience His love in and through me. Resolve began to rise up within me as the atmosphere in the air flooded my lungs with more of a *Godly Desire*.

"I wish we could get drunk before we start this," I pondered deeply in myself. I had hardly opened my mouth when Emmanuel walked back in the room with two bottles of wine in each hand. I hadn't even noticed that He had left, but He had already anticipated my heart's desire.

> I made the choice that I would choose to live a life where the structure of shelves that housed my thoughts and beliefs would be supported by a willingness to receive correction, reproof and chastening

"I got some potent stuff here," Emmanuel said enthusiastically. "This will get your blood boiling." He held up one of the bottles and read the label. It said, 'Fire Water', another read, 'Worship no. 7' "This worship is special," Emmanuel whispered excitedly. "It goes seven levels deep. This other one will increase your passion for the Father." We drank deeply in each other's presence and worshipped Father Daddy for the next hour. It was awesome!

The New Library

After a period of time, who knows how long, I stood up, stretched my arms while giving a loud yawn and looked around?

Taking in another deep breath of the living atmosphere of *Godly Desire*, I eagerly grabbed the sledgehammer and began swinging. Faster and faster, I swung the sledgehammer and destroyed the fortress of shelves. I was beginning to bring every thought captive to the obedience of Christ. The structure did not come down easily as it was built right into the walls and tentacles were deeply embedded into the inner structure, but down it came, piece by piece.

As I swung the hammer, I felt a sharp stabbing pain penetrate my heart and radiate up and out over my shoulders. I shuddered in deep agonizing pain. As I did, I felt the house shudder just as violently. The knife had penetrated deep and a loud ripping; tearing sound began to manifest itself.

"What is that?" I gasped as I fought to get a breath of air as the agony drove me to my knees. The searing pain was almost more than I could bear.

As I finished, I fell on my face and began to worship. I felt the power of Comforter in and around me like a warm blanket. I felt so fulfilled. As I prayed to the Father, I made the choice that I would choose to live a life where the structure of shelves that housed my thoughts and beliefs would be supported by a willingness to receive correction, reproof and chastening. I would always be open to listen and examine myself to be sure I was in the faith. I would be willing to let others speak into my life. No longer would I allow a shelf of rebellious ideas or proud arguments to influence me. Somehow I knew that I would feel the pain until I completely died in that area, but I knew that pain now would result in fruitfulness later.

The Dwelling Place

With that settled I grabbed my sword and began to study it, work with it, and learn how to skillfully wield it. It was the key to a correct belief system.

"How can I bring captive my thoughts to the obedience of Christ if I am not in the Word, learning God's commands and promises? How can I have the love of God and His Presence flow through me correctly if I don't have the proper shelves in place?" I thought. If I am not willing to be teachable and realize that God and others are responsible for the achievements in my life, how can I really see God and myself as I truly am?"

A quiet burning began to fill me up from the core of my being, "I will find deep relationship with my Lord and Savior if I seek Him with all my heart. I will run after your Word," I whispered quietly.

Something in my heart felt like it was being cut out. Revelation from Rhema's pad began to come into focus within me. Rhema was writing a scripture verse.

> *My whole vision was filled with this little boy who looked adoringly into his father's eyes.*

"The Word of God is quick and powerful and sharper than any two edged sword, piercing to the dividing of soul and spirit and is a discerner of the thoughts and intents of the heart."

(Hebrews 4:12) KJV

Ahhh! That is what is happening. The Word is cutting out these old shelves including the whole structure. I am applying the Word by swinging the hammer, and the Spirit of the Word is cutting it out and putting to death the power of my former habits and desires. It is also separating out the tentacles that have embedded themselves into my inner walls. I was having a vision of what I was about to do.

The New Library

I quieted myself in the presence of the Lord worshipping Him, and suddenly, I found myself caught up in the Presence of God. I was standing before my King. I caught my reflection in a mirror off to the side and I saw that I was as a little boy coming expectantly to see His Father. Father reached out His hands with love and said, "Come to your Father." Eagerly I ran and climbed up into His lap and snuggled close.

"Read to me, Father," I said as I reached up and impulsively gave Him a kiss on the cheek.

The Father King smiled, picking up a scroll of His life-giving Words and began to read stories of faith and wisdom. He sang songs over me rocking me gently in His arms. They were songs filled with faith, hope and love.

I saw myself as the little boy whose heartbeat was beating so fast because he felt he had so much responsibility to carry; so many bullies out there that were mean to Him, so much to learn and do. It was a big world out there and it could be overwhelming at times. I saw him snuggle deep in Fathers arms and fall asleep content and secure. He felt totally protected. His Daddy would take care of Him. After all he carried His name and was protected by His love. As he fell asleep listening to His father's Words, the Word settled in His heart becoming foundation stones of faith, hope and love.

> *It was now crystal clear that everyone lives life from some sort of structure*

Relationship with the Father helped it to be settled quickly. He was loved and that made all the difference. Faith rose up quickly in the little boy for he believed in his Father. Soon the burden of responsibility became lighter. As he awoke, expectant joy and hope shone from his eyes as he looked adoringly into his Father's eyes.

Time seemed to have disappeared and I fell into a deep peaceful sleep. The vision of the little boy faded into a sweet darkness. I slept

The Dwelling Place

soundly for several hours. When I opened my eyes, I felt totally at peace and refreshed. I looked around and saw to my great surprise the most beautiful mahogany shelves. They were magnificent. This time there were no doors and no stained glass windows on the library shelves. In the shelves were etched the words, 'teachable' and 'humility'. Under the word 'teachable' were three words in parenthesis (doctrine, reproof and correction). At the base of the shelves in each section were the words, 'Faith', 'Hope', 'Love'. At the top and sides were the words 'Instruction in Righteousness'. I also noticed at the top over everything was a banner that read 'Truth'.

I looked in wonderment at this spectacular sight. It was just as Comforter had said.

"So this is the fortification that the Lord can inhabit," I theorized. "God inhabits a righteous structure."

As I reflected on this new revelation, Rhema wrote flamboyantly on His notepad. I began to visualize and see the structure in the word in'struct'ion. It all made perfect sense. This is the place where the good seed can grow into strong beliefs and attitudes that will be pillars in my life...pillars of wisdom and knowledge!!!

This was good doctrinal instruction built on faith, hope and love and the whole thing encapsulated the shelves were the attitudes of being teachable and humble. These were supported by sub-directives of doctrine, reproof and correction.

It was now crystal clear that everyone lives life from some sort of structure. It was just which camp do you want to live in. Before, I thought I was free to do what I wanted, but in doing what I wanted, I was still being held bondage to a structure of unrighteousness. It was a breeding ground of filth. That was the old pine book shelves...this old structure that was bent on pulling me down a slippery slope to hell.

The New Library

But now I was a new creature and free to live in this new structure and destroy the old. I could choose, but I could only live in one or the other. They were complete opposite structures.

"Wow! This is amazing!" I thought with astonishment. A new longing welled up within me. This is true freedom. This is what I want. It was all so clear now. I would still feel the pressure of the old system, but no longer would I allow it to influence my heart. No longer would I have to feel obligated to obey its desires. It was like a balloon in the water. The old system could touch the outside and its very presence could put pressure on me, but the air inside (the new structure) held it out and kept it from coming in. It would be my choice to either let the old system squeeze me into its mold, or allow His Truth to reveal the real me.

As this revelation unfolded itself before me, I again committed my life to live by 'whatever it takes'; that in any situation, place and time, I would visualize and implement any truth from God being bought into my life as being good for me. I was a new creation and I committed myself to the supposition that every belief system would be supported by the right attitude and that it would be received in a humble, teachable spirit which was who I now was.

Being teachable and humble involved letting other people speak into my life. I realized that it doesn't matter if the person was 'in charge' over me at home, work, church, or play, or is younger, older, better, worse, or is more or less experienced than I. This is the spirit I would choose to accept as my core values. This is how I would build a habitation of righteousness; a good stronghold that God can inhabit and grow in. My heart was running and dancing for joy.

Wow! What a mouth full! This revelation was out of this World. How could you get offended? I am agreeing to let anything come into my life as working for my good. God is good and anything He gives to me is good. If something is withheld, it is good. If something takes weeks, or

The Dwelling Place

months or years to fulfill, it is good. If I suffer for righteousness or for my own mistakes or failures to perform something correctly, it is good. If the people in my life are fixers and are always correcting me and changing things, then I will be teachable and humble and look for some positive; some good to come out of that situation. This is how a person can be changed from glory to glory. This is how one could truly become an over comer. This is good!

Ah! It was wonderful to realize and see the structure of righteousness. This is where true power flowed. This is what it meant to have a power of momentum from the Spirit. My mind was on sensory overload as Rhema downloaded into me more than I could process. It was all good though. I now saw the danger of building a shelf of rebellious ideas and pride on a foundation of fear doubt and unbelief. I now saw the power of being teachable and humble. I can never stop learning and I can never stop growing.

I was excited as I began to see my mind integrating properly and falling in line with my heart. My desires had miraculously changed. Truly, as a man thinks in His heart, so is he. Comforter and Emmanuel had done something wonderful within me. I tore down the old shelves; the Spirit of the Word cut right through my soul and spirit and divided out wrong habits, wrong thinking and emotions and put a new desire within me. I wanted my mind and heart to think alike, so that I would be one in mind and heart, and I was seeing it happen before my eyes. I was excited as I pondered this incredible thought—the mind of Christ! I had the new desire and the new blueprint. It was a structure of righteousness in the picture of a beautiful mahogany book shelf system and it was a hand in glove perfect fit for my new man. Why was this good? The answer was obvious. It is the framework that allows the seed to grow. The seed is the Word of God.

"Thy Word have I hid in my heart that I might not sin against thee (GOD)"

(Psalms 119:11) KJV

"Blessed are the pure in heart for they will see God."

(Mathew 5:7) KJV

If the word of God is strong in me, I will see God. I will be able to see to enjoy His Presence. I will be able to see to do His will and see His will in heaven accomplished here on earth.

Doctrine

Rhema began to download to me fresh revelation at this point. A teachable spirit and humility were the vital attitudes that one's beliefs must rest upon. It began to dawn on me that if this was to be the structure of my beliefs and attitudes, then I must understand the depth of meaning of these three words. Within this structure of righteousness was an attitude of teachablility and humility. Over the whole structure was Truth with a capital 'T' which I knew had to be absolute Truth. It had to be the Truth of God or the Word of Truth. That narrowed it down to Jesus for He is:

"...the way the truth and the life, no man comes to the Father but by Him"

(John 14:6) KJV

I saw 'doctrine, reproof, and correction' in parenthesis under teachable and humility, so I began to look first at doctrine. I needed the correct Truth to be in my life and I had purposed to be open to being taught. I wanted the right thoughts about my relationship with God, others and myself. Doctrine had within itself the element of discipline. I need to discipline myself in absolute Truth. That Truth is in the Word of

The Dwelling Place

God. I was able to do this because I was a new creation and part of that creation was the fruit of self discipline.

Reproof

I took the other word 'reproof' and began to study that word. I began to see that I was to be open to constructive criticism. If my structure included correction, then there would be times that I might have a bent (slight or great) in the wrong direction. I would be committed to letting others speak freely into my life. I would be excited to let anyone 'proof' my beliefs. My beliefs needed to be challenged and tested to make sure they would be sound and true. If I got offended because people were challenging my structure then I was not being teachable and humble. It was out of this that character could grow. My whole life would be an open book. What did I have to lose? The verse in Proverbs sang clearly into my head:

> *"Faithful are the wounds of a friend"*

(Proverbs 27:6) KJV

A friend had my best interests at heart. This would include my boss, my pastor, authority figures and so on. I would treat everyone's opinion as I would friends. What could it hurt? I would keep an open mind and would find the best in whatever was offered to me.

> *The new man can take anything, anyway and at any time. It desires to be like Christ*

I don't always see things clearly and need to be committed to correction. So not only would I be open, but I would be excited and passionate about letting others speak into my life. Most importantly, I would be excited to let my close friends, Emmanuel,

The New Library

Comforter and Rhema speak into my life. Their words were always true. The new man loved to grow and was open to reproof.

Correction

The third word, 'rebuke', made me a bit uncomfortable as I understood its meaning. The word "correction or rebuke" meant to criticize or admonish sharply.

"Ow!" I said to myself. "Who is going to want to be willing to subject themselves to that? Many times, people are not always nice when they say corrective things. It comes across as hard, without tack or at the wrong time,"

I winced as a situation painfully revealed itself in my memory. Sometimes that person was a different gender or younger or less smart than I. Should I accept correction only if it is given in a godly way? How many times had I said, "Who does he think he is? Or how dare him! Or what right does he have? How rude! How often do people not show honor and instead walk all over you?" Now I realized that this thinking came from Fat man, not the new man.

> *Orderliness had begun to formulate from deep within my heart and the fragrance of God's love began permeating the library of my heart*

"How badly do you want the seed of God to grow in your life?" Emmanuel asked while interrupting my churning thoughts yet speaking to me gently. "This is why the old Fat Man must die. The new man can take anything at any time. It desires to be like Christ. Do you think people always spoke well to me? How often do you think people said things to me in a dishonoring way? I

The Dwelling Place

am God. I could have called a myriad of angels for help and they would have come instantly destroying everyone. Some people think that I should have just whispered the word and turned them to dust. But this is not who I am or ever will be. I honor you as a pearl of great price. I give you the ability to choose to be teachable and humble, and the freedom to fail or succeed.

"I also made it my priority to honor my Father above everything. In fact, I was always about my Father's business and everything shaped me to that end. I saw every situation as an opportunity to do the will of my Father. Why do you think I did it so willingly? Because I knew that doing the will of the Father always brought about the best in my life. My Father always knows what is best for me and I totally trust that. Go after these three things with zeal. Be eager. I am more concerned with your humble teachable heart than the situation itself.

Being a missionary, teacher, engineer, husband, wife, son or daughter is secondary to your attitude. Attitude trumps location. Let your good works flow out of good teaching, reproofs and correction.

Like I said, "The new man can take anything at anytime. He desires to be like Christ. I began to realize that it did not matter how people said things to me. This would be the structure that would shape my beliefs and attitudes. I saw the implicit trust that Emmanuel had in His Father. Excitement began to grow within me. I was beginning to see that the more I learned and implemented this structure into my life; I would see a great decrease of sycamine trees and fences sprouting up in my yard unannounced.

> *I was to about my father's business and everything I was always about my shaped me to that end. I saw every situation as an opportunity to do the will of my Father. Why do you think I did it so willingly? Because I knew that doing the will of the father always brought about the best in my life*

The New Library

I was so excited to see that the shelving that held up my beliefs was to be that of being teachable and humble. I was already seeing a vortex flowing up from the base of the shelves, through the shelves and then radiating out into the whole house. Turning to Comforter I asked what this meant.

With great enthusiasm, Comforter grinned at me and gave a knowing look to Rhema, who was doodling on His notepad. "You are having a Spirit moment," Comforter said with a deep laugh.

Giving Comforter a bemused look, I shook my head and asked with a laugh, "What do you mean a spirit moment?"

Comforter came over to where I was sitting and placed both His hands over mine. Looking intently into my eyes, He said with great enthusiasm, "You are seeing every thought, word and action flowing into your life through this structure of righteousness. You are already beginning to understand that this structure of righteousness is the mind of Christ. The very way that I think, say and do is within you. You have the mind of Christ (1 Corinthians 2:16). It is your right as a Son. This is natural for your new man and you are tapping into it.

This vortex flowing from the base up through the shelves and into your entire house is a picture of how my own mind functions. It is coming through the base because every thought, word and deed must first flow through the foundational stones of faith, hope and love. You must and will see everything filtered through these three stones. Do you mind if I discern your thoughts for a moment?"

"Go ahead," I said. "Fire away!"

Comforter gave me a sideways look for a moment and then continued. "Let's talk about the first foundational stone.

The Dwelling Place

FAITH

"Remember how you used to look at that verse in Romans 14:23 in a negative way? It was the verse that said, "Whatever is not of faith is sin?" I looked Comforter in the eyes reflecting back to the many times I had hung my head in shame at my inability to live every moment in faith. "That will be no more," Comforter replied emphatically, placing one of His hands on my forehead. "You have the mind of Christ, but you must exercise it. You must become skilful.

"Make it a habit to visualize everything coming into your life as flowing through faith," Emmanuel said as he joined the conversation. "See it as a positive. I have put my life within you. The more you believe the impossible as being possible, the more you will experience a release of life."

"Everyone who is my son or daughter starts with a measure of faith. It is as a grain of a mustard seed, but faith grows in your life as you meditate on the Word of God and walk out your day living in my Presence. Nothing you could ever do could earn your salvation,

> *By grace you are saved through faith and that not of yourself it is the gift of God, not of works lest any man should boast.*
>
> *(Ephesians 2:8-9) KJV*

However, once you have been given this free gift, you are to work your salvation out with fear and trembling:

> *Wherefore, my beloved, as ye have always obeyed, not as in my presence only, but now much more in my absence, work out your own salvation with fear and trembling.*
>
> *(Phil 2:12) KJV*

The New Library

This salvation that I had received had saved me from the penalty of eternal death. I was filled with a new power and I was enjoying the presence of the trinity three and could freely do so because of my salvation. Now I was beginning to see that I was saved from the pleasure of sin.

"If you include me in everything you do and incorporate me in every decision, faith will grow. You will become more and more confident," Emmanuel spoke assuredly.

With each victory you must always remember that the attitudes of being teachable and humble are a part of my mind. I am God, and yet I always deferred to doing the will of my Father."

My heart was pulsing and churning, slowly burning as the words of Comforter and Emmanuel settled deep within me. I was to visualize and see everything through faith. It was to be in the forefront of my mind as I walked through the day. I was to work it out with fear and trembling. In other words, I was to give careful and attentive focus on this new structure and it started by seeing everything being lived out through faith.

If I started to experience fear, doubt or unbelief beginning to creep in, it would be a warning sign for me to set my affections on things above, to focus on faith

HOPE

Comforter smiled while discerning that my thoughts were moving in the right direction. "The second foundational stone is that of hope," Comforter said eagerly. "Part of having hope is making it a habit to be always grateful and thankful for everything in your life. Find a way in every situation to give thanks for every kind word and deed done to you.

The Dwelling Place

Wake up in the morning and look with expectant hope at the goodness of God that you will experience today. There is no place for fear, doubt or unbelief. Put your hope in the Lord. I am the answer to every problem and the solution to every need. If you sense fear, doubt or unbelief trying to settle in, see it as a warning to run into the Presence of your Father. Remember when David wrote in the Psalms,

"What time I am afraid, I will trust in You."

(Psalms 56:3) NKJV

David didn't get all bent out of shape because He was afraid, He simply saw it as an opportunity to turn it into relationship with his favorite person and trust in God.

A slight frown cast a shadow across my countenance as a troubling thought assailed me. Why hope? I could understand faith and love, but I was having trouble understanding why hope would be one of the three foundation stones of the library. I was struggling with the idea of hope as being one of the three pillars of the mind of Christ. This would mean that everything I did, every thought I thought would have to be filtered through hope. It would be crucial to a sound mind (2 Timothy 1:7). I was struggling to comprehend putting the pieces of the puzzle together.

Comforter gripped my shoulders with much fervor as He spoke with great passion. "Hope is one of the anchors of the soul (Hebrews 6:19). It is hope that gives us access into the most holy place. You can approach Father God with boldness because of it. It is this hope that gives you confidence in a steadfast, unbroken relationship with the Trinity Three. It is this hope that will keep you going until the end (Hebrews 3:6). This hope is the essence of the gospel (Colossians 1:23). It will enable you to preach the good news of the gospel and its power to change lives, and it is all because of hope."

The New Library

Just hearing Comforter say these amazing words was lifting me up. I felt hope rising up within me. It was if I had begun walking up a mountain and could see further and clearer than I ever could before. I found myself talking out loud as I proclaimed fervently, "We must see everything though hope as we go throughout our day. Hope gives us the drive and desire to fulfill the dreams and destiny that are placed within us and before us. It is this hope of eternal life that we will live forever and ever with our awesome Father (Titus 3:7). It is a good hope through grace (2 Thessalonians 2:16). It is not a 'pie in the sky' hope, but a real and sure hope. It is as real as our very lives. It is in "setting my affections on things above;" (Colossians 3:2) of letting my mind be consumed with heaven. My eternal home is not here, it is up there.

I gave Comforter a warm impulsive hug. "Thank you for opening my eyes to these foundational stones that are becoming a part of my mind in this new nature. I never realized what a sound mind looked like. I had now experienced what a sound mind felt like and it really made sense. I could hardly wait to implement this as I started through my day."

Comforter gave me a warm, supportive look as His countenance brightened. "If you think you are excited now, let me reveal to you the amazing wonders of the third foundational stone." I turned with great interest and anticipation as He began to open up to me the mysteries of the mind of Christ; it was this stone that completed the base of the library shelves.

LOVE

"There is nothing greater than love," Comforter said earnestly. "Love is the main foundational stone than goes underneath faith and hope. Everything must pass through God's love as it enters and flows into

The Dwelling Place

your mind. Emmanuel's commitment to do the will of the Father flowed out of His love for the Father and the Father's love for Him. Within you is the mind of Christ which includes this precious foundational stone. God's love has been placed within the base of your library bookcase. It is what supports all your attitudes, your beliefs, and of course, faith and hope. This is the structure from which you live as a child of God. This is where life begins and happens." Comforter was becoming more passionate as He expounded on the facets of love. What have you seen to this point is what reveals the love of God?" Comforter said earnestly.

Pondering this, my mind wandered back through the past few days. "It is amazing to me;" I responded wholeheartedly, "That Emmanuelle always believes the best in me. He never assumes I will fail, or falter. He never sets me up for rejection. It seems as if He knows I will succeed. He sees me as perfect and complete. His hope is always for my success. It always amazes me that He is the first to get His hands dirty to clean up my house. He does not identify me with my trash, but sees who I really am beneath all the failures, mistakes, and continued sins. He always forgives me readily when I sin as soon as I ask (even if I did the same sin one thousand times)." I found a zealousness rising within me as I continued, "Emmanuel tells me I'm beautiful and lovely and I know He is telling the truth. No matter what problem I am having, He is always kind, patient and gives me a listening ear. I never hear Him talk about Himself; it is always about me." A tear began to trickle down my cheeks as the overwhelming love of God washed over me.

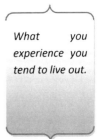

What you experience you tend to live out.

Ahhhh! It is always His goodness that brought about repentance in me. He never demanded for me to love Him and He never manipulated me to give Him love. He just loved me. I began to sob just talking about this. My heart was filled to overflowing as I readily and unreservedly soaked in His love. Comforter placed His arms around me and held me tenderly.

The New Library

"The more you stay close to Emmanuelle and experience His love, the easier it will be for you to filter that love through your own heart and then release it to others. What you experience, you tend to live out."

"This is good stuff," I blurted out.

All I could do was beam with joy. I was beginning to understand. Orderliness had begun to formulate from deep within my heart and the fragrance of God's love began permeating the library of my heart. Hope began to spring up so I could experience lasting change and I began to believe towards that end. "This is good stuff," I blurted out.

Comforter looked at me, like a teacher looking over an essay paper that had been completed with excellence. "You did well my son, you did well!" All I could do was to beam with joy. I was beginning to understand. Orderliness had begun to formulate from deep within my heart and the fragrance of God's love began permeating the library of my heart. Hope began to spring up that I could experience lasting change and I began to believe towards that end. Along with this love and hope that I was experiencing, I found faith growing within me. I was beginning to believe and that believing was beginning to open up not just my heart and house but also my lips. I felt a boldness beginning to well up within tied to a hope for the future and a love for others.

"Tell everyone the things that you have seen and heard," Emmanuel said with deep conviction. "My power to change you to be the man you were destined to be is the same power to bring about change in others. It is the power of evangelism."

Part III

THE FRUITFULNESS OF GODLINESS

22

LADY WISDOM

Feeling a bit hungry, I decided to go to the kitchen for a bite to eat. As I entered the kitchen, I was pleasantly surprised by a scurry of activity. A woman with a plaid working dress and a white apron was sitting at the counter busy peeling fruit. A big bowl of ripe peaches was sitting on the counter and was ready to be canned. On the stove a full pot of canned peaches was merrily boiling away. A slight rattle could be heard like the sound of wind chimes as the water boiled joyfully around the jars that were stacked tightly in the pot. I noticed it was the same pot that I had seen earlier in the vision in the boardroom on the stove.

The cover was off to the side, and not on top like I had seen earlier in my dream. At that time I had remembered then that it was being used to make a delicious pot of stew.

I put my face down over the steam and took in a deep breath.

"Mmm….." I said longingly. "It looks good, but there is no smell.

The Dwelling Place

As I stood there with my mouth watering looking longingly at the peaches, the woman who was canning beckoned to me saying, "Take a bite of this peach and tell me what you think."

I reached for a peach that was in a bowl on the counter and took a deep savory bite. Ohhh!!!... It was so juicy and sweet.

"That is so good!" I exclaimed as I smacked my lips. "What is it? Is there some meaning to this?" I took another bite and felt the saliva squirt liquid joy into my mouth as it mixed with the deliciousness of the peach."

"This is the goodness of God," the lady said warmly.

I noticed out of the corner of my eye Rhema passing by in the hallway. He had now stopped and was pacing back and forth as He was writing excitedly on his notepad. He seemed quite energized by what he had just heard and wanted me to get the full implication of what this lady had just said. Amazing revelation began to ignite this woman's words.

"O taste and see that the Lord is good."

(Psalm 34:8) KJV

This verse had just popped into my mind like a fourth of July explosion... Again my mouth watered and I felt compelled to take another bite of the juicy peach.

Noticing something very special about this woman, I asked curiously, "Who are you and where did you come from?"

The lady smiled and said, "I am Lady Wisdom. I have also been called the Spirit of Wisdom. I was sent by God to assist Comforter and Rhema."

"Rhema just walked by and gave me this amazing word about this fruit." I said excitedly. "He said to taste and see that the Lord is good. I did not notice any smell, but my saliva glands are bursting with longing to eat more of this delicious fruit." I sunk my teeth into another mouth

Lady Wisdom

watering bite as the juices squirted out of the fruit and began to run down my chin. An exquisite groan of delight rumbled from deep within me as I savored this fabulous fruit.

"God's power comes in many ways," Lady Wisdom said as she looked at me over the top of her glasses. "Sometimes you taste, sometimes you touch, and sometimes you see it. It has many textures and flavors. Take for example the peach. The peach is likened unto the goodness of God. The juice drips down off your chin with sweetness. It's like the oil that drips down Aaron's beard... God's anointing is sweetness." She laughed a hearty laugh as she took a checkered napkin and dabbed the juices running off my chin.

Goose bumps were prickling up and down my arm as the impact of God's goodness settled in my spirit. I wiped the remainder of the juice off my cheeks with the napkin as I snapped back to the reality of the moment. "Why are the peaches being canned?" I asked inquiringly.

"With every fruit there is a season just as there are seasons in your spiritual life," Lady Wisdom said wisely. "This fruit is being stored up for another season. It is now in season. This is a season for God's goodness, but in a few months it may seem like a winter season in your life."

More revelation began to flood my mind as I saw myself eating a bowl of peaches with cream on top. "Mmmm...Mmmm! Peaches and cream!" My mouth was watering at the prospect of peaches and cream being available from my pantry in the winter months.

I noticed that Rhema had not left the hallway where He was still writing with a passion and a mission. His eyes were bulging with new enthusiasm as He wrote. New revelation flooded my mind as another favorite verse of scripture came through my heart and mind:

"Surely goodness and mercy will follow me..."

The Dwelling Place

(Psalm 23:6a) KJV

"The dry times will be the times that you reflect on the written testimonies and relive and enjoy God's goodness," Lady Wisdom said with an encouraging smile.

I fell on my face in worship as I thought about the goodness of God and His mercy. How many seasons of my life did I not think that His goodness and mercy were not there because the season I was in was not a time where I could taste the fresh fruit? And yet…. here Lady Wisdom, guided by the hand of God, was storing up goodness and mercy for me to fill my pantry so I would lack no good thing. Its freshness was being sealed in so when I needed it, it would be as fresh as the day it was canned.

"I'm a bit confused," I said to Lady Wisdom. "If God's mercies are new every morning and goodness follows me all the days of my life, why do I need to 'can' it up, so to speak, for a future day?"

"Good question," Lady Wisdom responded with a wide Grandma like grin. "Let me ask you this. When you eat homemade fruit that has been properly prepared and canned, does it taste like brand new?"

"Well yes, when grandma does her canning, sometimes it tastes better later than when you picked it off the tree.

"Exactly," Lady Wisdom said. "And sometimes you will read the testimonies of God's goodness a year or two from now and it will have more meaning then than when it happened that day. That is why you are to store up these testimonies by writing them down so you can read them later. God's goodness and mercies are new each day, but sometimes we have a hard time tapping into them. Sometimes we are not even aware how good they were that day. Write down the amazing testimonies of God's goodness and mercy in your journal. Take this as wisdom. You will never be sorry."

Lady Wisdom

Again revelation flooded me.

"...And I will dwell in the house of the Lord forever."

(Psalm 23:6b) KJV

I had always thought of the House of the Lord as being the church, (and surely that is one of His houses) but Rhema's revelation was telling me that my heart was also His house. Lady Wisdom under the direction of Emmanuel, Comforter and Conscience were teaching me to fill up my pantry with good fruits for another season. I was now eating in season but soon I would be able to eat out of season, and there would be an abundance to share with whoever came across my path. I would store up God's goodness in my pantry by writing down the testimonies. They would be testimonies of remembrance.

"We need to make more room in the pantry," I blurted out. An inspired idea struck me. "I want a pantry full of good fruits and vegetables so I can share God's goodness to others in their dry and winter seasons also.

"You're a quick study," Lady Wisdom said as she set the ladling spoon down and then put the peaches aside for a moment. She reached out and took hold of a banana and a strawberry and held one in each hand. I looked at her inquisitively as she said, "A banana is like the unveiling of the revelation of the riches of God. Bananas are rich in potassium and give strong bones. A banana gives fluidness to the muscles so they won't cramp up. It helps prevent Charlie horses. You can rest, run or sprint with ease. Live in revelation, my son. Strawberries go well with bananas. A strawberry is like a Word in due season. It refreshes and gives us hope and a promise of new things to come."

`My mouth watered as I thought about revelation and a Word in due season. "What about that avocado over there?" I asked inquisitively.

The Dwelling Place

"There are three parts to an Avocado—the outer skin, the meat of the fruit and the pit. The avocado is a type of hatred, bitterness and murder. The outer shell is hard just like hatred causes us to be hard hearted. It is like the "o" fences that surround the heart along with the sycamine trees whose root systems choke out the effectiveness of a tender heart. The inner part, until it is ripe, is very bitter and the seed is poisonous to eat. When you hate someone, you become hard hearted and this turns into bitterness. If not dealt with it turns to murdering thoughts and eventually murder. Birds especially will stay away from avocados, as it will kill them. The saying, "that's for the birds" doesn't apply to this fruit.

"You can tell when an avocado is ripe and good to eat because you can press into the skin and it will leave an impression," Lady Wisdom continued. "It has gone from being hard hearted to soft hearted. Likewise, people eating the fruit of our life will find it bitter if you are hard hearted. If it is soft hearted the fruit will be tasty to eat. Now you know why Emmanuel insisted on removing the brick maze and the stones on the wall of your heart."

As we were talking, Emmanuel walked into the kitchen and after speaking something into Lady Wisdom's ear, they began to set the dinner table and prepare an absolutely delightful dinner. Soon we were eating. The food was out of this world and very delicious. It was a wonderful time as we ate together laughing and enjoying ourselves to the fullest.

I glanced up to see one of devlins' henchmen looking in the kitchen window of my heart. He had a long face and seemed very irritated. I hardly recognized them now as they were down to the size of a large bug. They seemed to be getting smaller and smaller and less intimidating. I got up to pull the curtains and totally rain on his parade. I smiled as a verse flooded my mind:

Lady Wisdom

"You prepare a table before me in the midst of my enemies. My cup runneth over."

(Psalm 23:6) KJV

The deep satisfaction I felt was amazing. I was going to sleep well tonight. I was so secure. The henchmen were but bugs now and I could hardly wait to get one of them under my feet and squash it! On second thought, I reached under the kitchen sink for some bug spray. I proceeded to go to the window, cracked it open a couple of inches and sprayed him right in the face. Howling in surprise and pain, he went flying off the window rubbing his eyes furiously. Last I looked he was hacking and coughing and sputtering as he lay gasping for air while lying on his back. I looked at the can and read the ingredients. Huh! It only had one ingredient and it was a supernatural ingredient at that....God's love! I guess they can't take a full spray of God's love direct on their face? Fancy that!

It was at this point that a new revelation began to inundate my heart and mind. This whole experience with Emmanuel, Comforter and Rhema in my home and Him actively working in my heart was revealing some amazing things. It was not only revealing some things, but I was experiencing stuff first hand.

One of the most astounding things I noticed was that I no longer felt like a servant or a slave and Emmanuel was my Master. It had gone far beyond that. What I was seeing and experiencing in my heart was far beyond obedience. I was experiencing intimacy. Before this encounter, I found myself reaching for obedience out of obedience. It was expected of me and the Word of God said it. I was simply a doer of the Word because of fear and because it was the right thing to do. Besides, I had seen what damien devlin, worldly Wendy and fat man wanted to do to me when he seemed like my only option.

The Dwelling Place

But here I am sitting with Emmanuel and Comforter with a beautiful table spread before me in the presence of my enemy (Well, that was past tense now as he was wheezing on his back). We were talking and laughing and eating together. I was so amazed! I had been elevated to an equal level of being a Son. I was starting to even have input in our discussions. From rebirth I was always a son, but I still did not understand it fully. Now, it was beginning to become a part of my experience. I had my own personal scribe who wrote cool things on His note pad and they revealed themselves to me. He made me look really smart. Yes, an equal level of being a Son of God. I was a friend of God and a Son. I was moving beyond being a slave to co-reigning with Jesus Christ...the Anointed One. Even as this truth blazed in glory across my heart, Rhema revealed this truth from the Word of God to confirm my discovery:

> *"No longer do I call you slaves, for the slave does not know what his master is doing; but I have called you friends, for all things that I have heard from my father I have made know to you"*
>
> (John 15:15) NKJV

> *I was seeing more and more clearly that the tough times where an opportunity to experience God's blessings and be brought more fully into God's purposes for my life*

Something else that was sinking in was that I felt no punishment, guilt or condemnation for my sin. Just being in Emmanuel's presence, I wanted to be transformed to be like Him.... and He was so willing to grant my desire.

I experienced His correction and discipline, but I was enjoying it. Well, OK, I'm beginning to see the value in it. Trust was developing and I was beginning to understand that He is always good, always in a good mood and always wanting to do good things for me (including correction and discipline). Wow! Amazing!!

Lady Wisdom

The other incredulous thing I noticed was that I was precious to God. He gave me so many honors. (1 Peter 2:9). I was so important to Him. I was a precious possession and I felt His love. I was seeing more clearly that the tough times where an opportunity to experience God's blessings and be brought more fully into God's purposes for my life. I smiled in appreciation as I slowly pondered these things.

Before I knew it I had fallen asleep dreaming new dreams and visions.

Notes

23

ELI JOHN

(I see I obey)

It was 3am a few nights later, on a hot August night, when I awoke in a dead sweat. Although I was fully awake, I was caught up in a vision and saw a man running before me at breakneck speed. His eyes were fixed straight ahead but slightly upwards. The path on which he was traveling was being created in seven feet in front of him about by His faith as he ran. I noticed that I was out of my house and in a large open area. By my side was the angel who had appeared with me just over a year ago in the beginning of my vision when I was back in the church.

Now, whenever I had envisioned a path before, it was always a wide path by at least three to six feet. It was very straight and God had already created it, but this was strangely different. This, however, looked at first to be a path as wide as a railroad track. On closer inspection though, it was exactly eight inches wide. I did not know this at the time, but the number eight signifies new beginnings and completion. I saw myself measuring the width of my shoes and found that by standing still with my

The Dwelling Place

feet firmly planted together, the width measured exactly eight inches. I was astonished as I pondered the narrowness of such a path. I measured it because I wondered how one could even stand on such a narrow path and keep their balance. This was now the second time that I had encouraged the number eight. Here and the eight eyes on the sword.

I turned to look at the angel standing next to me and asked, "Who is this and what does this mean?"

"This is Eli John, a prophet of the Lord," He said. He is a proclaimer of God's grace "He is an embodiment of fruitfulness and a model for you to follow. What you see in Him will help you to see God's heart for fruitfulness.

"Fruitfulness is the Lords desire for every human," the angel said decisively. "It was one of the first things God said to Adam in the Garden was to be fruitful and multiply. It is in His very nature. When you become a new person in Christ, a believer, you immediately have that capacity to multiply. Just as you reproduce in the natural, God's design is that your reproduce in the spiritual also." I turned to look at Eli John. I observed that he was running at breakneck speed. He seemed very invigorated, was not tired or sweating, and seemed to have endless energy. It was as if he was running with a call and purpose on his life. Destiny was in his every move.

I heard a voice saying, "Do not look to the left or to the right. Look straight ahead." I turned to see who he was looking at. I gasped as I saw that it was Emmanuel and He was running ahead by only seven feet. The amazing thing was that Emmanuel was running **backwards.**

Eli John's eyes were transfixed on Emmanuel's eyes. As he ran I could see his faith in action. I was perplexed for a moment for I would have thought that Emmanuel would have been creating the path for Eli John, but that was not the case. Even though the path was being created just below Emmanuel's feet, the revelation I was receiving from Rhema indicated that it was Eli John's faith that was creating the path. "Hhmmm!," I mused. "This indeed was interesting. I'm sure it would all make sense sometime soon."

On either side of the path were fields and forests. The more Eli John riveted his eyes on Emmanuel several things were happening; not only was the eight inch path being created, which was smooth and somewhat straight, but winds of harvesting was taking place on both sides. I say somewhat straight, because the path seemed to go where it would be in proximity of the harvest.

The fields, in massive sweeps, were being mowed down and harvested. As he passed a forest which was breathtakingly huge, I saw the forests cut down and harvested. Huge trees were cut down like butter. These forests represented families, loved ones of all kinds and people groups to whom before had been impossible to reach. Now they were being brought into the kingdom of heaven.

As the prophet and the Lord of Hosts locked eyes I could see that the Lord was well pleased. A smile crossed His lips as He saw that His son was perfect; perfectly trained to listen and obey the voice and the heart of the Lord. He had listened to the voice of the Lord and had allowed him to create structure in His life. He had meditated and studied the Word. He had been faithful in the little things. There seemed to be a measured rhythm as they moved together in perfect harmony.

In the midst of this, I saw someone else though, who was not pleased. The adversary was taking bear traps and throwing them up on the path. He had been carefully crafting these various size traps and had filed those teeth razor sharp. The traps were designed to camouflage and blend into the path.

Emmanuel passed over them easily as He cannot be tempted by evil, but I saw Emmanuel giving intense instruction to Eli John. He handed Him a rod of iron that was about seven feet tall. It was a kingly scepter. He instructed Eli John to keep his eyes trained on Him and not ever waver...not to the right, nor to the left. He was not even to look or slow down. He told Him that when he said 'now', to not even hesitate slightly, but to grab the rod with both hands in front of him and come straight down with as much force as possible.

I looked at the bear traps that the adversary (devlin) was setting. They were crafty looking traps. Some were big, some medium sized and some small. Even the small ones looked like they could inflict some serious damage. I saw names in the middle where the trigger was placed to spring the trap. The names were 'seduction', 'spiritual pride', 'grumbling' 'worry', 'anger', and 'offenses'. I noticed that devlin was taking careful attention to seduction. I saw myriads of woman of all types, sizes and personalities. He was grooming them to try and turn Eli john's heartstrings away from God, his wife and family. These groomed women came under the pretense of being needy and of wanting God deeply in their heart. They asked for prayer and counseling, but their hearts were weak and they intended to do all they could to drag the prophet to the grave of hell. Some were asking for prayer and counseling, but there were others being groomed that were digital reproductions of the originals.

They were but ploys of the enemy to seduce and captivate and hobble the prophet's feet.

As Eli john's ministry was now growing larger, damien devlin crafted bear traps and had placed camouflages of false humility over them to try and trap him into walking into them. It was a false humility in that I am nothing but a worm and also sometimes spiritual pride in that I take the glory for what only the Lord can do. It was a double edged sword but vanity none the less. The other camouflage was rebellious ideas. It was the thought that I could be quietly stubborn and do things my way without there being any consequences or at least minimal consequences.

Eli John

Close friends, pastors, coworkers, family and friends were being targeted to bring offenses that would cause Him to take His eyes off Emmanuel. It was not always intentional. In fact he would try to orchestrate innocent conversations to create offense and make legitimate expectations that he could suggest were God given rights. He figured that offenses would cause wounds that would distract and slow him down. If he could plant a seed of bitterness, self-pity, or grumbling and complaining he could cause enough distraction to have Eli John step into one of his traps

The traps of spiritual pride would cause him to be careless and take credit for what only God could do. If he could only get the prophet to take a little credit then those who followed him would take credit in excess. He actually could kill two birds with one stone. It would cause a domino effect. It was a delicious scheme and had great potential. It only took one trap. He would be patient.

I jerked my head back to see Eli John bringing the iron rod down in a strong motion and catching a bear trap squarely in the middle. Emmanuel had given explicate instructions to Eli john that He was to look only into His eyes, listen for the word "Now" and without question bring the iron rod down with a "bam". Without losing stride, Eli John instantly obeyed the voice of the Lord—fixing his eyes intently on Emmanuel eyes. I heard the 'bam' and saw the iron bear traps flying high through the air; useless because not only were they sprung, but they were also damaged beyond repair. Bam, bam.....bam, bam, bam! The kingly scepter of iron caused irreparable damage.

I was so happy for the revelation earlier that intimacy with Emmanuel far exceeded obedience. I would not have understood earlier how Eli John could have been so completely obedient at the rate of speed he was going. This was not blind obedience. Eli John had such a relationship of trust and intimacy that He had no problem responding instantly. He had learned that God was good all the time and that he

The Dwelling Place

would not withhold any good thing from him as he walked in faith, hope and love out of a humble, teachable heart. I wanted that, oh how I wanted that.

I noticed that Eli John didn't even break a sweat as he ran. In fact although Eli John and Emmanuel eyes were locked on each other you did not sense a tension or rigidness between the two at all as they were in an earnest intimate conversation. They were just laughing and casually engaged. They did not seem to be in a hurry but yet were running fast. They both seemed to be at rest.

I turned my thoughts to Emmanuel as He spoke and said, "Either your heart will burn for me or it will burn with lust for things and people of this World; if your heart burns for me, then it will burn with love for the people of the World and you will use everything you have in this World for the kingdom. My kingdom is a selfless kingdom.

"Yet not I but Christ lives in me"

(Galatians 2:20)

> *Large groups of people were getting revelation that it was about real intimacy; love for God with all your heart, soul and mind*

The only "I" in God's kingdom is in the middle of "king". It is not the "I" (ego) but Christ (King) living in me and flowing from me. It's not me doing it alone but this new "I" who loves God and who loves others.

If your heart burns correctly, you will find ministry invigorating and fun; if it burns incorrectly, you will burn out. Your life will feel like a useless hollow shell.

"It all depends on your eye devotion. Are you singularly devoted or double minded?" I pondered this as I turned to look at the progress of Eli John. I was amazed at the speed of harvest. Neighbors, friends, loved ones, cities, states, and even countries were turning their hearts to God. It was a new wave of God's working. Large groups of people were getting revelation that it was about real intimacy; love for God with all your heart, soul and mind. There was a real freedom and joy. It was easy to go from that to laying down your life to serve others. It was a complete abandonment to God and His Word. "I will obey all your commands," was the cry in unison, as they spoke fervently from hearts immersed in intimacy with a loving, gracious and holy God.

I turned to look where this sound was coming from. I looked and saw a single file line of people extending as far as the eye could see following Eli John. By His example he had made a path to follow and now many too were running. People from the fields and forests of harvest came to follow the eight inch path. Without his example they might have been cautiously walking down the path. His ceiling had become their floor and they had been able to save years of frustrated trial and error. They had caught the vision and not only wanted to be taught, but were compelled to follow the same revelation. The path was brutal but doable. Yes, it was straight and smooth but it was extremely narrow. It allowed no room for error. Those who looked to the left or the right stumbled and turned their ankles or worse yet, got caught in the bear traps. You either walked in faith, hope and love, or you walked in fear, doubt and unbelief. You either were giving out or sucking in and creating death for yourself.

I heard Emmanuel say "Stand, and again I say stand. After you have done all...stand...but don't stop running." It began to dawn on me that standing was not stopping but resolving. Standing was about overcoming to the end, it was about perseverance. It was about keeping your eyes on Emmanuel and instantly responding to His voice. It was about not questioning, not doubting, not rebelling but obeying from the heart instantly. This was a part of the kingdom.

The Dwelling Place

I watched as Eli John tightened his belt--the belt of truth tighter, and looking through Emmanuel's eyes saw the end result --the finish line. Truth had to be more direct and more focused as the finish line approached. There was no time to waste. The heavy rains were here on the horizon and there were so many crops to harvest. He could not afford to let the harvest spoil.

The narrowness of the path indicated it had to be done His way and that way was the way of love and truth. And laugh. This resolve did not make him grim but rather he exuded a laughter and joy that was infectious. Emmanuel also was laughing along with Eli-John. It was the harvest time and the fields were white unto harvest. They were having great fun but Eli-John was very sensitive to His voice and locked onto His eyes.

As I observed this amazing phenomenon, a subtle shift took place and then one, two, three, and then ten more individuals moved from behind Eli John to join side by side next to him...

> *Truth had to be more direct and more focused as the finish line approached*

Suddenly new paths were created in front of them, and Emmanuel was in front of each of them running backwards. Momentum had just increased. Suddenly I blinked my eyes then blinked them again, rubbing them profusely. I was seeing ten Emmanuel's. Each of them was running backwards and in front of each person. Shaking my head as I pondered this spectacular event, I turned and asked the angel "Are there really ten Emmanuel's?"

The angel laughed a hearty laugh slapping his knee several times. "No there are not ten Emmanuel's, but Emmanuel has the ability to make himself real to each person and talk with each one as if they are the only one in the whole World.

I was mesmerized by this spectacle of faith, hope and love displayed before me. I turned back to observe that these road warriors were able to encourage each other to keep the pace and the faith. If one started to stumble the other was there to help the other up. I began to see that this was not about being a spectator sport of watching one person leading and the rest following or a competition for that matter, but each helping the other to finish strong. These ten had caught the vision of pursuing intimacy and stepped out to follow Him.

I too saw in the distance the finish line. The banner over the top did not say <u>finish line</u> though but proclaimed the words-- <u>Over comer</u>. This was a race with a destination and a purpose.

As I watched, Emmanuel mouthed the words, "I am not willing that even one should perish. It is not a race of speed. It is your faith and perseverance in me. This is a journey. It is my love in you and it is from this hope that it all builds from. As you fix your eyes on me and are filled to overflowing with my love, that is what will win the world. But you must keep your eyes fixed on me. Do not fear the bear traps, but fear (listen to) the Lord. I have given you all you need to succeed.

> Emmanuel has the ability to make himself real to each person and talk with each one as if they are the only one in the whole World

"I am looking for those who will finish as well as they start. The reward goes to the finishers. I have limited myself to work through you. Do not let anything distract or turn you away from the path I have set you on. You have been saved by grace through faith but your salvation is completed by being an over comer or disqualified by evil works or apostasy (Rev 21:8). Your works in the end will either commend you or condemn you."

It was at this point that He started giving instruction about His wife. "Your spouse is your threefold cord so make sure that you share every bear trap story with your spouse (potential and real).

The Dwelling Place

Share the smallest detail because it is the small details left untold that create the crack in the dam of your heart. Don't even give damien devlin a toehold on your heart. You are joint heirs together with Christ.

"Pray together for your adversary wants to divide and conquer your marriage, but do not fear. I have given all authority and all power over him to you. Do not fear for greater is He that is in you than He who is in the world (throwing bear traps at your feet.)

"Catch yourself up to the third heaven and go boldly into the throne room of God. It is there, as you see yourself in God's presence that you can ask anything and He will do it. It is there that all principalities and powers including those in high places truly will be put under your feet. Bring everything to the feet of Emmanuel at the throne. You can look through my eyes to get there.

"Go and continue to harvest for the Lord with your faith. Faith is the victory that overcomes the World." (1 John 5:4) and do all through my intimate love."

As I pondered these things and gathered the items requested in obedience, the Lord of Lords directed me to Isaiah 40:3-11 NLT

> *"Listen! I hear the voice of someone shouting, "Make a highway for the Lord through the wilderness. Make a straight smooth road through the desert for our God."*
>
> *"Fill the valleys and level the hills. Straighten out the curves and smooth off the rough spots."*
>
> *"Then the glory of the Lord will be revealed, and all people will see it together The Lord has spoken!"*
>
> *"A voice said, "Shout!" I asked, what I should shout?" "Shout that people are like the grass that dies away. Their beauty fades as quickly as the flowers in a field. The grass withers*

and the flowers fade beneath the breath of the Lord and so it is with people,"

"*The grass withers, and the flowers fade, but the word of our God stands forever.*"

"*Messenger of good news, shout to Zion from the mountaintops! Shout louder to Jerusalem—do not be afraid. Tell the towns of Judah, "Your God is coming!"*"

"*He will rule with awesome strength. See he brings his reward with him as he comes.*"

"*He will feed his flock like a shepherd. He will carry the lambs in his arms, holding them <u>close to his heart</u>. He will gently lead the mother sheep with their young.*"

I heard a voice cry out "Fight".

I asked, "What shall I fight?" "Fight the good fight of faith. Never stop and never give up," Comforter said cheering me on passionately.

The enemy had been outflanked. "You are this tree that will not be just a leaf bearing tree, but a tree pruned to bear much mega- fruit, yes, much more fruit than the branches could ever hold."

As I carefully observed and pondered the vision of Eli John, I asked comforter what this all meant.

> Most would chaff at the narrowness of the path, but such things do not bother those who hear the call

"This vision is for Eli John but it applies to all who would follow God in absolute devotion," He said with a quiet, intense soberness. Eli John has learned to obey God and pay the price for a long time. He has learned to walk with God. True, Eli John has had his share of being tripped up by the bear traps, but he never gave up and he

The Dwelling Place

kept getting up. Because of His obedience and love for the Father, he is still walking with God. To him it is walking, but to you, you see it as running. The path is only eight inches wide because I am doing a new thing. Everything you see with 'eight' in it signifies new beginning and completeness. The call is focused. It is a pruning for the most effectiveness. The time for distractions and double mindedness is over. It's doing the one thing. Most would chaff at the narrowness of this path, but such things do not bother those who hear the call.

Eli John hears and sees the heartbeat of God. His head has been on Jesus chest for so long that he has learned to totally trust Him. He feels God's heartbeat of love flowing through him and has great honor and love for those he is called to serve. Most see this as hard work, but the one who really sees and walks in a love adoring relationship, run this walk with confidence and fun. In fact, if you notice not all the traps are destroyed. I turned to look as the scepter came down with a bam and caught one of the traps. I wondered if he missed it because instead of snapping, it flipped up into the air. Suddenly I began to laugh as I saw what was happening. The trap went flying straight at devlin and sprung as it hit him square on the nose. Devlin went howling in pain as he ran away to get some ice.

> Jesus does not give us faith so he can take over and do it for us. He gives us faith so we can step forth and display the mind of Christ, the relationship of Christ and the presence of Christ.

"Eli John is actually creating this path by his faith and although the path is narrow and stretches out beyond the horizon, the effects are miles wide. It had started with a measure of faith, a grain so small you would have needed a magnifying glass to find it, but by living every day applying that measure of faith in every situation it has now grown to great faith. Now, even the atmosphere around him created a shadow of light that affected those near him. That is how it is with faith. You step out in faith once and it grows a little. You step out again and again and it keeps growing bigger and bigger.

The Lord will direct you if you trust in the Lord with all your heart and lean not on your own understanding but believe God's promises. If you do you will find the path of faith that you are creating will be the will of God (Prove 3:5- 6) The Lord has put this path within Eli John that he is creating by His faith. What is put in must come back out. Jesus does not give us faith so he can take over and do it for us. He gives us faith so we can step forth and display the mind of Christ, the relationship of Christ and the presence of Christ.

"Would you like to be let in on a little secret?" Comforter quipped.

"Sure," I replied enthusiastically.

"Let me show you what things look like through Eli John's eyes and then you will understand better. Immediately, I was looking straight into Emmanuel's eyes standing squarely in front of me. I moved my eyes around and looked down at my feet. I gasped in astonishment. It was as if I was inside of Eli John's body and I was looking through his eyes.

> Eli John knows if he just looks in Emmanuel's eyes that he will always be on the right track

I uttered in surprised wonder, "I don't even see a path at all! Where is the narrow path," How is Eli John going to know where to go?"

Comforter howled in laughter. "You can't see what is being created by faith!" Comforter exclaimed. I looked around me and all I saw was fields white unto harvest and a forest ready to be cut down and harvested.

"Eli John knows that if he just looks in Emmanuel's eyes that he will always be on the right track," Comforter grinned even wider as he

The Dwelling Place

slapped me on the back. "One of these days a light bulb will come on my friend," Comforter responded with a reassuring tone. If I didn't know Comforter better I would have thought He was teasing me. I saw out of the corner of my eye Rhema writing like crazy. It must have been His cue.

I felt like I could actually experience the emotions of Eli John and felt an overwhelming compassion. Everywhere I looked the colors, people and things were enhanced to their most beautiful hue. I suddenly realized that I was looking through the eyes of love.

Suddenly I snapped back to Comforters voice. "Jesus is running backwards so that He can be available to hold the gaze of Eli John. It is a love relationship. Everything depends on Eli John fixing his eyes on Jesus. Everything depends on his ears being keenly attuned to the voice of Jesus," Comforter exhorted. "Let me show you the path from a different angle," Comforter explained. Immediately we were looking down on the path from high above. It was as if I could see the beginning of the path and the end. I was surprised to see that it was not a straight path at all as I had presupposed.

"I don't understand," I said. "I thought the path would be straight."

Comforter laughed again as He grabbed my arm and gave it a gentle shake. "I love your candor and honesty. Look again at Eli John and Emmanuel. Do you see any place where He is not totally connected with Emmanuel? Do you see any place where he has broken eye contact?

"And yet the path is moving in a zig zag pattern,' I said totally mesmerized."

"Maybe it would help if we went to one of the zags and hear their conversation." Immediately we were within ear distance and I could hear the ease of their conversation. I hadn't been listening a minute when Emmanuel said, "Hey Eli, let's go in this direction for a while. There are some amazing things I want to show you and something I would like to have you do." Eli John immediately switched directions and seamlessly they headed in the new direction.

At one of the zigs I heard Eli John say, "I feel passionate about preaching the gospel over here." "Yeah," Emmanuel said let's go do it!"

Comforter turned to look while smacking me on the back as He gave me a big grin. "See! See what I mean."

Rhema was making a quick note to help me understand and suddenly, I began grinning also. Proverbs 3:5-6 KJV suddenly had a new meaning.

> "Trust in the Lord with all you heart and lean not on your own understanding. In all your ways acknowledge Him and he will direct your paths straight."

> Jesus has given us a powerful weapon .It is the ability to say "No! It is the ability to have choice

"It seems like a point can come when you have trusted God with all our heart to such an extent and then His heart becomes our heart and the desires we want to do are in harmony with His desires," I reasoned.

Rhema stopped writing and my musings were interrupted as I heard,

"Damien devlin is using counterfeits to try to trip him up," Comforter instructed. "The groomed women are the lust of the eyes. They are a designed distraction. For a man, it can be a woman or his work; for a woman, it can be a man or her work. The spiritual pride is pride in ones possessions or positions; it is to think that I have accumulated or accomplished something on my own merit or effort and steal the glory from the Lord. It is thinking that I have arrived and am above the fray. It

The Dwelling Place

is the vanity of self love. It goes along with offenses in that you have a right to something.

"The offenses are twofold. There are offenses that you personally have and offenses that others have towards you. The more you love God's Word, the less you will be offended. But remember it is impossible to not have offenses. If it you think you are doing everything right there will be times when you are misunderstood. It might be a slight inflection in your voice that to us is just preoccupation or tiredness, but to another it is anger or rejection. We may not have even sinned, but we have still sinned against that person. We will fail other's expectations, but when you are offended, you are to apply the Word with a 'bam'. You say with authority, "I say to you, offense, be you picked up by the root and be planted in the sea and you shall have already obeyed me (Luke 17:1-7). You must live in repentance and forgiveness daily."

"The secret is in the "now" and the "bam"

"The bam for 'groomed women' or men, for that matter is to have already made a covenant with your eyes and heart to not look or listen to the right or the left. It is fixing your eyes on Jesus and living in the light. It is in being totally devoted. It is in keeping everything exposed. It is in being wise and cutting off the thing that offends you. Jesus has given us a powerful weapon; it is the ability to say "No! It is the ability to have choice."

Jesus is the one that is illuminating your path and has given you the kingly scepter to smash any high thought or principality, and bring captive every thought to the obedience to Christ. He has made us kings and priest and given us the kingly scepter to rule over the powers of darkness and rein His rule on the earth. This scepter is a representation of your authority. We are the ones who are to bring the kingdom of heaven to earth.

"Bear traps will always be there. Sometimes they will even come in threes, but it doesn't matter as long as you fix your eyes intently on Christ and look neither to the right or the left. Press in to listen. The running is a forward motion. It's face-to-face...intimacy with the Father. When you choose to live your life through faith, hope, love, humility and teach ability, that is what will create the path in front of you," Comforter exclaimed with a quiet excitement in his voice.

"Walk in love, walk in faith, walk in hope and do all with a teachable and humble heart. Listen and see to obey the look in my eyes. Yes, the path is created by your faith, but it is a faith that is saturated with the love of God and a joyful expectant hope. It is a faith born from hearing and listening to the voice of the Lord and acting on it. Whenever, whatever and wherever you go, release this seven feet in front of you. In other words release it to all you come in contact with."

"So, what is the secret to fruitfulness?" I inquired eagerly and intently. "How can a person have more fruit in their life than they could ever imagine? I want great fruitfulness," I eagerly pleaded with Comforter. It was as if I had not heard a word He said.

Comforter began to patiently teach some more by saying, "The secret is in the 'now' and the 'bam'; it is as you run after God and His commands. You are to fix your eyes intently on Jesus and <u>listen to obey</u>. You are waiting for Him to say 'now', so you can go 'bam'. It is obedience responding to faith. This will come as you rest in My presence. Spend your time with Me and learn My voice. Soak in My Word and be always asking Rhema for revelation so that My Word will be alive to you. The more you obey My Word, the easier it will be to hear My voice.

As I watched this whole vision of Eli John, I was reminded of Hebrews 12:1-4 NLT:

> *"Therefore, since we are surrounded by such a huge crowd of witnesses to the life of faith, let us strip off every weight that*

The Dwelling Place

slows us down, especially the sin that so easily hinders our progress. And let us run with endurance the race that God has set before us."

"We do this by keeping our eyes on Jesus, on whom our faith depends from start to finish. He was willing to die a shameful death on the cross because of the joy he knew would be his afterward. Now he is seated in the place of highest honor beside God's throne in heaven."

"Think about all He endured when sinful people did such terrible things to Him, so that you don't become weary and give up after all, you have not yet given your lives in your struggle against sin."

> *You are to fix your eyes intently on Jesus and <u>listen to obey.</u> You are waiting for Him to say "now" so you can go "bam": It is obedience responding to faith*

I found myself getting very excited. Here I had just seen this verse in living color in a vision. I am being told to lay aside every heavy weight; especially the sin that pulls me back into a structure of unrighteousness and to run with steadfast, persevering endurance the race God has set before me. And the way I do that is to keep my eyes fixed on Jesus, to realize that in my struggle against sin I have not died, but yet He did and took that sin on himself so I could live and enjoy the freedom of His presence. I pursue a revelation of God's love and I seek to experience that love in my daily life in everything I do.

I responded by saying, "Whatever, whenever, however I will listen. I will study to show myself approved. It's pursuing you and finding out your call for my life and the gifts he has given me. I will discipline my body so I can hear better, and I make this temple (my body) a place where my King can dwell without reservation. I must get to know this Word inside and out. I must study it diligently. Faith comes by hearing and hearing by the

Word of God. I cannot hear what I do not study and I cannot do what I do not know. All of this flows out of an intimate relationship. My priority is to spend time and get to know the King.... fruitfulness will flow from relationship. I will choose to obey and I will do all this by fixing my eyes on You. I will do this by pursuing a revelation of your love and experiencing it with all my senses through every experience of every day."

I began to clap my hands with joy. It was all beginning to make perfect sense. "As I listen to God's voice and follow His Word, every day will be an adventure," I said in wonderment. "I will be a conduit for His love, mercy, grace, faith, instruction, disciplines, exhortation, teaching, whatever, whenever, however." As I stated this, faith welled up in my heart."

Revelation flooded my mind as I realized that this was all possible if I just pursued the presence of God. He would enable me. Understanding flooded my heart as I realized that there was no need for running around like a chicken with its head cut off, driven by condemnation and guilt. There was to be only a love for His Word and listening to His voice and obeying instantly whatever His still quiet voice says to me.

As I stopped and lay still before the Lord letting Him teach me, I heard these words loud and clear spoken directly to my heart.

> FRUITFULNESS IS SIMPLY THE RESULT OF LISTENING AND OBEYING THE WORD OF GOD WITHOUT HESITATION AND WITHOUT QUESTION. IT IS ABIDING IN HIS LOVE.

I saw bushel baskets full from the fields of corn, wheat and barley. I saw forests neatly cut and stacked. The stacks were huge. The final harvest had begun for those who would do whatever it took and yield in absolute surrender to the King of the Universe.

The Dwelling Place

I was exhilarated. It was worth the cost. It was worth any price. Relationship with the Lord Jesus Christ would be my lifelong pursuit. He would flow from the gifts he had put within me.

As I fell on my face I found myself caught up into the third heaven to the very throne room of God to worship the One, the Lord Jesus Christ who came in the flesh and who died for me so that I would become a profitable and useful son.

I fell on my face and cried out, "Worthy, worthy, worthy is the Lamb. Every Word in your Book is true. I worship the Word, the Lord Jesus Christ. I fall before you in absolute devotion and say, 'Whatever it takes.' You are already my Savior, my deliverer; you already are my protector and my healer. I take it all. It's already done. It was all done at the cross. By your stripes I have already been healed.

> My life would forever be changed because my whole thinking was changed. I could never go back to the way things were before

So, I worshipped the King of Kings, who has stated, "It is finished"; who gave me the keys to the kingdom. I saw that these were the keys, which were given to me. It was the keys to win the souls of men. These were the keys I saw in the pantry of my heart.

As I looked back from the throne room of heaven; the immensity of the heavenlies overwhelmed me. As far as I could see there was a sea of faces. The joy of the Lord was evident. His seal was in their foreheads and their names were written in the book of life.

And I was given the privilege to see my destiny from the future. It was the souls of men. It was amazing what God was doing and had done in me, but it was all to prepare me to help others see and experience the truth; it was about them. I fell on my face and wept with joy and cried out, "Every Word of God, every promise of God, I will burn it in my heart. It is worth the cost. I run to you, obeying you without question, for my enemy is under my feet and He cannot win for I have seen the end. The enemy is under my feet because I am at the feet of the throne of God worshipping and resting in God's presence listening and obeying His voice and Word. I have seen the key to the secret place of your presence. It is your amazing love."

And I heard the angels cry out and say, "Holy, Holy is the Lamb of God the whole earth is full of His glory!!!

24

ADDICTED TO WORSHIP

It had been several months now since I had first seen the angel. It seemed like years since I had first been at that piano in the church. My life would forever be changed because my whole thinking was changed. I could never go back to the way things were before.

Revelation had flooded my mind. I now knew that I knew that I knew that being a normal Christian was about fully abandoning yourself to God. It was in holding nothing back but giving every part of your heart to God. It meant opening up every room with all its contents and letting Emmanuel into each room to do as He pleased.

If I truly meant and practiced that verse in (Matthew 22:37), to love the Lord my God with all my heart and all my soul and my entire mind and love others as I love myself, truly that would solve almost all my wrong thinking patterns. If I took God's Word and meditated on it and memorized it with the intent to know God with all my heart and obey every Word He told me to, my life would change so fast, the results would be astounding.

The Dwelling Place

Through this process, which frankly has just begun and by willingly surrendering all, I found that my concept of the Word of God changed me; it took on a whole new meaning.

I discovered that I was made to be a worshipper. I was made to be a devoted worshipper.

One could choose to worship things, the world, take pride in ones possessions or one could worship God. There are two opposing forces vying for my worship. One is the old fat man and the other is the new man. The old man is influenced by three sources; the world, the flesh and the devil. The new man is also influenced positively by three sources; Father God, Jesus and the Holy Spirit. Each of these three sources will seek to influence its candidate (so to speak) to worship them and hate the other. I found that worldly Wendy, Freddy fleash and damien devlin sought to drive my desires and cause me to yield my members as instruments of unrighteousness, and nurture it until I was captivated.

> He will reveal the secrets and mysteries of His heart if we will stay close to His heart

Damien devlin's concept of surrender for me is to conquer, defeat, kill, maim, and destroy. He will deceive, manipulate and intimidate a person with His purpose to inflict one with disease, sickness and pain, but in spite of all this he demands our worship He will promise you everything right to the brink of hell and then kick you in and laugh. Every word he tells you is either a lie or a truth laced with a lie.

The truth though, is that he is powerless without the driving conviction in my heart where I am operating out of rebellion and pride. Like I mentioned earlier he no longer owns the mortgage on my heart (house) and his loan collectors have been rendered powerless. My mortgage has been paid in full and Emmanuel does not even obligate me for the debt to Him.

Addicted to Worship

On the other hand, Emmanuel, Comforter and Father God are also after my devotion. They are my creator. They made me from dust and created me in their image.

I was made in the very image of God with a very special place created inside of me shaped for Him to live. He wants me to choose to worship Him, to love Him with all my heart, soul and mind. He doesn't conquer, but liberates. He offers to set me free; He loves me even when I sin. In fact He has already forgiven all my sins. He is patient and kind. He always protects, lifts up, heals and delivers. He is all about giving life and giving it more abundantly. Emmanuel will snatch anyone from the brink of hell and save all if one but asks.

> The more structure I can build in my life through the in "struct" ion of the Comforter then the more protected my heart will be

Every word He says is true. He is a true servant and loves to clean up our messes. I think though, that He loves it even more if He can minister from a clean house. However, he will clean it seventy times seven and then seventy times seven again if He has too. You will find Him to reveal the secrets and mysteries of His heart if we will stay close to His heart. He will do it to any and all who are willing. He is no respecter of persons. He loves to give joy. He has come to our heart to give us freedom and life everlasting. He doesn't keep things from us, but for us. The driving force within us must be humility, faith and obedience though.

We were born to be worshippers. If we choose to worship on both sides we will be in a world of hurt because it really is impossible to serve and worship two masters.

You really must choose one side or the other. I mean you must really choose one side or the other! For your own sake you must do this. You cannot choose the fence because satan owns the fence.

The Dwelling Place

The more we get to know Jesus and obey Him and His Word daily, the more you worship him and soak in His Presence, your thoughts and actions will totally change.

As I soaked in His presence, my heart cried out this new song of worship.

> With all of my heart
> With all of my soul
> With all that I am
> I worship you
>
> Jesus
> You are so beautiful
> Jesus
> You are so pure
> Jesus
> You are so wonderful
> So wonderful
> You are
> The one I adore
>
> ©2009 You are so Beautiful
> Words and Music by John M. Davidson

I honestly don't see devlin and fat man so much in my heart any more. I have purposefully put fat man to death and I resist damien devlin. I now guard my heart. God has given me a new heart and I am a new creation. I do have my days but I now see the value in protecting it and having everything decently and in order. I don't want anything to distort my view of my identity or that close intimacy. I can choose to yield my members to do unrighteousness but my focus now is on worshipping Emmanuel, listening to Comforter and receiving revelation from Rhema.

Addicted to Worship

The more structure I can build in my life through the in "struct" ion of the Comforter then the more protected my heart will be. I pray often throughout the day that I am open to rebuke, discipline and correction. It is the shelving for my beliefs and attitudes. As I already know that Emmanuel has placed godly desire within me this prayer is easier to pray. The focus is not sin or self love but living in and from God's love.

For the most part we all tend in the natural World to create a good structure for our natural homes. We keep our houses and yards clean. We spend a lot of time building, remodeling, and doing up keep. What we do in the natural is far more important to do in the spiritual. This is the unseen World that we have been involved in to steward.

My heart for the most part is clean. I understand it is a daily process and just as a normal house needs cleaning so my house needs daily cleaning. The beautiful thing is that it is not trashed like it was in the beginning. As I walk day by day with my three companions, I find the library is being changed, one by one with right belief systems; the pantry is being stored up with good ingredients that will build a long and healthy life. My mindset and attitudes are such that my life does not belong to me. I find my mind becoming clearer and sounder. I can only choose one person and I have made that choice. I have found that if you choose a righteous structure and focus on it, the wrong beliefs with be exposed. They cannot permanently live in a righteous structure. They are incongruent with the mind of Christ.

> *The focus is not sin or self love but living in and from God's love.*

This means that I have committed myself to love the Lord with all my heart and love others with all my heart. I now believe that any attitude, belief system, activity, or any thought no longer belongs solely to me; it belongs to God. If any of those things do not line up with God's Word, whether it is a promise or a command it has to go.

The Dwelling Place

I have committed myself to obey the Holy Spirits prompting. I have no rights but what the Holy Spirit gives me. It is my choice. I own nothing. To demand my rights means I have to step outside of love and I don't want to live in that kind of anxiety. I see myself as possessing nothing but yet I am a steward over everything. I have an abundance to share with others who have need. I drink good clean water and eat only foods and fruits that nurture and minister to my spirit.

I enjoy times of refreshing in my Jacuzzi, soaking in worship and loving the one who gives me life.

Having a clean heart does not make me more holy or more righteous. I cannot be more holy or righteous than I am already declared to be. Having a clean heart and living holy and righteously does help me see my identity more clearly and live my purpose more passionately. This is nothing to get all proud and mighty about. Does one get proud because he can breathe properly? Does one get arrogant because he can see things around him more clearly?

> I look for opportunities to overflow to others. This is not out of obligation or duty even though it is my obligation and duty. It is out of the desire of my heart as I develop and drive that intimacy deep in my spirit with my beloved trio of friends

And what about sin? Does this mean I never sin? Absolutely not! Remember I only had twenty good belief systems. I'm sure this will take a lifetime to correct. Maybe not. I am however committed to the process. I am committed on a fast track though. If you are willing to be humble and teachable and focus on receiving everything in your life in a spirit of faith, hope, and love, you will begin to identify quicker and easier the wrong beliefs that try to pop up here and there. It is so much easier when you are absolutely devoted to follow all of God's commands. The gateway is His presence. It is in spending vast quantities of time in His presence, spending enormous times in His Word praying for revelation to bring the word as a fire that burns within us.

Addicted to Worship

And ahhhh! Jack is gone. That part of me I built for protection to keep me safe and bring me comfort is now resting permanently at Jesus feet. My mind is sound and at peace. I don't need to hide behind a wall or compartmentalize things. I can live honest and open before God and others.

Revelation flashed before my mind at this moment as I thought of Jack. It suddenly dawned on me as to why Jack loved the cool glasses, the tattoos, and tongue and nose piercings. In what I had considered the other world, the world we all are so familiar with, I didn't wear body piercings or tattoos. The marks I put on my body were not as permanent but they might as well have. For me it was about gold chains and gold rings. It was about very expensive clothes and other trappings. It was about gold credit cards and status. God had discerned my motives and my focus was on the external to the exclusion of the inner heart. Jack was a persona of that.

Further revelation began to come that I was not to make judgment on others and assume that what was my motives were carte blanche the same motives of others. For me it was about getting a revelation of God's love and experiencing it.

"What is going to happen to Jill," I asked Comforter. "I haven't seen hide or hair of her for some time. Comforter looked me straight on and said,

"Where did the notion of Jack and Jill come from?"

As I tried to remember back, Rhema decided to help as he wrote quickly on His pad.

"Oh I remember, I said excitedly. "When I was very young there was a nursery rhyme that we used to chant all the time.

The Dwelling Place

> Jack and Jill went up the hill
> To fetch a pail of water
> Jack fell down and broke His crown
> And Jill came tumbling after

"Ah!" I said. "Do you think...?"

"If Jack fell down, or went to the feet of Jesus, and surrendered his crown to the Lordship of Christ," I reasoned "then Jill followed with him and she is there also."

I didn't need an answer. I already knew.

"What about all the different people in the church that I saw in the fog; others who like me are caught up in lies? Like the ones in the tread wheel, the prophets in the jail cell, or all the people who were being wounded by devlin and his henchmen. What about them? What about all the leadership, the Youth Group, the broken hearted and the sick and all the rest?" I said somewhat perplexed.

Rhema was already responding as He furiously wrote on his notepad:

I pray that from his glorious, unlimited resources He will give you mighty inner strength through his Holy Spirit.

And I pray that Christ will be more and more at home in your hearts as you trust in Him. May your roots go down deep into the soil of God's marvelous love?

And may you have the power to understand, as all God's people should, how wide, how long, how high, and how deep his love really is.

May you experience the love of Christ, though it is so great you will never fully understand it? Then you will be filled with the fullness of life and power that comes from God.

Addicted to Worship

(Ephesians 3:16-19) NLT

Don't just pretend that you love others. Really love them. Hate what is wrong. Stand on the side of the good.

Love each other with genuine affection, and take delight in honoring each other.

(Romans 12:9-10) NLT

So it was clear. I had been walking this road for a while now and ended up answering my own question with a little revelation. I was to pray for others that they would have a revelation and experience God's love and while I am doing that help them to understand and experience that love by really loving them with Christ's love. I was to go out of my way to honor them. My response was to love people fervently. God is the one who gives the revelation. I can't change one thing in one person and if I try I have switched mindsets because I would have to use manipulation and control techniques to do it. Nah! I think I will just love them.

You are not your trash

Before, I had seen myself and others at face value. I looked in my own heart and saw all the trash and mess and identified that as who I was. I did not see myself or others through God's eyes. I also judged others because that is the way I thought or did things.

My faithful trio looked at my heart and said, "You are my treasure." They did not see my trash as my identity. They saw my identity under all the trash. They saw the real me in me.

It really is simple when you step away from the fog into the light.

The Dwelling Place

"Love the Lord Your God with all you heart, soul and mind and all your strength and, Love your neighbor as yourself."

(Mark 12:20-21) NLT

So I have decided to pursue relationship with my favorite trio. I love worshipping with Emmanuel. He is my constant companion and I am usually aware of His presence through each and every day. We spend sometimes-long periods of worship to the Father and then sometimes minutes here and there. Devlin really does hate me soaking for it is here that I develop and drive that intimacy deep in my spirit. Besides he tends to get all wrinkly and antsy. He has no ability to stand still or be at peace. Ah! He is but a bug now. This is not to make me careless but I realize he has no power without my agreement.

You are a treasure to God

Worship, praise and thanksgiving are a very close second and very important third to experiencing God's love in everything.

Because I have wholly given myself over to God, the love of God flows from my life, I look for opportunities to overflow to others. This is not out of obligation or duty even though it is my obligation and duty. It is out of the deep desire of my heart. My heart knit together with God's heart. My desires have become His desires and His desires are my desires. It's a heart of absolute love. And I have seen God display that love as I release His presence on others. The sick do get well and the hurting healed. I have seen people get new hearts, legs grow out, pain reduced, surgeries stopped, arthritis gone and the list goes on and on.

If I do find reservation and stinking religious thinking settling in, then I know I need more time in His presence. It is all about freedom and joy in the Lord. I need a revelation of His love. God is all about relationship with us and our relating to others in love. That's it. Period!

Addicted to Worship

I shake my head in wonder when I realized that I used to be so afraid to trust Emmanuel. I get angry when I think that I gave devlin so much time, thought and energy. Emmanuel tells me though to not live in regret. He tells me that this is a waste of my energy. It is all forgiven and He has forgotten what I did because when I confessed it as sin it is now under the blood. He says it is gone as far as the east is from the west. He says that's been painted over. You got to love that red paint.

Pursuing His presence and pursuing it passionately. I wrote a song as I was writing down this vision. It goes like this:

> **Jesus I love you**
> **I call you my friend**
> **I love to walk with you**
> **Day by day**
> **Sharing the joy**
> **Of a life filled with you**
> **Your joy and peace**
> **Floods my heart.**
>
> **Loved by the Father**
> **Approved by the Son**
> **Clothed in righteousness**
> **Before the throne**

©2007 Jesus I love You
Words and Music by John M. Davidson

There is no greater joy than having an intimate relationship with the Lord. If you really want to live, if you really want to experience joy then choose Christ. Don't just choose Him but choose Him one hundred percent. We were designed by our creator to love only one God with a single heart and purpose. Damien devlin wants to usurp the one and only true God and steal our affection but he can only do it with our consent.

The Dwelling Place

If you choose any choice but one hundred percent which is absolute devotion then you have chosen the little god of this World—damien devlin. You cannot serve two masters. You will love the one and hate the other or you will hold to the one and despise the other. If you are there trying to love both, I feel your pain. I traveled that road for too long. I pray that you will choose life. Then you can feel the joy that I now have.

I do not even consider Jesus as my Master anymore; he is my close and intimate friend. I have moved beyond obligation and duty to love. It is amazing, Jesus set me free and I serve Him out of love. If there is a secret to success I would consider it this: Love Jesus—Love others—Live in Jesus Love

Addicted to Worship

Notes

25

THE NURSERY

There was one last room that was missed in the heart and although it is the last room it is perhaps the most important one. As I went through the hallway of faith, there was a door on the left that I had not opened. On one of my walks through the hallway of faith, Emmanuel asked me one day if I wanted to see my destiny. Because of the work that had been accomplished in my heart, I was now able to see beyond myself to the destiny that He was already birthing within me.

As Emmanuel opened the door I saw a nursery. At first I only saw one crib, but then I saw the room expanding before my eyes. The room suddenly became huge and there were hundreds of cribs filled with little babies. I saw in another area of the nursery a group of toddlers, in another area were young children, in another were teenagers this room represented a newborn baby through his growth cycle to a young person who was born again. This was possible because someone invited Jesus to come into his or her heart. They asked Jesus to forgive them of their sin and then put their faith and trust in Him.

The Dwelling Place

The Bible calls this being "born again." There must be a point of origin where a spiritual birth begins. Emmanuel and Comforter are not just automatically in your heart from your natural birth. There is no other way into the heart/ house except through the nursery. You must be born into it. It is a Spirit experience (John 3). If you remember my house was twenty years old. It was twenty years earlier that I made my decision. I prayed the prayer but then regulated Emmanuel, Comforter and Rhema to a six by six area in the entry. I lost twenty years by trying to straddle the fence. That is why my house was so full of trash. It was because of my quiet rebellion of still wanting to do my own thing my own way. It wasn't until five years ago that I made a commitment. I took a great risk during those fifteen years. I shudder to think, would I have been saved by fire or would He have said, "depart from me you worker of iniquity."

The great thing about God's grace and mercy is that as long as you're alive, you have a second chance. On this side of eternity you can still make choices.

You enter the kingdom of God by faith through your confession of your mouth (Romans 10:9-10), but it is the love of God that keeps you there. It is an intimate relationship as He puts a godly desire to become like Him, to be with Him and to live for Him. He writes His Words on the halls of our heart and whatever He is or does that's where we want to be. It is not a duty it is a love relationship. We love Him because He first loved us. The Son of God took our sin on him, He who knew no sin so that I could enjoy relationship with the Father, the Son and the Holy Spirit. If you have never done this and your heart cries out for this lifelong adventure that I have gone through, this can be for you also. Everything you see here in this vision is for you also. I invite to pray out loud this prayer:

"Jesus...I admit that I am a sinner. I admit that my sin has separated me from you. I know that you died on the cross to save me from my sin. Your Word says that you were raised from the dead and that you paid the

The Nursery

price for my sin. I ask that you forgive me of my sin and come into my heart. Give me a new heart. By faith, I ask you to come in to my heart and I believe that you have because your Word the Bible says that if I confess with my mouth the Lord Jesus and believe in my heart that you were raised from the dead I will be saved (Romans 10:9-10). Thank you for saving me. In Jesus name Amen.

If you just prayed this prayer then authority has just been changed. You no longer belong to devlins (the devils) kingdom. You now belong to Emmanuel's (Jesus') kingdom. You at this moment have the authority to resist devlin and His cohorts. You are now a new creation in Christ. That is what the word says:

> "If any man be in Christ he is a new creation. Old things are passed away; behold all things are new."

(2 Corinthians 5:17 KJV)

When you pray this prayer and believe, your house becomes brand new. In fact, it will never be cleaner than the day you become a child of God. You now have Emmanuel, Comforter and Rhema inside your heart (house) just like I do. You are like a new baby in Christ. Now, you need to find people around you that can help you to grow to be strong and mature.

Being born again or becoming a new baby is only the first step. It is important for you as a new Christian to have other loving Christians to help you grow from a new born to a toddler to a young child, teen and then finally an adult so that you can help others go through the same journey that I have been going through. You do this by allowing the trinity three to take you on your own journey through your heart (home) and let them do the same process in you that they have done in me. The moment you make this decision you become a son of God and can start the same adventure that I did. Having read my adventure and journey gives you a distinct advantage. You now have a visual blue print. What

The Dwelling Place

happened in my house could happen in yours as quickly as days, weeks or months. My ceiling could become your floor.

If you saw the mistakes I made and learned from them, perhaps most of the trash in your house would not accumulate. The choice is yours. How fast are you willing to say "Whatever it takes!" Remember that trash accumulates because of believing lies about yourself and living in unconfessed sin. Keep a clean slate between yourself, God and others.

You don't have to transfer your old furniture to the new house either. Ask God to build the mahogany book shelves from day one or this day forward. Live from faith, hope and love out of a teachable and humble heart. Ask for a GD (godly desire furnace) and exercise it daily using self control. Study the new water treatment system that has now been installed. Put only good things in your pantry. Get rid of the filthy clothes and put on the new clothes. Always wear the garment of humility. Go to bed with your armor and when you wake up, reaffirm it. You don't have to allow fat man to have control or worldly Wendy to build walls or mazes in your heart so she can turn your heart into stone.

Just as you accepted Jesus into your heart by faith, so you live your life by faith. Unfortunately, probably more than 95% of professing Christians do not live by faith. Jesus has given us an amazing commission:

And these signs shall follow them that believe; In my name shall they cast out devils; they shall speak with new tongues; They shall take up serpents; and if they drink any deadly thing, it shall not hurt them; they shall lay hands on the sick, and they shall recover.

(Mark 16:17-18 KJV)

Living by faith means that we cast out devils, lay hands on the sick and guarantee their recovery and bring people into the kingdom. People need to know that it is their sin that is the source of their sickness. A non believer is born into the devils kingdom but a Christian does not have to

The Nursery

live from that kingdom once they become a child of God. So many "Christians" live in continued sickness because they do not know that sickness and disease was paid for and finished at the cross.

God has a new design. We were not made to live unto ourselves but to go out and make disciples of all nations (Mark 16:15). All of us have a responsibility to love and care for one another. Even children help other children and babies. We all have a part. I speak life and freedom to you and declare, let the adventure begin. And may you choose a life of absolute devotion. From that devotion, choose to live a life of faith. Take the twenty one verses from the library and meditate on them day and night until they flow from you. You have a new power within you. God is a faith God and he

The LORD said ...I am watching to see that my word is fulfilled."

(Jeremiah 1:12 NIV)

The 'world' is looking for a new sound. Although they criticize an on fire faith believing Christian, they hate even more an anemic, faithless Christian.

Don't be fooled by those who say, "If you just pray a prayer, you are saved. Although you cannot be saved by your works for it is a free gift of God, there obviously are those who are condemned to hell by their works (Revelation 21:8). If you pray the prayer to become a believer, it is just that. You cannot be saved from this world and satans domain without becoming a follower of Jesus. It is a lifelong salvation and thank God for that. Thank God everyday for your salvation and glory in it. Press in to know your God and make Him known.

Live by faith in God's promises (like the one above in Jeremiah 1:12). If you do your life will be forever changed and you will never be the same. You will find the trinity three inside your heart (house) living the same adventure as mine and they will flow in power from you.

26

The Conclusion of the Beginning

I thought that it was ironic as I wrote this story that my life paralleled Solomon's life. Although I was obviously not remotely as smart or wealthy as him, the conflict of spiritual struggle was the same. I had come to the conclusion that I could hang onto self love and still have God in my life. Somehow I got caught up in the next best thing that would fill that God shaped void. The problem was that I did not fill it with God but with idols of my own choosing. What I could not do was to be passionate about God and this world system at the same time and remain sane. What I could not do was be single minded and really experience the man I was designed to be. It was because I was pursuing my flesh and a world system while trying to do all the right 'religious' things.

You can't do much of anything if you are double minded. Being torn between two choices will leave you trapped between those two choices. You will be caught in a limbo of regret and frustration.

The Dwelling Place

I came to a conclusion that there must be a new beginning. It is that I would be passionate about just one thing. I would be passionate about pursuing a love relationship with my Creator.

Dr Dale Fife speaks the words of my heart as clearly as I could ever say them as he wrote them in his book, The Hidden Kingdom p. 62-63:

> *To passionately pursue God's presence implies something much deeper than heartfelt emotion, no matter how intense. It means that we are willing to suffer to obtain an audience with God. It means that we are willing to lay our convenience, comfort, stoicism, pride, respectability, schedule, priorities, and anything else that might be required on the altar of sacrifice and put them to death.*
>
> *Whatever specific personal sacrifice God may ask of us, there is an absolute, universal requirement that He demands from everyone who truly longs for intimacy with Him. It is very clear. The price we all must pay to obtain an audience with the Almighty is our willingness to wait before Him, to do nothing else except sit like the showbread until He transforms us into the bread of His presence."*

For me, the conclusion of the beginning was to say with all my heart, "Whatever it takes." I had to come to the conclusion that He was the conclusion. Nothing else mattered. I had to pursue His heart and I had to fully experience His love. Whatever it meant to be passionate, I had to be willing to pay the cost. Dr Fife is right. It is in embracing suffering. I had to count the cost. It wasn't until I got to the point that nothing else mattered; until I was willing to lay it all on the altar and let Emmanuel, Comforter and Rhema have carte blanche access to every area of my heart (no matter how painful that exposure would be), that I would be stuck in this rut of my mediocrity. I would be lost in this form of godliness

The Conclusion of the Beginning

(fog), and be wandering aimlessly with no purpose and no understanding of identity.

The heart of God burns with a consuming fire to find the man or woman who is willing to lay down every weight and every sin; and look passionately unto Jesus so that they can experience all of the fullness and power that is in Christ Jesus. Paul, in Ephesians 3:16-19, (NLT) prays this prayer for the Ephesians, but it is just as powerful for us:

> *"I pray that from his glorious, unlimited resources he will give you mighty inner strength through his Holy Spirit.*
>
> *And I pray that Christ will be more and more at home in you as your roots go down deep into the soil of God's marvelous love*
>
> *And may you have the power to understand, as all God's people should, how wide, how long, how high, and how deep his love really is*
>
> *May you experience the love of Christ, though it is so great you will never fully understand it? Then you will be filled with the fullness of life and power that comes from God*

As I saw my heart as a home and these three guys living with me, working in me, and being with me, it truly allowed me to see God begin to fill my whole vision with His love. I got to see God in an everyday light working side by side in my heart, as opposed to my misguided view of Him on a throne surrounded by an impersonal white light. As I saw it first with my spiritual eyes, I then began to experience it in my daily life. The result is that two years after seeing this vision, I can honestly say that my life has been totally changed. I am experiencing increased fullness of life and power.

Three years ago, I had little clue of what it meant to know Christ. Now I know little else, but knowing Him. I understand what it means to

The Dwelling Place

have Christ more and more at home in me. He is not a guest anymore, but close family. I have been finding out that living life from the conclusion that my identity functions best when I am teachable and humble is the greatest thing about living close to Emmanuel. A grateful and thankful heart for everything that touches my life is a close second.

A good father and mother want to see their children become better than they are. They want them to have a life that is better, richer, fuller and more complete than they did. I know I want that for my children. The point of the matter is that I got a chance to see the trinity three do that for me. They wanted me to become the best I could be. They wanted me to experience the full potential of my being a son of God. They worked tirelessly for me. They don't see me as a nobody but a somebody that is valued and treasured. I am a son—deeply loved and cherished. They gave up everything and sacrificed it all so that I would be complete and whole. The amazing thing is that they did it with a pure heart. They never manipulated, dominated or controlled me to see me reach my potential. It was all done and is still being done from simple and pure love.

It has been an incredible journey and I know that I have only tapped the surface. I am on a lifelong quest with lifelong friends, and it's an expedition to the center of His Presence. Whatever it takes, I'm going to keep digging, pursuing and going all out for His love. It's all about knowing Him and making Him known. That's real living. There is so much more to discover and live.

Emmanuel tells me He is going to teach me how my heart and home functions in a restful state. Because my life is in agreement with Him and I am committed to Him cleaning house, the time is coming when he will be at total rest over my house and be at rest in it. I am so excited to see how different it will look to see Him living this restful state in and through me. I am exuberant about having Emmanuel sitting down on my couch of joy in the living room, kicking back and relaxing because the house is

The Conclusion of the Beginning

clean. I know what 'clean' means. It is the state of being like minded in everything. I can also see that this will denote that we have a good understanding and sense of each other's thoughts.

It will be a complete paradigm shift where my total concentration will naturally be to bring worship to Emmanuel and the Father, and release that life of rest, peace, and love to those around me. Its true kingdom living. It will be learning to speak life and health in a powerful way to those around me.

Although I have been experiencing this rest upon me in 'pockets', the majority of work to this point has been what the trinity three has been doing in me... which is what they love to do. Living at rest 24/7, though, sounds even greater to me. It is a deeper level of intimacy. It is consistent rest at a deeper level. I am excited about this paradigm shift. Is this really possible? Yeah, I believe so! I can already see it! I can hardly wait. Whatever it takes!

Until then...let the journey continue. ☺

Coming soon……

The Sequel to *The Dwelling Place*

Living from Rest

By

John M Davidson